"[Ameisen has] discovered the treatment for addiction."
—Jean Dausset, M.D., winner of the 1980
Nobel Prize in Medicine

"[Ameisen] is as deft with the medical basis for baclofen's efficacy as he is unsparing in his personal account of alcohol's terrors."
—Joel Turnipseed, *Minneapolis Star Tribune*

"[A] moving story . . . Compelling."
— Steve Heilig, *San Francisco Chronicle*

"This book is the riveting story of a sensitive and talented doctor whose life lapses into alcoholism. It is also the story of the dazzling discovery of a cure that could soon be within reach of all. If you or someone close to you suffers from alcoholism or drug dependence, you must read this book."
—David Servan-Schreiber, M.D., Ph.D.,
author of *The Instinct to Heal* and *Anticancer*

"Dr. Olivier Ameisen is a remarkable medical researcher who shares his journey from profound alcohol addiction to sobriety in this fascinating book . . . This book is to be recommended. It provides ample literature [for physicians] to strongly consider baclofen for patients who fail to respond to treatments in our conventional current repertoire. It is also a useful educational resource for those who work in the addiction field and for people who seek to gain a greater understanding of alcohol dependence." —Claire McIntosh, *Alcohol and Alcoholism*

"This engaging account [gives] interesting insights into the toll this disease can take and shows how . . . it was possible to fight back . . . It may be useful against other addictions."
— Clare Wilson, *New Scientist*

"Brave, insightful and sure to be significant." —*Publishers Weekly*

"I couldn't put it down. It's already changed a great deal about the way that I think about addiction, as well as the way I think about finding a cure . . . Coming from a well-respected doctor, the spiral downward into addiction is even more striking. [Ameisen] conveys a life of desperation in a simple, direct manner that is incredibly captivating . . . Incredibly well-written and very affecting, not least for its message of hope."
— Scienceblogs.com

"In this remarkably candid memoir of crippling alcoholism, cardiologist Ameisen's passion for curing addiction is palpable, at times gritty, and, in the end, hopeful."
— Donna Chavez, *Booklist*

"This is a wonderful book. Ameisen may be responsible for making a signal discovery—much like, but better than, that of George Cotzias [the first to show that L-dopa could alleviate Parkinson's disease] in that so many more patients may be involved."
— Jerome Posner, M.D.,
George C. Cotzias Chair of Neuro-oncology,
Department of Neurology,
Memorial Sloan-Kettering Cancer Center

Franck Ferville

Olivier Ameisen, M.D.
HEAL THYSELF

Olivier Ameisen, M.D., inaugurated the position of official physician to the prime minister of France. He came to the United States in 1983 to join the prestigious cardiology team at New York Hospital and Cornell University Medical College, where he became associate professor of clinical medicine and associate attending physician. He currently devotes his efforts to the treatment of addiction and lives in Paris and New York.

HEAL THYSELF

HEAL THYSELF

A Doctor at the Peak of His Medical Career,

Destroyed by Alcohol — and the Personal Miracle

That Brought Him Back

Olivier Ameisen, M.D.

with Hilary Hinzmann

SARAH CRICHTON BOOKS

FARRAR, STRAUS AND GIROUX / NEW YORK

Sarah Crichton Books
Farrar, Straus and Giroux
18 West 18th Street, New York 10011

Library of Congress Cataloging-in-Publication Data
Ameisen, Olivier, 1953–
    Heal Thyself : a doctor at the peak of his medical career, destroyed by alcohol, and
the personal miracle that brought him back / Olivier Ameisen with Hilary
Hinzmann — 1st paperback ed.
      p. ; cm.
    Originally published as: The end of my addiction / Olivier Ameisen. 2009.
    Includes bibliographical references and index.
    ISBN 978-0-374-53220-8 (pbk. : alk. paper)
    1. Ameisen, Olivier, 1953 — Mental health.   2. Alcoholics — United States —
Biography   3. Physicians — United States — Biography.   4. Alcoholism —
Chemotherapy.   I. Ameisen, Olivier, 1953– The end of my addiction   II. Title.
III. Title: Doctor at the peak of his medical career, destroyed by alcohol, and the
personal miracle that brought him back.
    [DNLM: 1. Ameisen Olivier, 1953–   2. Alcoholism — drug threrapy — Personal
Narratives.   3. Autoexperimentation — Personal Narratives.   4. Baclofen —
therapeutic use — Personal Narratives.   5. Physician Impairment — Personal
Narratives.   6. Physicians — Personal Narratives. WM 274 A498h 2010]

RC565.A4685 2010
616.86'10092 — dc22
[B]

2009042262

Designed by Maggie Goodman

www.fsgbooks.com

10 9 8 7 6 5 4 3 2 1

In memory of my parents

It is harder to crack a prejudice than an atom.

—ALBERT EINSTEIN

Miracles only happen in the soul of one who looks for them.

— STEFAN ZWEIG

CONTENTS

Appendix

In the months since this book was first published in the United States, France, and the United Kingdom, support for baclofen has grown as I had hoped but had never dared to expect it would. Patients have shown my book to their doctors, doctors have shown it to their patients, and increasing numbers of addiction specialists and general practitioners alike have begun using my discovery.

Hundreds of patients in Europe and in the United States have already written directly to me, or have posted on blogs and Internet forums, that they have now been cured of alcoholism and other addictions, although the disease of addiction is still officially labeled "incurable." Some of their physicians have also contacted me to say how glad they are that they at last have a reliable, successful treatment to offer patients suffering from addiction. A large number of cures and a very high success rate have been documented by addiction specialists: nearly all of the 135 patients treated at Hôpital Paul Guiraud in Villejuif, near Paris;

nearly all of the 67 patients treated at the University Hospitals of Geneva; nearly all of the 53 patients treated at the Victoria Infirmary in Glasgow, Scotland; and nearly all of the 78 patients treated by physicians affiliated with major academic medical centers in the United States.

Dr. Jonathan Chick, coeditor-in-chief of *Alcohol and Alcoholism*, one of the most important medical journals in the field of addiction, has publicly supported use of the treatment I have discovered. This is an unusual step for the editor of a medical journal. Dr. Chick has told the media, "We are fairly convinced that . . . [baclofen] can correct the addictive process in the cells . . . It seems there are no dangerous side effects."

Thus, this book no longer reflects only a personal experience. It now represents many other patients, whose numbers are growing exponentially and whose cures are as successful and complete as my own.

—Olivier Ameisen
July 1, 2009

NOTE TO THE READER

In the depths of a desperate struggle with alcoholism, I found a medicine, baclofen, that both freed me of all craving for alcohol and resolved the underlying disorder, overwhelming anxiety, that made me vulnerable to addiction.

By completely suppressing my addiction, baclofen saved my life. I believe it can save and improve the lives of many others by completely suppressing their addictions, and I have written this book to that end. It is in effect an extended self-case report on the etiology and course of my illness, including the severe anxiety that troubled me from early childhood, my descent into alcoholism in New York City and Paris, the fortunate circumstances that made me aware of baclofen before alcoholism irreversibly damaged my health or killed me, my decision to test baclofen on myself and then to break my anonymity as a physician with addiction and publish the results, and my efforts, in both concert and conflict with some of the world's leading addiction researchers, to further understanding of this valuable medicine and make it available to others.

In what follows I draw on my personal experiences with the aim of illuminating common themes in both the experience and treatment of addiction. For reasons of privacy I have changed some names and identifying details.

This book is not a self-help manual, and it is in no way meant to be a guide to self-treatment. Addiction is a serious illness, and anyone suffering from it should seek qualified medical advice and care. Likewise, baclofen, a prescription drug, should be taken only as prescribed and closely supervised by a licensed physician.

—Olivier Ameisen

HEAL THYSELF

1. Moment of Truth

I CAME TO MY SENSES and took stock of where I was: in a cab, with blood streaming down my face and spattering my trench coat. I looked out the window and in the glow of the streetlights saw the cab was on Lexington Avenue in Manhattan, waiting for the light to change at 76th Street. The church on the corner reminded me it was Sunday, and I looked at my watch. It was almost midnight. The few people on the street were buttoned up against the late winter chill, but it was warm in the cab.

My apartment was not too far away, on East 63rd Street between York and First Avenues, but I needed medical attention. I asked the driver to take me to the emergency room at New York Hospital, at 68th Street and York Avenue. He seemed oblivious to my condition, and I wondered what had happened. Had the cab braked suddenly so that I hit my head, or had I been injured in some other way before I hailed it? I knew I'd been drinking, but not where or how much.

As the cab pulled up in front of the hospital emergency room entrance, a memory of the evening began to come together. Around 8:30 p.m. I had visited my friend Jeff Steiner, the CEO of Fairchild Corporation, to ask his advice on running my cardiology practice, which I'd started two and a half years before. I'd been introduced to Jeff in the late 1980s by a mutual friend, another physician.

Although I'd intended not to drink that evening, I felt insulted when Jeff's butler offered me a choice of teas. "Why doesn't he offer me an alcoholic drink as well at this hour?" I thought. "Is this a judgmental message?"

I asked for and drank a glass of Scotch, then made a show of declining a refill. Much later I learned that Jeff was not aware that I had been drinking heavily. He'd known me only to have a few drinks at large parties, here and there, over the years. But my mounting concerns about my practice finances had changed that.

The standard expectation is that it will take a new medical practice two years to break even. Mine broke even in four months. And almost three years later, in March 1997, there it remained— hovering a little over the break-even point.

Staggering into the emergency room, I thought, "They will see I'm drunk. That's not so good. But at least I know the place is well run and will fix me up right." I had been associated with New York Hospital and its partner institution, Cornell University Medical College,* ever since I arrived from France in the fall of 1983 to do research and clinical fellowships in cardiology. Thirteen and a half years later, I was a clinical associate professor

*As the two institutions were then known; in 1998 they became New York-Presbyterian Hospital and Weill Cornell Medical College.

of medicine at Cornell and an associate attending physician at New York Hospital, in addition to running my private practice.

Inside the emergency room, I passed out again. When I came to, one of my ex-students, Matt, now a resident, was standing over me preparing to stitch the wound in my forehead. So as not to be left with a scar, I asked him to use Steri-Strips instead. He did and then left me to lie quietly for a few hours so I could sober up enough to walk home safely. He was plainly even more embarrassed to treat me in my drunken state than I was to need treatment. I cringed at the thought of my appearance in the ER being discussed around the hospital, then pushed the thought out of my mind. Matt was not the kind of person to talk about it; that was some comfort.

Lying there, I ran the video of the evening in my mind. "Run the video of what happens when you drink" was something I'd been hearing in Alcoholics Anonymous, where I was still very much a newcomer.

My conversation with Jeff Steiner had been frustrating for us both. Although he was eager to help, there was a mismatch between his expertise and my problems. What I really needed was a small business adviser, not a big corporate dealmaker.

As I left Jeff's apartment, my mind whirled with conflicting thoughts. My cost-blind practice style might function better in France's universal health care system than in the United States, I thought, and I wondered if I should relocate back to Paris, where I was from. But I loved my life in New York. In 1991 I had acquired U.S. citizenship, and it pleased me to be a citizen of a country with so many shared ideals with my country of origin. If not profitable, my practice was at least busy and my work enormously rewarding. My patient roster included wealthy and celebrated people along with Harlem church ladies on Medicare or Medicaid and the indigent, and I liked that mix. And my social life was wonderfully stimulating—more so than I could imagine having anywhere else. No, I wasn't eager to leave.

But my practice could not continue indefinitely at this rate, and the constant anxiety created by financial worries was growing into a source of full-blown panic. I struggled with a deep sense of failure, and I lived in fear that the world would see that my accomplishments were nothing but a sham, a house of cards that could collapse at any second.

This was not a new feeling to me. Throughout my life I had been plagued by anxious feelings of inadequacy, of being an impostor on the brink of being unmasked. I had been seeing therapists for a long time before I started drinking. To be honest, they never were much help with my anxiety. Nor was the Xanax they prescribed me.

The one Scotch at Jeff's made me aware of how thirsty I was. I went to a Chinese restaurant, intending to have a meal as well, but wound up eating nothing and drinking one double vodka after another. And then . . . I found myself bleeding in the taxicab.

It wasn't my first blackout drinking. But the blackouts were getting more common, whole stretches of evenings expunged from my memory. And this was the first time I'd come out of a blackout with a physical injury. Until then blackouts had only been sources of intense mortification as I wondered what embarrassing things I might have said or done.

The next morning I thought briefly about amusing tales I could concoct to explain the bandages on my forehead. Deciding that I was too hungover to go to work, I had my office assistant reschedule the day's patients. As my drinking had increased, I had scrupulously honored my first duty as a doctor—to do no harm. I stopped driving. And I never set foot in my office or the hospital when I was not completely sober.

Still, I resisted seeing myself as a problem drinker. All I really needed, I thought, was to learn to drink better. This delusion was encouraged by a well-meaning friend and an equally well-meaning but I think even more misguided therapist, both of whom undertook to show me how to be a moderate wine drinker rather than a binger on Scotch or vodka. I even began AA with the thought that it might give me tips on managing my drinking better rather than stopping completely.

Not everyone thought I was a candidate for moderation. The two friends who escorted me to my first meeting didn't think so. One was a longtime AA member, a poet and a writer and a very beautiful woman who looked a bit like Katharine Hepburn. She used to say, "I want you to see me before I lose my looks." She still has those looks today. When we met, she had been sober for many years, yet she told me, "I am an alcoholic." That struck me as very strange, and I was embarrassed to hear her say it. People with diabetes or hypertension didn't identify themselves by their illnesses. Why should people with alcoholism?

Of course, I thought that because I did not want to admit—to myself or anyone else—that I might be alcohol-dependent. And so I was terrified to go to a meeting. But my friends each took me by an arm, and escorted me from my apartment on East 63rd Street to the major AA meeting place in the neighborhood—the 79th Street Workshop, in the basement of St. Monica's Catholic Church, on 79th Street between York and First Avenues. It was my first step, taken reluctantly, toward facing my illness. But it was a vital one.

It is hard for everyone who attends AA to get past the potential embarrassment of being seen as an alcoholic. Shortly before I went to AA for the first time, my shrink began encouraging me to go. I said, "What about anonymity? My office and my apartment are right in the same neighborhood. What if a patient or somebody else I know sees me?"

He said, "Don't worry. Anyone inside will be an alcoholic and won't say anything."

"But what if a colleague sees me entering or leaving the place?"

"It won't happen."

It did happen. But after I started going to AA, I told him, "AA is a great place. Have you been to a meeting?"

"No."

"You refer people. Maybe you should know what it's like. Will you come with me to an open meeting?"

"No."

"Why not?"

"Because somebody might see me."

There is a moral stigma to addiction, and it is prospective shame that drives people to resist admitting they have a problem. It leads physicians to miss or delay a diagnosis of addiction, too. Only a couple of months earlier, I had brought up AA in a session with my shrink. "Oh, you're not an alcoholic," he said dismissively, "but you could become one." Then he changed the subject away from alcohol and drinking.

Later on in my alcoholism, when I knew more about the course of the illness, I wondered how he could have missed the signs of its onset in me, and could even have turned a deaf ear to my first outright call for help. The responses of my physician colleagues at New York Hospital–Cornell puzzled me, too. When I would discreetly ask around about how to help "someone" with a drinking problem, they'd ask, "Is the person close to you?"

If I said no, they'd say, "You don't want to get involved. It's a minefield."

If yes, "Well, I really don't know what to say. It's very complex . . ."

Recent studies have shown that, at least among physicians who are not specialists in the field, a missed or delayed diagnosis is the rule, rather than the exception, in cases of addiction. One study videotaped doctors and patients and found that when patients mention addiction issues, doctors tend to change the subject as quickly as possible.[1]

I didn't know what to make of this phenomenon when I first encountered it. But it has dawned on me that doctors are uncomfortable with the subject because they don't have a reliable treatment to deliver or recommend.

The lack of reliable treatment also explains the moral assumptions attached to addiction. Whenever medicine has lacked a means to cure an illness, it has blamed the patient's lack of moral virtue, positive thinking, and willpower. In the nineteenth century, tuberculosis was associated in novels and operas with characters of dubious morality or sanity, at least insofar as the establishment was concerned. Think of Fantine, the unwed mother turned prostitute in Victor Hugo's *Les Misérables*; the deranged revolutionary Kirillov in Dostoevsky's *The Possessed*; or the courtesan Violetta in Verdi's *La Traviata*. Susan Sontag memorably exposed a similar dynamic at work in relation to cancer and AIDS, respectively, in *Illness as Metaphor* and *AIDS and Its Metaphors*.

I very much feared moral judgments about my drinking, and no one was judging me more harshly than me. "I am supposed to be an intelligent person with willpower. I should be able to control my urge to drink. When people find out about my drinking, they will finally see what a fake I am," I told myself.

What further complicates the picture is the fact that some people are able to halt their compulsive behavior with the help of twelve-step programs like AA and commonly prescribed medications like Revia, Campral, and Antabuse. But for the vast majority of people with addiction, these are not enough. They weren't for me. Which is not to say that AA didn't help me. It did. It was a critical resource without which I might not have survived until I found an effective medication in baclofen. It taught me a great deal about accepting my illness and about my fellow sufferers and myself, but it couldn't stop my cravings or the uncontrollable anxiety that led me to drink.

I was terrified of living without alcohol. Without it, I would be an anxious wreck. Admitting my problem drinking to most of my friends and my colleagues terrified me, too. I feared being ostracized, and since I felt that drinking should be under my control I felt ostracism would be justified. (Naively, I assumed that very few physicians had a drinking problem. I didn't yet know that about 10 percent of physicians, like roughly 10 percent of the general population, will become dependent on alcohol at some point in their lives, that many more in each group are problem drinkers, and that according to the British Medical Association, physicians are three times more likely than the general population to have liver cirrhosis from alcohol abuse.)[2]

Through the next two months after my appearance in the ER, I clung to abstinence. I called my new AA sponsor regularly, and worked overtime in my practice so that I had no free time for drinking. And in June, I went off to the Swiss Alps, which, since my childhood, had been a magical place for me. But hiking in the mountains and quiet evenings after a good dinner failed to restore my spirits as usual. I had been sober for sixty-three days, but there was no peace in me. My drinking had threatened my career, even my life. I needed to talk to someone about it.

I decided to call André Gadaud, whom I'd met in 1984 when he became France's consul general in New York. After other high-level diplomatic postings, André had become the French ambassador to Switzerland. He was also what they call in AA a "civilian," that is, a non–problem drinker. We'd always had a great rapport, and I thought sharing my secret with him might help me.

André generously offered to drive from the French embassy in Bern and meet me for lunch at the Hotel Quellenhof in Bad Ragaz, a luxurious thermal resort town. As we sat down to lunch, André said, "Let's order champagne and have a toast, since we haven't seen each other in several years."

"I'd rather not have champagne," I said.

"Why not? It's been so long!"

I did not know how to say no, so I gave in. It felt impossible to refuse champagne when it was proposed by a French ambassador, and then it felt equally impossible to reveal that my drinking had become a serious issue. I worried that André would assume

I was not exercising enough willpower and lose respect for me. It seemed better to keep quiet and not risk ruining our visit or possibly even our friendship.

After lunch, during which I restricted myself to only one glass of champagne, André and I walked for hours in the mountains, talking about everything except my problem, before he had to drive back to Bern. That evening, I went to a pizzeria for dinner. When the waiter asked if I wanted a drink, I immediately started craving alcohol. The glass of champagne at lunch had reactivated the whole cycle, which I knew would be hard to fight.

The craving became stronger, growing in my chest, in my throat. Some cravings are more violent than others. Although cravings have an emotional component, the physical part was the hardest to bear for me. An AA acronym, HALT, sums up the states—Hungry, Angry, Lonely, Tired—in which cravings strengthen. I was experiencing all four. I was jet-lagged, lonely and angry because my friend had left without my being able to mention why I had called, and hungry because my food was very slow to arrive.

Just to take the edge off, I ordered a double vodka tonic, assuring myself that a single drink would forestall a major binge. It almost worked. After dinner, I felt somewhat soothed. But as I walked back to the hotel, I passed a bar and the craving struck again with irresistible force.

I entered the bar and ordered a double vodka tonic. Another customer came over. "I heard you play the piano here last summer," he said. "You were terrific. Would you please play again?"

As I sat down at the piano, a wave of anxiety swept over me. What if I didn't play well? Another vodka tonic materialized, offered, I was told, by the customer who'd asked me to play. After gulping it down, I felt great—relaxed, personable, happy. I played with confidence; people danced and applauded. After two more vodka tonics, I returned to my hotel and fell into a peaceful, refreshing sleep.

I awoke feeling good, but in the late afternoon I went out and bought a bottle of vodka. And I drank it, launching myself on a binge.

With great effort, I ended the binge and managed to dry out in time for my flight home to New York.

My failure to stay sober on vacation frightened me. I called my office assistant, Erdie, and told her to cancel all appointments.

"For how long?" Erdie asked.

"Until the end of the summer," I said.

"But why, Doctor Ameisen?"

I hesitated a moment, and then said, "Because I'm an alcoholic, Erdie."

She laughed and said, "But seriously, Doc, why?"

"I am serious, Erdie."

Over the next several weeks, I decided, I would either manage to arrest my downward slide or ease myself out of my practice until I regained control.

Almost immediately, I began drinking heavily every evening. Finally, I managed to wrench myself out of the abyss and stop. I grew ill, vomiting and aching all over, but as usual staved off acute withdrawal with B vitamins, gallons of fluids for hydration, and Valium. I was usually well supplied with Valium, which my physician prescribed for my anxiety, and since I had started bingeing, I had always made sure to have some on hand so that I could detox myself.

Detoxing from alcohol takes around five days. A day into this regimen, I called my girlfriend, Joan, who proved immensely empathetic and encouraging, even though we were having a rocky time over my inability to make a long-term commitment.

The next morning, August 19, 1997, I realized I had run out of Valium and could not remember when I had taken the last pill. With Joan's help, I searched the apartment repeatedly, desperate to find at least a couple of pills, but there were none in the bathroom medicine cabinet, on the nightstand by my bed, in the kitchen drawer, or anywhere else. The doctors I knew and trusted were away, and I could not imagine explaining to another doctor why I needed a prescription on an emergency basis.

Joan did not understand my concern. "Why do you need Valium so badly?" she asked.

I explained that withdrawal from alcohol can easily become a medical emergency with delirium tremens (the DTs), seizures, loss of consciousness, hallucinations, major spikes in blood pressure, and even death. The risk of serious, and potentially lethal, medical consequences is much higher in acute withdrawal from alcohol than in withdrawal from any other drug of abuse.

I also explained that in the days before Valium and similar drugs existed, people were detoxed using diminishing doses of alcohol. If I could get out to a liquor store, I could halt the progression of my symptoms. But my arms and legs felt like they were made of rubber; I was so exhausted that I could not even stand. Terrified of what might happen, I begged Joan, "Please, buy a bottle of vodka and bring it to me."

She refused. Looking back, I suppose I could have written Joan a prescription for Valium that she could then give to me. But I was horrified by the thought of doing something that would compromise my ethics.

I said, "I'm having a medical crisis. Either I drink or risk a negative neurological event, like a seizure."

Joan knew that I was a good doctor, but she also knew the depth of my dependence on alcohol. A tall business executive, Joan looked me in the eye and said, "I'm sorry, Olivier, but I can't bring you liquor."

I gave up the fight. "Something is going to happen to me," I said. "When it does, you must call EMS and have them take me to New York Hospital. I don't like going to my own hospital in this condition, but they will take good care of me there."

"Isn't there anything else we can do?"

"You can bring me liquor, or we can wait for the bad things to happen."

We waited.

Half an hour later, I felt a strange sense of agitation mixed with relief. I wondered if this was the "aura" that precedes a seizure. And then I lost consciousness except for a vague impression of medical personnel milling in the lobby of my building or on the street, and a bit later someone pulling a privacy curtain around me in the hospital and whispering, "He's an attending," shorthand for attending physician. Then I lost consciousness again.

When I awoke, I was attached to several IV tubes and a urinary catheter. A young medical student, a bit pompous but sweet, appeared and questioned me about my "malady." I liked his choice of words so much that instead of asking for an experienced nurse or an intern, I let him draw arterial blood gases. This was a long, very painful process, because I was his first live patient.

My next visitor was Professor John Schaefer, an outstanding neurologist originally from Australia, whom I knew very well and greatly admired. With matter-of-fact kindness and no hint of moral judgment, he explained that I had suffered multiple seizures, which had been controlled with intravenous Valium. I had been kept heavily sedated for two days and I was continuing to receive Valium intravenously to treat acute withdrawal.

The seizures were so violent that they produced rhabdomyolysis, a breakdown in muscle tissue that is toxic to the kidneys and is measured by the level of CPKs—creatine phosphokinase isoenzymes—in the blood. The same thing can happen to people who suffer what is known as crush syndrome, from traumatic injuries in a car accident or being trapped in the rubble of an earthquake. Only recently, a colleague told me that on seeing my chart in the intensive care unit, he assumed I must have been in a massive car crash, because my CPKs were extraordinarily high. Rhabdomyolysis explained the urinary catheter and another of the IVs; they were to make sure I was getting enough fresh fluids to prevent renal failure.

"You almost lost your kidneys, my boy," John said. His characteristic jovial "my boy" cheered me up and made me feel I could talk to him about the real problem, that I had subjected my body to this trauma by excessive drinking. (Perhaps fortunately for my state of mind at the time, he only told me much later that I was admitted to the hospital in "status epilepticus," an ongoing seizure state that put me "near death.")

"You are going to have to report me—" I began.

"On the contrary," John said. "I'd like to commend you. I know you haven't seen patients all summer. Too many doctors continue to practice for years when they are—and know they are—alcohol-dependent."

"I am going to resign as associate professor and associate attending physician here."

John shook his head. "Are you crazy? You don't resign because you have an illness."

"I know alcoholism is a disease. But in my case, that's not what it is. I know I should be able to control my drinking, but I have not succeeded so far. I guess it's a weakness on my part. Do you understand?"

"No," John said. "It *is* an illness. One you will have to recover from and then you will come back and work normally. To help that along, you should begin seeing an expert in these matters. With your permission I would like to call in a friend of mine, Professor Elizabeth Khuri, as a consultant. She is right next door to the hospital at Rockefeller University and also has an office here. Would that be okay with you?"

"Can I tell her . . . ?"

"You can tell her anything and it will not filter to anyone here at the hospital, including me."

"Okay, then, I will be glad to see her. Thank you. Thank you for everything."

"Glad to be of service, my boy. I will check in on you in the morning. For now, just get some rest."

"John, given the risk of infection, don't you think this urinary catheter could be removed now?"

John laughed. "You must be feeling better if you've got the energy to resent that imposition, and you are right about the infection risk," he said. "I'll tell the head nurse about the catheter. Now get some rest, and you'll be back to normal in no time."

I wondered if things would ever be normal again for me. One fact was clear and could no longer be denied: I had become an alcoholic.

2. A Remedy Gone Wrong

THEY SAY that alcoholism runs in families. Not mine. Unlike most French families, we never had wine with our meals, and my parents rarely drank, at home or on vacation. Two or three times a year I might see them with a small glass of Scotch in the evening, and there was a sip of wine once a year at Passover. That was it.

But I have come to believe that it isn't addiction that recurs through the generations so much as it is dysphoria (the opposite of euphoria)—a chronic, underlying distress that predisposes people, to varying degrees, to addiction and other compulsive behaviors.

In addiction medicine, it has long been recognized that people addicted to various substances and compulsive behaviors frequently experience symptoms of anxiety, depression, and/or other mood or personality disorders. (Medicine classifies anxiety, mood, and personality disorders in separate but related categories for precise diagnosis; I sometimes use mood disorders as a catchall term, in the commonsense way of speaking of anxious and depressed moods.) The concept of dual diagnosis and comorbidity—the presence of two or more diseases, or morbidities, at the same time, with one seen as "primary" and the other(s) as "secondary"—is a vital one, for both treatment and research. At the same time, though, the nomenclature of "dual" and "co-" can be misleading. It implies either that the addiction and the mood disorder originate together or (and this is what tends to be assumed by treatment protocols) that they are associated without cause and effect.

This assumption follows from the fact that anxiety or depression, say, is far less likely to bring people to medical attention than addiction is. Thus the primary diagnosis will almost always be addiction, and the secondary diagnosis will be anxiety, depression, or another mood disorder. My doctors, for example, diagnosed me as suffering from "alcohol dependence with comorbid anxiety."

It is certainly true that addiction generates its own cycles of anxiety and depression. But as I always thought, based on my own case and my observation of others, and as the best recent scientific evidence has confirmed, there is usually an underlying disorder, a preaddiction morbidity, that sets the stage for addictive behavior. To put it more directly: the anxiety, depression, compulsiveness, or other underlying disorder comes first.[1] I was troubled by anxiety long before I became an alcoholic. Yet everyone who treated me for alcoholism turned out to be deaf to that fact, no matter how often I repeated it.

I told all my doctors, "I use alcohol as a tranquilizer. If you rid me of anxiety, I'll stop drinking."

My doctors all told me, "You're anxious because you drink. Stop drinking and your anxiety will subside."

There may have been no alcoholism in my extended family in Europe and America. But there was a streak of anxiety and nervousness in my mother (with good reason, given her experiences) that became part of my nature and nurture.

Both sides of the family were of Polish Jewish origin. My father, Emmanuel ("Maniek" to my mother and his closest friends), hailed from Kraków. When he was a teenager, his violin teacher wanted him to go to Berlin to train as a concert violinist with one of the great masters of the time. But my father, a true walking encyclopedia with a passion for learning about everything from ancient Greek to opera, from astronomy to zoology, chose to study engineering.

In 1932, at the age of twenty-four, he went to the Institut Polytechnique de Grenoble (the Grenoble Institute of Technology), as it is now called, the French equivalent of MIT. He arrived not speaking a word of French but was soon fluent in the language, although he always spoke it with a slight accent, and he completed his studies with distinction. Then he went to Paris, where he looked up his father's brother, who had changed his name from Edward Ameisen to Edward William Titus. It was a strange act for a Jew to adopt the name of Titus, the Roman emperor who destroyed the Temple in Jerusalem. But Edward Titus made a habit of defying convention.

In 1908, in London, Edward William Titus had married Helena Rubinstein, and begun helping her grow what would become one of the great cosmetics empires. Only four-foot-ten, Rubinstein was notorious for her tyrannical ways. Yet after going to work for her, my father gained her trust with his engineering expertise and management skill, and rose to a senior position in her French operations (despite the fact that she would divorce Titus in 1937 because of his many infidelities).

At the start of World War II, my father volunteered for the French army, although he was still a Polish citizen. After seeing combat in northern France, he was captured in 1940 by the Germans and sent to a prisoner of war camp in Pomerania. Within a few days he was identified as a Jew and sent to a forced labor camp. When the labor camp was liberated by General George Patton's troops in the last months of the war in Europe, he returned to Paris and set about rebuilding Helena Rubinstein's French business, becoming the company's managing director.

When the war began, my mother, Janina ("Yanka") Schanz, then only seventeen years old, was already at the Jagiellonian University in Kraków, in the same philosophy class as Karol Wojtyla, the future Pope John Paul II. Her father had a successful textile factory in the southern Polish town of Bielsko-Biala. Samuel Schanz was under no illusions about Nazi Germany's view of the Jews. His brother had already emigrated to Palestine, and Samuel went and bought land there. But his wife, Anna, refused to leave her familiar surroundings. Like so many others, she could not believe that what was happening to Jews elsewhere would soon happen in Poland.

Displaying her characteristic strength of will, my mother managed to secure visas to Argentina for her parents, herself, and her younger brother, Zev. But my grandmother again refused to leave, insisting that all would be well. Escape soon became impossible. Arrested by the Germans in the Kraków ghetto after having survived the Warsaw bombardment, my mother and her family were taken to the concentration camp at Plaszów, where they found my then-twelve-year-old cousin Steve Israeler, who, just before being captured, had seen his parents and five brothers and sisters killed by the Germans. Soon after, they were split up. My grandfather was sent to Mauthausen. Bidding farewell to my mother, he said, "I will not survive, but you and your mother and brother must."

My mother survived Auschwitz-Birkenau. My grandmother walked out of the camp at Skarżysko with a broken hip from a beating. My cousin Steve survived Flossenburg, and my uncle Zev survived, too: he was on Schindler's list.

My mother and her brother and mother and Steve made their way to Paris—where, looking for help, they turned to their distant relative, Helena Rubinstein.

Not long after, my parents were married. Around the same time, my grandmother, my uncle Zev, and my cousin Steve emigrated to America. My older brother, Jean-Claude, was born on December 22, 1951; I came a year and a half later, on June 25, 1953; and our sister, Eva, followed on September 8, 1957.

Seeing the confident affection between our handsome, athletic father and our beautiful mother, it was easy for my brother and sister and me to think that the happy ending was complete. Certainly my father never told us a sad story. Although his voice sometimes took on an edge of intensity, he recounted grueling night marches in the rain and mud, the lottery of death on the battlefield, and life as a prisoner of war as if they were episodes from an adventure story. He delighted us with his description of how teaching himself to play an accordion got him out of peeling potatoes, because both the other prisoners and the guards were so entertained by his playing.

To the outside world, my mother showed the same lack of

distress. In the 1990s she participated in the Survivors of the Shoah Visual History Foundation archive, which Steven Spielberg established after making *Schindler's List*. In her videotaped interview, she says little more than, "The Germans were not very refined. They could have been more polite."

But when my brother and sister and I were little, she spoke very differently to us. She sobbed with grief and anger as she recited the horrors her family had witnessed and endured. When she lamented, "The Germans murdered my father," or described how she dreamed of eating oranges, only to wake up and remember that she was in Auschwitz, my heart ached.

She often expressed the fear that after the survivors died, no one would remember or believe what had occurred. When I was grown up, I asked her if she had ever considered seeing a psychiatrist about her experiences. She said that she had once consulted a young Jewish psychiatrist. When she told him about watching German soldiers tear still-living children limb from limb, he said, "You have a lot of imagination." That was the last she had to do with psychiatrists until late in life, when she hoped that one of them might help me recover from alcoholism.

It has been suggested that children of Holocaust survivors are at increased risk of post-traumatic stress disorder (PTSD), severe anxiety, and depression because of the atmosphere in which they were raised. Some research has also pointed to genetic factors. A Mount Sinai School of Medicine study found a "higher prevalence of lifetime PTSD, mood, anxiety disorders, and to a lesser extent, substance abuse disorders . . . in offspring of Holocaust survivors." Although "PTSD in any parent contributes to risk for depression, and parental traumatization is associated with increased anxiety disorders in offspring," the study found that maternal traumatization has a greater impact than paternal traumatization. It noted that the children of women who survived the Holocaust are more likely to have low levels of the stress hormone cortisol, which would make them less emotionally resilient, and that the "tendency for maternal PTSD to make a greater contribution than paternal PTSD to [offspring's] PTSD risk . . . paves the way for the speculation that epigenetic factors may be involved." This could occur through a change in gene expression known as genomic imprinting, in which the genetic contribution of the father or mother outweighs that of the other parent.[2]

Do my early childhood experiences explain why I became anxious? An alcoholic? The old nature versus nurture debate remains undecided. A scientist looking at the impact of nurture on a category of medical problems and vulnerabilities might point to animal studies of "learned nervousness," where, for example, the offspring of a nervous female monkey will imitate her behavior and themselves exhibit nervous behavior for the rest of their lives. But from observations of my family and others, it is clear to me that nature also contributes—vitally, but to varying degrees—to different family members' genetic predispositions toward anxiety. For example, no one has more joie de vivre than my cousin Steve, and I could say the same of other Holocaust survivors and children of Holocaust survivors I have known.

It should be said that anxiety is not necessarily an undesirable trait from an evolutionary point of view. Anxiety about survival helps avoid danger and motivates discovery, invention, and technological development. The question to ask about the allegedly disproportionate achievement of Jews in business, the learned professions, and the sciences is probably not whether they have higher-than-average IQs, which I doubt, but whether they have higher-than-average anxiety about being killed in recurring episodes of virulent anti-Semitism.

Every human trait exists on a continuum from mild to pronounced. An anxiety response somewhere in the middle of the spectrum that can help alert one to danger and drive an appropriate reaction is surely useful. I believe this was true of my mother's somewhat above-average anxiety, which she medicated with up to two packs of cigarettes a day. But at the extremes the trait loses its survival value, shading off into delusive overconfidence at one end and paralyzing panic at the other, neither a promising condition for decision-making and action.

Even when we were children, there was a marked difference between my older brother and me. I remember so well a particular moment when Jean-Claude was six years old and I was four and a half. The family was going to the Alps for skiing, something we did regularly. We were going by train, and were all in the station waiting room except for my father, who was seeing to the luggage.

Jean-Claude asked, "Maman, may I hold my ticket?"

I piped up, "May I hold mine, too?"

My mother hesitated for a moment, looking, I thought, more at me than at Jean-Claude. Carefully she gave us our tickets, one little pasteboard rectangle each. "Don't lose it," she said as she gave me mine.

Jean-Claude inspected his ticket happily, and put it in his coat pocket, but I couldn't let go of mine. I revolved it in my fingers, held it first in one hand and then in the other, with increasing concern about what to do with it. If I put it in my pocket, it might fall out. I couldn't give it back to my mother while Jean-Claude still had his, and I wondered how he could be so calm.

My mother was tapping her foot nervously while she held two-year-old Eva in her arms. "What is taking your father so long?" she fretted. "We will miss our train."

My mother put Eva down at her side and snapped her purse open, searching for a cigarette. Just then my father came striding up, calmly, with his usual smile on seeing us, and my mother visibly relaxed. She slid the cigarettes back in her purse. We walked to the platform and boarded the train with time to spare. I was calmer, too, when I saw my father, but I still held my ticket tight until the conductor came around, punched the tickets, and handed them all back to my mother. It was only then that I could relax and give myself over to the pure pleasure of our vacation adventure.

I didn't intend to become a doctor. I loved the piano, and dreamed of becoming a professional musician. My music teachers told my parents that I had enough talent, but that I should not leave school without passing the *baccalauréat*, the exam that is a prerequisite for university-level study in France. The final year of high school is devoted mainly to cramming for this exam, which takes two to three days to complete and which comes in three forms, depending on the student's preparation: science and math, economics and social sciences, and literature and philosophy.

In the middle of my second year of high school, I told my mother that I wanted to take the literature and philosophy *baccalauréat* early. My mother and I went to see the director of my school, Georges Hacquard. He loved my piano playing, and told my mother, "If he wants to become a pianist, by all means, he should try. He is the best musician we have ever had in the school." So he wrote to the Ministry of Education that I was ready to take the test and requested permission for me to do so.

Weeks passed, and an official wrote back in the usual bureaucratic way and turned us down. I didn't accept that as an answer. I saw the chance to escape school for good, and I wasn't ready to let it go. I called the Ministry of Education and asked for an appointment with the Minister of Education, Edgar Faure. In retrospect, I am amazed by my chutzpah; it was not at all how I usually behaved. And Edgar Faure was an exalted figure. He had been prime minister of France twice in the 1950s and had held many other positions at the highest level of government. But he was also known to write mystery novels under a pseudonym, and my parents said he had a reputation for open-mindedness, so I thought that if I managed to see him I might win him over.

I got as far as an undersecretary. He told me, "We hear you are brilliant, but we cannot make exceptions."

I asked my mother to write to Faure. I had more confidence in her powers of persuasion than in my own. I looked up Faure's home address in *Who's Who*, and took my mother's letter there myself. I rang the doorbell, thinking Faure himself might come to the door, but a small, chubby butler opened it and took the letter.

Six days before the *baccalauréat* we received a letter saying I could take the exam, which I passed with honors. According to the Ministry of Education, it was the first and only time a student had passed the *baccalauréat* without completing the last two years of high school.

———

Passing the *baccalauréat* wasn't the ticket to being a musician that I had hoped. My parents were not prepared to see me spend all my time playing the piano at sixteen years of age without a thought for my future. They wanted me to enter an academic program that would prepare me for a good, worthwhile career in France or another country. They had seen democratic countries elect dictators or be conquered by them, and they had seen what people become in war. "Never again," the leading sentiment of the immediate post–World War II years, was for them a hope, not an expectation. In such a world, my parents felt, a Jew always needed to be ready for emigration. A law degree was usually only accepted in a person's home country, whereas a credential in architecture or engineering provided more options. A medical degree was best of all, a Jew's passport, a highly portable credential likely to be recognized anywhere in the world.

I resisted.

I had spent the summer playing piano at a neighborhood restaurant, La Closerie des Lilas. It had been a fixture of the Montparnasse scene for decades, a meeting place for artists and intellectuals from Pablo Picasso, Gertrude Stein, and Ernest Hemingway to Jean-Paul Sartre and Simone de Beauvoir. Playing there for a few francs a night was heaven. I strung classical pieces and pop and folk songs together as the spirit moved me, or as requested by the patrons. One evening a waiter told me that the Surrealist poet Louis Aragon was requesting the first movement of Beethoven's *Moonlight* Sonata, and I happily complied.

I turned sixteen that summer, but I looked older. So people in the restaurant naturally sent over drinks from time to time. I refused them all, and the restaurant staff learned to tell patrons "Thanks, but no thanks" on my behalf. Shortly after my birthday in June, however, I decided to see what liquor tasted like and I accepted a drink with a patron's compliments. I felt no effect whatsoever, and I thought, "Is that all there is to it?" It was many years before I experimented with alcohol again.

I would have been happy to go on playing in cafés and restaurants indefinitely. My parents did not consider that an acceptable option. They were willing to see me train as a concert pianist, however, if a good authority vouched for my potential and I devoted myself to disciplined practice.

My piano teacher was one of the best in Paris, and other excellent musicians had praised my playing. But I had not passed the test of playing for someone who really knew the concert stage and its demands. With chutzpah that, again, rose up in me because of my desire to be a musician, I conceived the idea of writing to the great virtuoso Artur Rubinstein to ask if he would consent to see me and hear me play.

As before, my mother wrote a letter. Although he surely received many such requests, I thought it was normal for him to respond, as he did, saying, "Telephone me at Kléber-4183, I fly tonight for a concert in Rome." After all, who could resist my mother, even in epistolary form?

I went to see him on a beautiful morning in September, at his mansion at 22 Square de l'Avenue Foch. I arrived punctually at 10:30 a.m., almost overcome with nervousness. A butler ushered me to a room filled with Impressionist paintings and a magnificent Steinway. Half an hour later Rubinstein arrived in a black robe with red piping—I half expected him to be in concert attire— and said, "Let's talk."

I had no voice. I was paralyzed with shyness. He said kindly, "Go to the piano." I sat down at the Steinway, my fingers trembling.

"What do you want to play?" the maestro asked.

My dream was to play Chopin for him, but I thought if I played Chopin he would think it was because my technique was not good enough to play Liszt. So I began a Liszt rhapsody, reluctantly, because I wasn't good at it, no. 11 in A Minor. Rubinstein stopped me after a few bars. "Look, first, you should play it a little differently. But I cannot judge somebody on Liszt. Could you play Chopin?"

That was all I needed to hear. I played Nocturne no. 16 in B-flat Major. My fingers were doing whatever they did. I could not control anything. The music was going along, but I felt horrible. At the end of the piece, he said, "You are a very brave man."

I thought, "Oh, my God, what did I do now?" I wanted to disappear.

He said, "This piece is so musically difficult that I haven't played it in thirty years. Horowitz played it. Ignatz Friedman played it. And since Friedman played it so well, I decided never to play it."

I thought that meant, "Here is the door." But he said, "You played that with such passion. You remind me of me playing for Paderewski when I was fifteen. Can you play another nocturne?"

I played the Nocturne no. 15 in F Minor. And then he came and sat beside me and made up chords. That captured my mind, his fingers and mine on the same keys. That and the fact that he was like me, or rather I was like him. I could see that he was making things up, but very well. And he saw that I was making things up, too; he was no fool.

He told me, "You are doing what I did when I was young. Nowadays audiences want every note. What I fooled the Europeans with didn't work in the United States. I had to practice very hard to be recognized there."

He asked me to play some more, and I played a few of my own compositions. He said, "I love what you composed. Your influences seem to be Wagner and Rachmaninoff." I adored Rachmaninoff and took that as the greatest praise I could ever have received. Of Wagner I had only heard the prelude to *Tristan and Isolde*, but I didn't dare tell him that.

I said that I was starting medical school, and that I wondered if I could study both medicine and piano.

He said, "No, that used to be possible at the time of pianists like Moriz Rosenthal"—a pupil of Liszt's who studied philosophy at the University of Vienna in the 1880s—"but nowadays you have to practice like a maniac."

He continued, "You are a fantastic pianist; you are one of the best. You remind me not only of me, but of Samson François. He played for me on that same piano."

The comparison took my breath away. Samson François was my favorite among the younger generation of pianists.

Rubinstein went on, "You must perfect your technique. You need to practice Czerny, Scarlatti, Bach, and Mozart. You should abandon medicine and start right now."

Hearing "You must perfect your technique" crushed me. The praise went in one ear and out the other, while the criticism echoed over and over in my mind. I told myself later, "If that's how it is, I'm not going to become a performer, because it's too much work." I didn't want to do scales. And I had difficulty reading scores: that would be a terrible hindrance and embarrassment in a conservatory program or in trying to work with professional musicians.

The die was cast. I would become a doctor.

A few weeks later, in October 1969, I began medical studies at one of the University of Paris's teaching hospitals, Hôpital Cochin, a fifteen-minute walk from home. I was only sixteen years old, two or three years younger than everyone else in the class. I was painfully conscious of not fitting in. But then chemistry captured my imagination, thanks in large part to a brilliant teacher named Jean Durup, and I became engaged intellectually in what I was doing. I saw aesthetic beauty in how chemical bonds formed and how different arrangements of atoms and molecules created different substances. My mother had pushed me into a field that I would soon come to love.

The following year my older brother, Jean-Claude, followed me into medical school. (Eva also studied medicine in due course. Jean-Claude became a distinguished immunologist and Eva a fine surgeon.) Thereafter Jean-Claude and I often prepared for our exams together and throughout medical school we had a great intellectual partnership, the closest and most stimulating that I have ever had with anyone. But this also meant that in my mind I carried the burden of Jean-Claude's prospective progress, as well as my own. Having taken the exams before, I had to be sure that he knew what to expect. My anxiety left me unable to sleep, and I was soon exhausted from insomnia.

Desperate for more rest at night and less anxiety during the day, I went to our family doctor, Dr. Gilbert Meshaka. He listened to me carefully and prescribed a two-week supply of Tranxene, a tranquilizer that belongs to a family of drugs called benzodiazepines, or benzos, that includes Ativan, Valium, and Xanax. That helped me get through the ordeal of exams, and thereafter

Dr. Meshaka prescribed Tranxene or another benzo intermittently when my anxiety became unmanageable.

In 1977 I completed my basic medical training. Having passed the medical internship test, I did internships in neurology, internal medicine, and cardiology. In French hospitals then there was usually wine on the table in *la salle de garde*, the room where interns and residents ate meals and took catnaps when they were on call. One day at lunch I decided to have a drink. It ruined the rest of the workday, and I concluded that alcohol did not agree with me.

After my internships, I did a residency in nephrology at Saint-Cloud Hospital in the western suburbs of Paris. Saint-Cloud had one of the best-known alcoholism treatment programs in France, and I sometimes admitted patients when they arrived to enter the program. They all had a similar look, pale and grim, that I later saw among my fellow patients in detox wards and rehab centers in the United States, not to mention when I looked in the mirror during binges, after I became an alcoholic.

What puzzled me as a young physician, however, was that the criterion for admission was a minimum period of abstinence from alcohol. It seemed there was only help for those not in the most immediate need of it. I wondered about those alcoholics who were in even worse shape. But I never stopped to question the requirement of abstinence before treatment and its implicit assumption that alcoholism was largely a question of willpower.

After much debate, I decided that cardiology was the medical specialty for me. France had a strong tradition of research and training in cardiology, and I did a cardiology residency in Paris. But I wondered how the field looked from an American perspective. Ever since I had seen the Statue of Liberty at the age of fifteen, I had harbored a dream of spending at least a year in America, and my heart was set on New York, the city of Woody Allen, Leonard Bernstein, and Carnegie Hall.

I arrived in October 1983, for a fellowship in the cardiology division of the department of medicine at New York Hospital–Cornell University Medical College, where I worked under and with Drs. John Laragh, Jeffrey Borer, and Paul Kligfield. Laragh was the head of the cardiology division and had recently been on the cover of *Time* magazine for working out some of the mechanisms of hypertension. This cover story popularized the concept of hypertension as "the silent killer." Jeff Borer and Paul Kligfield were also enormously talented and productive people, and Jeff headed up the hospital's division of cardiovascular pathophysiology.

The research project that Jeff Borer and Paul Kligfield were running, and which I joined, was an effort to refine the accuracy of the heart stress test. False normal results were common with the stress test, meaning that serious heart disease was routinely being missed. Over time we developed a new form of the test that took the individual's heart rate into account, and we published a number of papers on the ST/HR (ST segment/heart rate) slope. This innovation enabled very precise differential diagnosis of mild, moderate, or severe coronary heart disease.

As part of this work, I often read EKGs and twenty-four-hour monitors known as Holters in a windowless room in the heart station. The room had only one door, and I sometimes experienced a rising sense of anxiety as I sat there. It wasn't claustrophobia.

Rather, if someone came in suddenly, there was no way for me to dart out without being seen. That was a problem not because I was avoiding work, but because I felt subject to scrutiny without notice and I was always ready to think that I would then be found inadequate. I was sure that the only reason people were nice to me was that I was a novelty, the French guy.

One day Paul Kligfield came around with a woman from the Payne Whitney Psychiatric Clinic and said they were interested in heart rate variability in people with panic attacks. It was the first time I had heard the term *panic attack*, which was not yet widely used. When they told me the diagnostic criteria for susceptibility to panic attacks, I realized I fit the bill.

To calm stage jitters before a talk, some of my colleagues used beta-blockers, which reduce symptoms such as heart pounding and shakiness. Beta-blockers did nothing to ease my anxieties, however. Valium and Xanax worked somewhat better. But I never liked how I felt on benzos, and it is best not to take them too much because they induce dependency and impair memory and other cognitive function. The result was that I sometimes paged myself out of meetings in order to avoid possibly revealing the extent of my anxiety.

Day to day, I worked most closely with Paul Kligfield. We developed a friendly rapport, and when I lived in a sublet on West 60th Street we usually walked part of the way home together. I actually walked a few blocks more than necessary, doubling back uptown at 57th Street, because I enjoyed our conversations so much. On Friday evenings Paul often invited me to join other colleagues and him for a beer. I did so a few times, confining myself to soft drinks, but the point of a bar is booze and I soon stopped going.

During my first years at New York Hospital–Cornell, a few of my research colleagues encouraged me to make research my lifelong career. They said, "You'll have a good salary, you'll have manageable hours, and you won't have to put up with patients calling you in the middle of the night to ask if they should take Tylenol or aspirin. We're allergic to patients."

"But I like seeing patients," I said.

They thought I was crazy, but I really enjoyed treating patients. The ability to help people with their heart problems gave me tremendous joy and satisfaction. For that reason I was keen to do clinical fellowships and an accelerated residency at New York Hospital–Cornell—accelerated because of the residencies I had already done in France. I wanted to start treating patients again. That was the best part of medicine for me.

Interestingly, I never experienced anxiety during patient consultations or panic during medical emergencies, because they took all my attention off myself and engaged my mind solely on the patient's problems. In fact, being on the front lines of cardiac care was the best antipanic medicine for me. I functioned best in crises when quick decisions had to be made to stabilize or save a patient.

I continued to do research for several years, but in the summer of 1986, on completion of only one year of a normal two-year American clinical fellowship in cardiology, I was promoted to assistant professor of medicine at Cornell University Medical College and assistant attending physician at New York Hospital. My workload became about a third research, a third treating patients, and a third teaching.

This was the beginning of a golden period in my life. I was doing a job I loved and I was exactly where I wanted to be. The next year my social life also took a turn for the better. I began seeing another physician at New York Hospital. And I began playing the piano regularly at parties.

Through the woman I was seeing, I met Murat Sungar, who was then Turkey's consul general in New York. Murat was an enthusiastic musician, and he loved the songs I wrote. He began arranging them, and we began recording them in rough and ready fashion with a soundboard that I bought but that Murat was much better at using.

Murat gave great parties, glittering affairs that brought together the elite of Turkey's diplomatic corps and expatriate community among other guests, and he pressed me to play at them. Playing for a trusted friend in private, or in public at a recital or in a restaurant or hotel lobby, where people were free to come or go, respond to the music or not, wasn't difficult for me. But playing in a social setting, where I would have to confront the reactions of fellow guests, triggered all my anxiety about being inadequate and an impostor.

Just attending Murat's parties made me feel tongue-tied and shy. I tried to put up a good front and chatter away like other guests, but inside I was a bundle of raw nerves. I discovered that one or two shots of Scotch—although I hated the taste and almost had to hold my nose to get it down—produced a remarkable relaxation effect. The alcohol calmed my anxiety as benzos had never done, and without any of the benzos' unpleasant side effects. It also raised my sense of self-esteem. I felt calm, expansive, lucid, completely at ease. I could chat enjoyably with a perfect stranger.

When much later I began attending Alcoholics Anonymous meetings, I discovered this was a standard refrain: "I never felt okay in myself," "I never fit in," or "I never really relaxed"—until they started drinking. With a couple of drinks I could play the piano with confidence in my ability to entertain. At Murat's delighted behest I transformed his parties for an hour or more into a combination cabaret and concert hall, stimulating the other guests to dance, sing along, or listen raptly as I played their requests and my own favorites. As soon as I arrived at one of his parties, or before long at parties given by other friends, people began asking me to sit down at the piano and play.

And so it was that I became an occasional moderate social drinker, and I remained one for many years.

After I went into private practice, however, for the first time in my working life I did not have a guaranteed income, and I became increasingly concerned about my finances as my practice hovered above the break-even point for month after month. I worried about my age. I was now over forty, and I felt that time might be running out for me to marry and have children. I feared that I would never achieve a big enough income to support a family. Or to provide the kind of lifestyle that my father had provided thanks to his successful business career.

Beyond that I feared I would lose everything and become completely impoverished and homeless.

The logic of anxiety is that it can latch onto any idea, rational or irrational, and lock it into a feedback loop that keeps strengthening in intensity and irrationality. If this feedback loop is not broken soon enough, it becomes impossible to reason with the fear and dread that it generates. The fear and dread may take no specific form, but rather be an overwhelming sense that horrible things are going to happen.

Until this period, my anxiety had been a background hum that I could turn down for days or even weeks, if never entirely switch off. It flared up from time to time, but then subsided thanks to a change in circumstances or a medication like Tranxene or Valium. But over the next two years, my anxiety became a more and more insistent distraction, and I ceased to be able to turn the volume down.

I began to have paralyzing panic attacks that made me feel like I was losing my mind. The attacks began innocuously enough with a twitching in my calf muscles. This sort of twitching of bundles of muscle fibers, or fascicles, is called benign idiopathic fasciculation. A fluttering eyelid tic is a common example. The fasciculation is benign because it will cause no harm in and of itself, and idiopathic because it has no known origin. In my anxious moments, however, the fasciculations increased until they felt like worms under my skin. The next symptoms were tightness in my chest and internal trembling. I felt as if I couldn't breathe and would suffocate. And then unstoppable panic took over my whole being.

I was already seeing a shrink, and he referred me to a psychopharmacologist, who tried me on a vast range of medications at different doses. Nothing helped.

Worn out by accumulating stress, I began increasing my intake of the one drug that brought relief: alcohol. Talk about a slippery slope. The more I drank to ease my anxiety, stave off panic, and counter draining insomnia, the more I had to drink for the same effect.

At this point, alcohol ceased to be a means to relaxation and became an end in itself. I managed okay during the morning and the middle of the day. But every afternoon the craving for alcohol welled up in me like a flood tide. I resisted the craving for as long as I could, a day, two days, a week or more, but then it captured me and I binged.

I was an accident waiting to happen. When, in August 1997, I wound up in New York Hospital with acute withdrawal seizures that nearly killed me, it was devastating—and a great relief. I thought, "I am no longer hiding my drinking from anyone. Now I will get proper treatment and recover."

3. Under Treatment and "In Recovery"

PHYSICIANS ARE NOTORIOUSLY BAD PATIENTS who often inhibit their recovery by trying to run their own cases. In the last days of August 1997, as I recuperated in New York Hospital from massive seizures suffered during acute alcohol withdrawal, I wondered if I had been adding to my problems in that way, despite my best efforts not to do so.

For the previous nine months, despite recurring denial of the extent of my drinking problem, I had been trying to find someone who could run my case and manage my treatment for anxiety and alcohol dependency. A daisy chain of referrals sent me to a number of highly regarded and credentialed specialists, none of whom ever proposed a comprehensive treatment plan, although some of them did not hesitate to criticize the way my referring psychiatrist treated me. By default, I was forced to coordinate my care as best I could on my own.

From my psychopharmacologist I received prescriptions for tranquilizers, benzos like Valium and Xanax. Saying they were helpful for anxiety as well as depression, the psychopharmacologist also prescribed selective serotonin reuptake inhibitors, or SSRIs, like Prozac and Zoloft. We tried them at various dosages alone and in combination. None of the permutations were effective, and all of them had unpleasant side effects.

The psychiatrist I was seeing for alcohol dependency knew I was taking these medications, and he also prescribed Antabuse (disulfiram). Antabuse, which stays active in the body for five days, blocks the liver from breaking down alcohol, so that if you drink on it you almost immediately experience the nastiest symptoms of severe intoxication: accelerated heart rate, flushed skin, shortness of breath, nausea, and vomiting. Keep drinking and you could die. Taking Antabuse is a form of aversion therapy, the idea being that the fear of becoming very ill or dying will scare the patient enough not to drink.

Aversion therapy with Antabuse has not worked well in general, because it does not affect the craving for alcohol and patients know that if they stop taking Antabuse for five days it will clear their systems and they can drink again safely, so to speak. It has been shown effective only in a minority of patients. Very few problem drinkers can stick to an Antabuse regimen, and I was not one of them. Instead, like many people who try Antabuse, I played games with it. When I was looking forward to attending a party on the weekend, I stopped taking it at the beginning of the week so that it cleared my system. In one instance I simply succumbed to mounting craving and drank even though I had the medication in my bloodstream, which flushed my face and made my heart pound. When I reported this to my psychiatrist and said I thought it was dangerous for me to be on Antabuse, he agreed and immediately took me off it.

I tried acupuncture and hypnosis therapy, both of which had zero effect, and I consulted a highly recommended specialist in cognitive behavioral therapy (CBT), which I was told could help me avoid and resolve emotional experiences that triggered drinking. He seemed more interested in turning me from a binge liquor drinker into a moderate wine drinker.

Progressively, I increased my attendance at Alcoholics Anonymous meetings, read about AA's history and philosophy, and tried unsuccessfully to advance through the famous twelve steps. I always found benefit in the wisdom of AA, but fearing that my religious agnosticism might keep the program from working for me, I also tried Rational Recovery (RR).

RR appealed to me greatly. Its central premises are that alcoholism is not a biological disease but a voluntary behavior and that the individual can overcome it with his or her own intellectual resources. In my experience, however, the "power within" celebrated by RR and the "higher power" of AA both proved puny in the face of the overwhelming power of my anxiety-driven craving for alcohol. Either I was seriously lacking in willpower and/or spirituality, or my alcoholism had a fundamental biological component that would have to be addressed medically.

Determined to miss nothing that might help, I maintained a regular exercise regimen and did yoga to promote relaxation and reduce anxiety. I got real benefit from both and in the big scheme of things they supported my overall health, but they could not themselves resolve my lifelong chronic anxiety or my more recent heavy drinking.

When I was not in the midst of a binge, the effort to avoid drinking consumed all my time and energy. Every day I went to AA at least once, did self-hypnosis several times, and spent hours on the phone with AA contacts and friends. I saw my primary psychiatrist and an acupuncturist three or four times a week each, visited the CBT therapist once a week, and went to the psychopharmacologist once every two weeks.

I confided my drinking problem to a good friend and colleague at New York Hospital, Boris Pasche, a talented young cancer researcher from Switzerland with M.D. and Ph.D. degrees from the Karolinska Institute in Sweden and postdoctoral training at Harvard. Boris, who has since joined the faculty of Northwestern University Medical School, where he directs the university's Cancer Genetics Program, is also an expert in homeopathy. He treated me without charge, and we experimented with various herbs and minerals alleged to bolster mood, support liver function, moderate craving for alcohol, and so on. There were no positive results apart from the substantial benefit of Boris's friendship and support.

Boris told me that a medicine to reduce craving for alcohol had recently come on the market in Europe. It was called acamprosate, and based on what he'd read, he said, "it sounds like exactly what you need." Acamprosate (sold under the brand name Campral) was already available in France, and I asked my mother to send me some. Alcohol withdrawal triggers the release of excitatory neurotransmitters, especially glutamate, and acamprosate was thought to hold promise because it blocks glutamate receptors in the brain. I took acamprosate in accordance with the manufacturer's directions for its use, and found that it had no effect on my symptoms.

My experience with acamprosate, like that with Antabuse, turns out not to have been atypical. Later on in rehab, I learned to say,

"I am a good person with a bad disease," but lying in New York Hospital in August 1997, I felt confused by the failures of the treatments, and I was inclined to blame myself for them. Although John Schaefer buoyed my sagging spirits when he was adamant that alcoholism is a disease, not a flaw, I still could not shake a sense of shame. And it was dismaying, to say the least, to learn from John and from Elizabeth Khuri that there was no proven protocol for recovery from alcoholism. Medications, twelve-step programs, and rehab simply did not offer definite solutions either in themselves or in combination with one another. There seemed to be no way out.

Still, I knew I was in the best hands. I had complete trust in Liz Khuri's world-class expertise as an addiction researcher at Rockefeller University, and her warmth and compassion were an especial help during terrible times.

"I am a good person with a bad disease." That is exactly how Liz and John acted toward me. They always greeted me with a smile and looked me in the eye when we spoke. Unfortunately, that wasn't the case with most of the other physicians I saw during this thirteen-day hospital stay, including those I knew and had a good rapport with. Although I'd try to speak to them—about my drinking, or any other topics—they resisted the contact. Certainly they never looked me in the eye, which is what they would have done had my medical problems resulted from any other form of illness. It was striking how strained their manner was. In addition, none of my close working colleagues came to see me, even though we all always visited colleagues who were in the hospital for other reasons besides addiction. I don't doubt some of them behaved this way thinking it would avoid embarrassment for me, but if so, their intentions backfired: I became ashamed that doctors were too embarrassed by the disease of addiction to treat me like a normal human being.

Science has established that in all human cultures, as well as in many other social animals, there is this common truth: to shun is to shame. This fact should long ago have altered how the majority of physicians treat patients with addiction. It hasn't.

We live in a world that assumes everything is fixable—by experts or money, or a combination of both. And if the "experts" can't solve a problem, well, then either the problem doesn't really exist or it falls to the sufferer to fix it alone. We like to see ourselves as strong creatures, up to meeting all life's challenges. We flatter ourselves that willpower can overcome all obstacles.

That was the heart of Rational Recovery's appeal for me. The fantasy that I could think and will myself into freedom from addiction was enormously attractive. Reflecting on my past as I recuperated, I could see that I had exerted significant willpower in my life: taking the *baccalauréat* early; auditioning for Artur Rubinstein; becoming a good cardiologist.

But at the same time, based on what I had seen in AA meetings, there was no shortage of willpower among alcoholics, some of whom functioned at a high level in demanding professions and other circumstances. (Not to mention the willpower that all addicts show in obtaining whatever addictive substance it is that makes them feel better.) What AA and Narcotics Anonymous assert is that willpower, no matter how strong, is inadequate against severe addiction. That too made sense to me. I was finding much wisdom in the first of AA's original twelve steps: "We admitted that we were powerless over alcohol—that our lives had become unmanageable."

There was one thing the alcoholics I met in AA seemed to have in common: they all said they drank to relieve lifelong emotional pain, usually connected with an anxiety, mood, or personality disorder. I found this remarkable.

The fact that every alcoholic seemed to have a preaddiction morbidity like my own encouraged me to think that alcoholism must fundamentally be a biological disease. And because it was a biological disease, it couldn't just be addressed by willpower or positive thinking: it had to be addressed medically.

In the last days of my hospital stay, I began to hope that the worst was behind me. Taken out of my daily routine, with its triggers for anxiety and drinking, and inspired by my talks with John Schaefer and Liz Khuri and their confidence that I could achieve a full recovery, I felt a deep inner quietness and clarity of mind. In his books Bill W., the cofounder of AA, described these sensations as heralding the spiritual awakening that ushered him into lifelong sobriety. I had heard similar accounts in AA meetings.

The next time Liz Khuri came to see me, I told her about my experiences and said, "I have always considered myself an agnostic, but I think I'm feeling a spiritual awakening. It makes me feel that I will never drink again."

Liz said, "The sensations you're describing fit the model of all that we know about spiritual awakenings in people with addiction. It could be some kind of miracle, and after what you've been through, you deserve it. Remember what I keep telling you; you're a child of the universe, and maybe the universe is looking out for you now."

With cautious optimism verging on outright confidence, Liz and I prepared for my discharge from the hospital after a thirteen-day stay. I would continue to consult her on an out-patient basis at her Cornell office, and I would also see John Schaefer again in a month for routine follow-up.

Before I left the hospital, I told John that I would be happy to give a talk at medical grand rounds at Cornell to share my experience with other doctors and encourage those with a dependency to seek help.

"It's a noble offer, my boy," he said, "but you should only do that after you've been sober for five years and you know you're out of the woods. Plenty of doctors still think alcoholism is a weakness, not a disease, and some of them will try to use whatever you say against you. It's best to keep a low profile until you know you're well."

John Schaefer's warning aside, the next week was a joyful one. My spirits rose day by day, as I looked forward to resuming my normal life, and before long my cardiology practice, without the burden of alcohol cravings. I delighted in playing the piano and in Joan's company, and we spent a wonderful weekend at a Victorian resort hotel on a lake in upstate New York.

And then, without knowing why, I drank.

In retrospect, I was becoming overexcited about the future, and with that nervous agitation came renewed anxiety about making my practice pay and about making the lifelong commitment to Joan that she wanted. In any case, for whatever reason, the binge was on, and despite my protests, Joan overreacted and called EMS. It was an understandable decision on her part, given the seizures I had experienced in acute withdrawal only three weeks before. When EMS arrived, I was furious, but too tired to argue, and soon found myself being detoxed in the ER at New York Hospital.

Liz Khuri now advised that I should go straight from the ER into residential rehab. She thought of the Betty Ford Clinic in California, but it was full up. There was room at Clear Spring Hospital in the New York suburbs, so that was where I reluctantly agreed to go. I felt pushed into rehab, but more than that I felt bitterly disappointed in myself for drinking only days after a spiritual epiphany.

At the same time, I hoped that rehab would be the answer I needed. In AA some people said it was helpful, and some said it was not.

Joan drove me to Clear Spring. I arrived with only the clothes on my back and in a state of bleak depression. My credit cards were in my wallet in my apartment in New York, and the hospital required a $5,000 deposit before I could be admitted. Joan generously used her credit card for the deposit, trusting that I would immediately repay her when I was discharged, which I did.

Clear Spring was the Ritz of rehab, a beautiful place with the amenities of a five-star resort. It drew affluent patients from the New York metropolitan area and across the country, and a number of celebrities and wealthy people were in residence, as I soon learned.

We have all become used to seeing celebrities caught in the glare of the paparazzi's flashbulbs as they go through the revolving door of rehab. After several extended stays of my own in rehab, I would suggest that this is not because celebrities are particularly lacking in willpower, spirituality, or positive attitude. The truth is that every addicted patient receives not as much rehab as he or she needs, but as much as he or she can afford. But perhaps that is getting ahead of the story a little too much.

For the first couple of days at Clear Spring I was continuing to detox, and then I saw Dr. R. for an intake interview and assessment. To my surprise the interview did not involve a thorough discussion of my medical history and my drinking, and it was all over in ten minutes. Dr. R. prescribed Luvox (fluvoxamine), an SSRI, and naltrexone, an anticraving agent like acamprosate. Dr. R. said, "Luvox is good for compulsive behavior like alcoholism, and the naltrexone will get your cravings under control." (I continued to take both medications for some time after I left Clear Spring, but they did nothing to alter my drinking.)

A few days after our first meeting, Dr. R. saw me again briefly to ask how I was feeling on the medication. In a three-week stay at Clear Spring, these were my only contacts with an M.D. But I thought I was in expert hands at last and should trust the process. And my stay at Clear Spring was restful and restorative. In the absence of a proven treatment, the main benefit of rehab is that it provides an addicted patient with a much-needed respite from alcohol or another addictive substance or behavior.

For alcoholics, the daily routine at Clear Spring began with taking turns reading from *Living Sober* and other AA-approved books. Later there were classes in coping skills such as how to refuse a drink, AA meetings, and a good deal of free time, in which I took walks, talked to fellow patients, and played a beautiful piano they had there. One of the people my piano playing attracted was a clarinetist for one of the country's leading symphony orchestras, a very pleasant guy who was being treated for depression. We had many good conversations, but I imagined that he thought I was a low-life drinker, whereas he had been diagnosed with a respectable disease.

In this regard I told Dr. R. and everyone else at Clear Spring, as I told all my caregivers, "My fundamental problem isn't alcohol, it's anxiety. If my anxiety is resolved, I won't drink."

Dr. R. responded, as all my caregivers did, "If you stop drinking, you won't be so anxious anymore."

After three weeks at Clear Spring, I was prepared to give her the benefit of the doubt on the subject. Thanks to the routine of rehab, removed from daily stresses and strains, I felt remarkably calm and peaceful, if not as inspired and hopeful as I was in the last days of my admission to New York Hospital. The counselors at Clear Spring all told me I was doing great and predicted that I was on the way to a full recovery from alcoholism.

A month later I was back. Once I was out of the rehab cocoon, my anxiety, and following that my craving for alcohol, returned in full force despite the Luvox and naltrexone I was continuing to take as directed. Said a counselor with almost maternal concern, "You've lost weight."

My second stint of rehab at Clear Spring had lasted a week when a physician came and spoke to me in the morning. With great earnestness he said, "You need to stay here longer this time. Your first stay with us was too short, and that's why you relapsed. What you absolutely need for your health is to stay for two months or so."

"That seems like a very long time, Doctor," I said.

"In the context of your whole life, assuming you are able to enjoy a normal life span, it's a very short time. And I am only recommending this because you have an extremely severe addiction, and your life depends on treating it with all the seriousness it requires. I am not exaggerating in the slightest when I say that for you this is a matter of life or death."

"What do you mean? I'm going to die if I don't stay here for at least two months?"

He looked at me with grave concern and said, "Consider the state you were in when you arrived a few days ago." He gave me an encouraging smile and said, "I won't press you more on this right now. Carry on with the rest of the day's activities, and we'll discuss it again tomorrow."

Late in the morning, the sky clouded over and it began to rain steadily. At lunchtime the doctor approached me again and said, "There's a problem."

"What's the problem?" I asked.

"Your insurance won't pay for you to stay here any longer."

"Why not? They paid last time."

"We checked and double-checked. You are maxed out on their coverage for addiction treatment. Are you willing to pay out of pocket?"

"How much is it?"

He hemmed and hawed for a moment, looked around to see if any other patients were within earshot, and then almost whispered, "At your current level of accommodation and treatment, it is a little over five hundred dollars a day."

It was a shocking amount. "I'm not sure I can afford that much." I wondered how much the celebrities and wealthy people in the private bungalows were paying.

"Then you have to leave."

"When?"

"Right now, today. The insurance will pay only through this morning."

"But is that safe? You said my treatment here was a matter of life or death."

"No, no, that's not what I said at all. Don't be dramatic. These things are not black-and-white."

"But you told me that if I don't stay, it will be terrible for me."

"Let's not exaggerate," the doctor said.

"But how will I get back to New York? I don't know if I can reach anyone to come pick me up."

"There is a train station not so far away. You can walk there and get a train to the city."

I was trembling with anxiety. I pointed outside the window and said, "In this downpour? Can't I stay tonight and make arrangements to leave tomorrow morning? I can pay for one night at least."

The doctor stood up, straightened his white coat, and said, "This is a hospital, not a hotel. I'm sure you'll do very well." Then he turned on his heel and left without another word.

I got my things, a few changes of clothes, and put them in the paper shopping bag in which Joan had brought them to New York Hospital.

I didn't know what to do. Once again I had no credit cards, and only a few crumpled bills that were in my pocket when Joan called EMS. I doubted there was enough for both a taxi to the train station and a ticket to New York. A counselor I had a nice rapport with passed by and said, "You're leaving us already?"

I explained the situation and he said, "I am sure some other patients will be leaving today. Maybe you can catch a ride with one of them to the station or even all the way to New York City."

I waited through the afternoon. Around six o'clock an eighteen-year-old kid I had talked to earlier in the week came into the reception area with his things. Other patients said he looked like a young James Caan. He was finishing a rehab stint, by no means his first, for a cocaine problem. His parents were coming to bring him home to New York City, and when they arrived they kindly offered to take me along in their black Mercedes.

We left without any dinner around seven p.m. I was full of rage and thought, "I'll show these rehab idiots. I'm going to get home and have a nice big drink." My fellow patient's parents were going to drop me in front of my place. There was a liquor store around the block, and realizing I had just enough cash, I said, "Oh, leave me at the far corner, please."

I went into the liquor store and bought a bottle of Stoli. That began a binge that lasted, like all binges, until I could no longer drink because I felt so horrible. After I detoxed myself with Valium, I called my insurance company and learned that my coverage included $15,000 for addiction treatment and that this was a total rather than a yearly figure. Three weeks at Clear Spring in September and one week in November had consumed all $15,000.

I was already paying for my alcoholism-related visits to doctors and other therapists to the tune of $2,300 a month out of pocket, and from now on I would also have to pay for any ER visits, detoxes, and rehab stays myself. Because I was not practicing medicine while I was ill, only a few more stints of rehab, at least at Clear Spring prices, would exhaust all my resources.

For that reason, and because I was outraged by the abrupt, callous shift from "You must stay in rehab here a long time if you want to live" to "If you can't or won't pay, get out," I contemplated suing Clear Spring and was referred to a successful malpractice lawyer who was described admiringly as "a real shark." He grilled me like he was cross-examining me in court and then said I had an excellent case. But he wisely asked if I was willing to burn all my bridges as a cardiologist at New York Hospital by waging a lawsuit while I was still ill with alcoholism. Hearing that, and recalling John Schaefer's advice to keep a low profile until I had at least five years of sobriety, I decided not to sue.

As part of keeping a low profile, I also decided that when I had to go to an ER to detox, I would no longer go to New York Hospital. Fortunately in a big city like New York there were many other options. Joan agreed that if she ever felt she had to intervene and call EMS again, she would make sure that I was taken to another hospital besides my own.

Another step I took at this time was to put all my expenses on automatic bill payment. I wanted to streamline things as much as possible, so that I could concentrate on getting well and not worry about having my phone or the electricity turned off because I was bingeing and forgot to pay the bill. People in AA told horror stories about things like that.

Hoping that it would help me break free of the binge-drinking cycle, my mother urged me to come to Paris for a visit. Liz Khuri agreed that this might be helpful, and she gave me the name of a Paris psychiatrist, Dr. T. I went to see him shortly after arriving in Paris, and I found a very congenial and sympathetic man with a thick beard who looked like the great nineteenth-century founder of Zionism, Theodor Herzl.

Dr. T. made no secret of the fact that he had himself been a narcotics addict, and I felt it was a great help that he understood craving from the point of view of the addicted patient. He was also a child of Holocaust survivors, and on that basis he refused to charge me. He was completely nonjudgmental. He agreed to let me conduct an experiment, although he predicted it would be useless: I would drink before and during a session to see if that enabled me to talk more freely about emotional issues that triggered drinking.

My sister-in-law, Fabienne, drove me to the appointment; there was a bottle of Scotch on my lap. The experiment was a total failure. I certainly talked to Dr. T. freely, but we hit on no great insights or undiscovered issues.

Talk therapy in individual and/or group sessions is a standard part of addiction treatment. There were regular talk therapy sessions at Clear Spring, every AA meeting was a form of group therapy, and I had been seeing shrinks for anxiety long before I started drinking. But it is hard to analyze yourself and take appropriate action, if indeed there is any appropriate action to take, when you are in the grip of anxiety and panic or when your brain is pickled in alcohol. Later I learned that AA and CBT are most effective for addicted patients, although the results even then are not remarkably positive, after at least six to eighteen months of abstinence.

In the best circumstances, talk therapy can be a frustrating process of chasing symptoms. For those born with temperaments that include, or dispose them toward, serious anxiety, mood, or personality disorders, identifying triggers for anxiety and depression does nothing to address their biological origins and mechanisms. I don't mean to say that talk therapy has no benefits, only to note its obvious medical limits.

During our talks Dr. T. repeated several times, "Addiction is a spiritual problem. Why can't you get spirituality?"

"I don't understand," I said. "Please tell me how."

"You'll grasp it in time."

"Meanwhile I'll die waiting for spiritual enlightenment."

Instead of brushing that off, Dr. T. said sympathetically, "Yes, that is possible. But we must try our best to get you well just the same." He advised me to go into a private rehab clinic in Paris for the rest that had been cut short in my second stay at Clear Spring.

I had lived outside France for so many years that I no longer qualified for government-paid health care, and the private clinic was expensive, if not as costly as Clear Spring. Although I paid part of it, my mother bore most of the bill, which left me feeling bad. But I stayed there for almost four weeks in November and December, and the rest did me good.

Before I left Paris, I paid a call on my old boss, Raymond Barre. In 1980–81, as a young doctor doing obligatory national service in the French army, I had been chosen to inaugurate the position of physician to the prime minister and cabinet of France. Barre was then prime minister, and we had formed a very warm relationship over our shared love of classical music. When I applied for cardiology fellowships in the United States, I did so with the benefit of Barre's handwritten letter of recommendation.

Raymond Barre did not know that I had become an alcoholic, and I was relieved that I was in good enough shape to see him without looking ill. At the end of a long chat he said, "You know, *cher ami*, we must initiate the procedure for you to receive the Legion of Honor for your contributions to the image of France abroad and to cardiology. My secretary informs me that next year it will be fifteen years since your M.D. thesis, and that is the earliest date a physician can receive it."

I was stunned. My guilty conscience made me want to blurt out, "But if you haven't heard, I am now a hopeless drunk and a total failure. Don't embarrass yourself by proposing me." But I kept quiet out of my own embarrassment and shame, and I left Barre's office thinking that in the process of assembling a dossier to submit me for the Legion of Honor, he would learn about my alcoholism in some other way and drop the idea.

Returning to New York in mid-December, I wrestled with the notion that addiction is a spiritual problem. It occurred to me that I knew an expert on spirituality, my friend Elie Wiesel. When Elie won the 1986 Nobel Peace Prize, the judges saluted him as "one of the [world's] most important spiritual leaders and guides."

Elie had become a good friend many years before, and we spoke a lot on the phone about this and that. He and his wife, Marion, lived near me on the Upper East Side, and Elie often invited me for long chats on Saturdays. Afterward, Elie and Marion sometimes asked me to stay and observe Shabbos with them or to spend the rest of the weekend in the country with them and other friends.

Elie did not know about my problem drinking. To talk to him about spirituality and addiction, I first had to get my nerve up by having a couple of drinks. I telephoned him in Florida, where he and Marion were spending a winter vacation.

"Elie," I said, "I am an alcoholic."

"What?"

"Yes, and I was told I need spiritual guidance. Can I ask you for some advice?"

Elie said, "I am devastated to hear this . . . just devastated . . . just devastated. You should seek medical help, Olivier."

"I have the best medical help there is. I am surrounded by that. But I have been told alcoholism is a problem of spirituality. Jung said it is due to a spiritual vacuum. I don't know what that means. I don't understand it. Can you help me?"

Elie said again, "Ah, you should see a doctor." Throughout the rest of the conversation, one of the briefest we ever had, he kept repeating those words and saying, "I am just devastated, just devastated."

I was devastated that Elie had no spiritual guidance for me. But in hindsight I do not think it was fair to expect him to explain the spiritual nature of addiction. Addiction is undoubtedly a crisis of the human spirit. But insofar as that is true, it seems to me that the spiritual crisis of addiction is a late-stage development of a process with fundamentally biological origins and mechanisms. Surely there is no way to analyze the preaddiction morbidity of a lifelong mood disorder, such as the very anxious temperament I was born with, in spiritual terms.

At the time of my phone call to Elie Wiesel, however, I did not have any of this hindsight perspective. I was simply bewildered about the nature of my alcoholism and desperate to seize any opportunity to defeat it.

Over the winter of 1997–98 I stayed sober when I could, and strove to limit the health impact of my binges when I couldn't. The key time of the day for me was late afternoon. That was when my craving for alcohol began to build. Some days I fought the craving successfully, although the struggle left me feeling awful.

Craving can be an elusive concept, because it has physical, emotional, and mental symptoms that come in waves over the course of hours and days, but for me it was a brutal fact of life. At its worst, research has shown, craving for an addictive substance models the hunger for food that starving people feel, releasing the same hormones and activating the same brain areas. The

National Institute on Alcohol Abuse and Alcoholism (NIAAA) has stated that craving for alcohol can be even stronger than hunger or thirst, and that once alcoholism takes hold, the brain perceives alcohol as indispensable to survival.

Thoughts about an addictive substance or behavior can insinuate themselves into an addicted person's consciousness in even the calmest moments and quickly preoccupy the whole mind with anxiety about obtaining it. This is a harrowing experience mentally and emotionally as well as physically, because it is charged with shame and self-loathing for even experiencing the craving.

Craving could propel me into a near-trance state, in which I set out to buy liquor as if someone else were controlling my body and directing my steps. When craving defeated me, I could only hope, pray, and strive to do a better job of resisting it the next day.

I've already mentioned the AA acronym HALT, or Hungry, Angry, Lonely, Tired, the four situations that most foster and exacerbate craving. Eating food does attenuate craving. But at that time I didn't know how to cook for myself, and ordering in food or going out for it did not offer the quicker and much fuller relief of alcohol.

I went to many AA meetings, and twice achieved the AA goal of "90 in 90," ninety meetings in ninety days. Often I went to two, three, or even four AA meetings a day. My sponsor constantly urged me to attend more meetings and said, "There is a chair with your name on it."

Unfortunately AA meetings could trigger powerful cravings for me because of the constant mention of alcohol. Other people in AA said they also had this problem. At the 79th Street Workshop, the last meeting of the day was at ten p.m. Sometimes as I sat there listening to the word *alcohol* being repeated over and over again, I knew that craving had won, and I slipped out to buy a bottle before the liquor stores closed at eleven.

Partly out of denial that I would need to drink more and partly as a safety precaution, I always bought only one bottle and never stockpiled bottles at home. It was all too easy to binge to the point of a lethal blood alcohol level. My other great fears were a fatal gastrointestinal bleed or passing out and suffocating on my own vomit, both also not uncommon occurrences for alcoholics.

When I woke up in the middle of a binge, I checked my eyes in the mirror to make sure they weren't yellow from elevated bilirubin, a sign of serious liver stress. As I did so, I often vowed not to drink that day, and I sometimes succeeded in ending the binge or at least interrupting it for a day or two. Other times I told myself, "You're not strong enough to fight the cravings today. Go with the flow and try not to drink too much." I thought of this as not swimming against the tide, waiting until I could summon more strength for the struggle to stay sober.

The daily question in a binge was how much I would have to drink until I could fall asleep and give my mind and body some rest from anxiety and cravings. If I hadn't had enough, I woke up after only a brief sleep, still thirsty for alcohol.

During the winter, I might wake up in the middle of a binge and see that it was five o'clock and dark outside. Then I wondered, "Is it five a.m. or five p.m.?" Five p.m. meant D-Day, victory, and 5 a.m. meant despair. I went to the window and looked outside into the dark. A fair number of people in the street meant it was five p.m. and I could go down and buy a bottle. Empty streets meant it was five a.m. and there were five hours to get through until the liquor stores opened.

If there was a little liquor left in the apartment, I could sip it and surf with some discomfort to the next bottle. One morning I woke up around seven a.m. needing liquor, but there was none left. Over the next hour, the idea began to grow in my mind that the doorman might have liquor. I went downstairs and asked him, "Do you happen to have any liquor behind the desk?"

Of course he said no, and he would have risked being fired if he either had liquor there or told me that he did. I said, "Ah, you see, it is a little awkward. But the French ambassador to the UN will be here at nine a.m. He's coming directly from the airport. I don't have any liquor in my apartment, and the liquor stores don't open until ten a.m. Are you sure you don't have any liquor you could let me have to greet him with a toast? Of course I will replace it as soon as the liquor stores open."

He told me no, and I went up to my apartment for a restless wait. A little before ten a.m. I went down and told the doorman, "The ambassador was delayed, fortunately, so I can go get something at the liquor store. If he arrives while I'm gone, please tell him I'll be right back." That is the level to which I fell.

Usually I managed my drinking better and woke up with a hangover, but not an unmanageable thirst, so I could spend the morning and early afternoon recouping. I drank lots of coffee, read the papers to stay current with what was going on in the world and exercise my mind, kept myself as well groomed as possible, went to the gym to restore the muscle tone and cardiovascular fitness that I was losing because of drinking, went to my doctors' appointments as often as I could, and attended AA meetings.

Following the advice of AA, I called my sponsor and other people throughout the day, drinking or dry, for support and human contact. I usually drank just before I called my sponsor, because he was sure to encourage me not to drink. He was a good guy I could call from anywhere at any time. I called him drunk in the middle of the night once that winter and said, "I'm finished. My life is over. I'm a zero. I might as well commit suicide."

He said, "Okay. So you want to end your life?"

"Yes, I am calling to say goodbye. My only worry is that I'll screw it up and I'll be worse than dead, paralyzed in a wheelchair."

"In that case I have a suggestion," my sponsor said. "Go to the Thirty-third Street station on the Lexington Avenue line, and when the express train hurtles through, throw yourself in front of it. That way you won't miss."

"Very funny."

"So why don't you go to a meeting?" my sponsor said. "It will help."

Although in depressed moments I sometimes contemplated suicide in a very matter-of-fact way, I was not ready to die, as my sponsor knew. I told myself and others that I did not want to die until I had seen India, a lifelong dream that I still have not fulfilled. Plus I was convinced that right after I died, a cure for alcoholism would be discovered. So I always held on grimly to life and a faint hope of recovery.

My sponsor was a much traveled, much married man, who had lost a good professional career to drinking and who now worked in a very different field at a much lower level. He had several years of sobriety as a narcotics addict as well as an alcoholic, although in accordance with twelve-step practice he only discussed drinking with me. We had a good mutual understanding, but he could be rather doctrinaire, and later that winter he fired me as his "sponsee" because I insisted on going to France for the bar mitzvah of Jean-Claude and Fabienne's son, David.

He said, "Don't go. You're not ready. I've spent hours discussing this with *my* sponsor. If you go, I know you will drink, and when you come back I won't sponsor you anymore."

"What if I go and I don't drink? Will you sponsor me when I come back?"

"No, because I won't understand what has happened."

I ended up going and being with my family. And I didn't drink. But that spelled the end of my relationship with that sponsor, and it was a little while before I found another one.

There are times in a binge when the alcohol induces euphoria and it feels possible to do anything, although of course this is a delusion. I heard tapes of myself playing the piano when I was drunk, rather than just having had a few drinks, and my performance was nothing to write home about. But the euphoria was a great relief while it lasted.

The end stages of a binge turned everything sour with gastrointestinal distress. When I felt the point drawing near where I literally could not drink any more without vomiting, I began detoxing with Valium to prevent acute withdrawal.

Often enough Joan called EMS despite my protests, and they took me to the emergency room. I wound up in the emergency rooms of many different hospitals, except New York Hospital. But the one that EMS took me to most frequently was at St. Luke's–Roosevelt Hospital at 59th Street and Tenth Avenue, which was more or less directly across Manhattan from my apartment on East 63rd Street and which had, and has, a nationally recognized alcoholism treatment program.

All the hospitals followed the same routine, and none was nicer than the others. Hospitals don't treat detoxing alcoholics with the same concern and compassion that they show other patients.

The one thing I wanted to avoid was starting to withdraw from the alcohol while I was still in the waiting room, so I drank until the moment EMS arrived. Then it was a matter of sitting in the hospital for hours feeling weak and awful—I had painful heartburn while withdrawing—with an IV for hydration and periodic doses of a benzo to prevent withdrawal from going into an acute phase. If I wanted to pee, I needed to ask for a urinal. A hospital once detoxed me with phenobarbitol, which made the experience almost pleasant, but every other time I got Valium, which simply kept the experience from becoming a nightmare.

Once people are diagnosed as intoxicated, hospitals don't let them leave until their blood alcohol level falls below a certain point. Otherwise if they walk outside and are hit by a bus, the hospital can be sued for negligence. A couple of times, I got fed up with waiting and snuck out early. On one occasion in the emergency room at St. Luke's–Roosevelt, I discreetly took out my IV and slipped away.

From start to finish, a visit to an emergency room to initiate detox took at least six or seven hours and cost around three hundred dollars for blood tests and so on. It cost much more if I was admitted as an inpatient and stayed four or five days for complete detoxification. Because my insurance coverage for alcoholism had been used up at Clear Spring, I had to pay those bills myself. And in an urban hospital detox ward, one can find oneself locked in for the night with some strange and frightening people.

All things considered, I preferred to administer my own detox treatment at home, taking Valium to prevent acute withdrawal, hydrating myself by drinking lots of fluids, using Prilosec for heartburn, and taking B vitamins, especially B_1, to prevent Wernicke's encephalopathy, a potentially deadly syndrome strongly associated with alcohol abuse and characterized by unsteadiness, visual impairment, and a confused state of mind. One night in March, however, Joan called EMS and they took me to the ER at St. Luke's–Roosevelt. In the detox ward a few hours later, I talked with another alcoholic named Andrew. I learned that he was a research engineer and was leaving soon to go into rehab at High Watch Farm in Connecticut.

"It's where Bill W. wrote *The Twelve and Twelve*," Andrew said, using the AA shorthand for the book *Twelve Steps and Twelve Traditions*. "It's very spiritual. There is a chapel that always makes me feel very peaceful and serene. The surroundings are beautiful, and the food is great."

"It sounds nice," I said, thinking it would be good to give my body an extended break from bingeing and try again to find some spirituality. I was enjoying Andrew's company, and he struck me as knowing what he was talking about. But I figured I could not afford to go to rehab, and I did not want to reveal that money was a concern. Then I decided there was no need to feel embarrassed talking with a fellow alcoholic, and I asked, "Is it expensive?"

He named a figure less than a third of what Clear Spring cost, and I realized that I could afford to try rehab at High Watch Farm. The director of evaluation and services for St. Luke's–Roosevelt's alcoholism program, John Bellamy Taylor, also knew High Watch Farm and gave it a great recommendation. I decided to go there after I finished detoxing in the hospital.

Unlike Clear Spring, with its glitzy patient roster of wealthy people and celebrities, High Watch Farm served a middle-class and working-class population, with a number of Medicaid patients, including ex-cons who were trying to get over heroin addiction. And as at every other rehab I went to except Clear Spring, at High Watch Farm no one had a private room. I was assigned to a room with a young black man named Charles, who was there for cocaine addiction.

I did not know what to make of Charlie at first, but he turned out to be a great guy. He was from a poor neighborhood in New Haven, and he was very devoted to his mother and his church. We had lots of good conversations in the evenings.

In general the spirit of High Watch Farm was as friendly and restful as Andrew said, and I felt much more at home there than at Clear Spring. The first time I heard the song "Amazing Grace" was in High Watch Farm's chapel, and its words of hope, and even more its serene and haunting melody, moved me to tears. It echoed in my mind as I walked outside into the Connecticut countryside and saw an early spring snow shower dusting the trees.

The basic routine was much the same at High Watch Farm as it had been at Clear Spring. There were AA meetings, classes on coping skills such as refusing a drink without embarrassment, lectures, and therapy sessions. The major difference, apart from the lack of rich people, celebrities, and private rooms, was that we all did a few chores every day. I didn't mind that at all. It was a pleasure to do simple, necessary things with the other patients.

As commonly happens for patients with addiction, I experienced no craving in rehab, thanks to a calm, highly structured routine with no triggers for emotional stress and no cues for drinking. I began to feel good, but a fragile good, and I accordingly prolonged my stay twice to a total of three and a half weeks, until spring arrived in earnest and the flowers began to bloom.

On April 9 I received a telephone call from one of my dearest friends, Maurice Blin, president of the French-American Chamber of Commerce in New York. "Congratulations, Olivier!" he said. "I am holding *Le Figaro*, which reports the Easter list of recipients of the Legion of Honor, including you."

"You are kidding," I said. That President Jacques Chirac had signed a decree naming me a Chevalier of the Legion of Honor seemed absurd. "If he could only see me," I thought.

The thought stayed with me long after I left High Watch Farm, gaining extra force when I received a letter informing me that President Chirac was awarding me the Legion of Honor from his personal reserve of crosses.

At first I did not tell anyone at High Watch Farm about the award. Eventually I told one person in confidence, and of course word spread quickly among the other patients and staff. Their congratulations warmed my heart but also dispirited me, because I felt I didn't deserve the award. The whole thing seemed crazy.

A few days after Maurice's call, Joan came to pick me up and drive me back to New York. I was overwhelmed with emotions, positive and negative. The High Watch Farm staff sent me off saying I should be the mayor of the facility because of all the friends I had made and the insightful support I had given people in group therapy. They said they were sure I was going to stay sober. I felt like a total fraud.

I decided that there was no reason to call my new sponsor that day to say I was home from rehab. I could call him the next day to say that I had just come back, and he would be none the wiser. In the meantime I could celebrate completing rehab with one double vodka tonic. I deserved a drink.

That is how the alcoholic mind works. I had one double vodka tonic, and then another and another and another. Within hours of leaving High Watch Farm, I was bingeing once more.

I had been through the rehab-relapse cycle four times now and I saw the pattern. The break from normal stresses in rehab induced calm and encouraged hope that the worst was over. But rehab was not the real world. Once I was back in a normal environment, the lack of a cure for alcoholism and an effective medication for my preexisting anxiety tripped me up sooner or later, usually sooner.

Celebrities who go on television after rehab with shining eyes and talk about their spiritual awakenings and newfound commitment to sobriety are not speaking falsely. They are simply describing the genuine experience they had in rehab. They have indeed found inner peace, as I had in each of my rehab stays. But it is a fragile peace, and strong emotion, positive or negative, can trigger the unrest of a chronic dysphoria, and all one craves is relief from it.

As I've said, the average celebrity can simply afford more rehab than the average noncelebrity. Even at High Watch Farm rather than Clear Spring rates, my money would not last long if I kept going into rehab. At the same time, if I could not periodically dry out thoroughly in rehab, my body would not last long, either.

According to my physicians, I had a robust constitution. It had taken four men to hold me down when I was admitted to

New York Hospital with seizures. Several times in emergency rooms and hospital detox wards, doctors or nurses told me that my blood alcohol level was so high when I was admitted that it was a miracle I was still alive. Sooner or later, though, my luck was bound to run out.

At one hospital, I ran into a nurse I secretly knew from AA. When it was time to go home, she gave me a lift. She offered to take me to a meeting, but I told her I wanted to go home. She knew why.

"Olivier," she said, "with your luck, you won't die easily."

"What?!"

"You're going to be much more miserable. You'll be homeless. You'll break god knows what."

I said, "If you want to scare me, you've succeeded. But I can't go to a meeting now. I'm not ready."

As I took stock of my situation after my first post–High Watch Farm binge, the thought nagged at me that what I was hearing from my physicians and in rehab must be medically incomplete. Recovery from addiction could not solely be a question of spiritual awareness, moral virtue, and willpower. There had to be a biological component that could be treated medically. That left me exactly where I was when my alcoholism developed. All I could do was hold on and hope for a cure.

WITH HIGH WATCH FARM behind me, I settled into a routine of debilitating binges punctuated by grueling abstinence. In the morning, except in the midst of a binge, I attended the outpatient alcoholism program at St. Luke's–Roosevelt Hospital. The program was a by now familiar mix of classes in coping skills, group therapy, and AA meetings. When the program finished at noon, I went for lunch to a coffee shop where I could watch the Bill Clinton–Monica Lewinsky scandal play itself out on CNN. In the afternoon and evening, I went to the gym and to AA meetings, called my sponsor, AA contacts, and friends, and fought the craving for alcohol that increased as the hours passed.

During this time I had two sorts of conversations with the counselors in the outpatient program at St. Luke's–Roosevelt and my own physicians. If I drank, they asked, "Why do you think you relapsed this time?" I never had an answer that satisfied them or me. In hindsight there was no satisfactory answer. The question only makes sense if alcoholism is not a biological disease in any way but strictly a spiritual problem. It is like asking the cancer patient, "Why did your cancer come back? Did you adopt a negative attitude?"

At the time, however, the question shamed me and deepened my self-loathing for my inability to stop drinking. If I suggested that my fundamental problem was anxiety, both physicians and counselors said, "If you stop drinking, your anxiety will disappear."

On the other hand, if I had achieved a few days or a week or two of sobriety, the physicians and counselors said, "You're doing great."

And I said, "But I feel awful."

The truth was that despite its toxicity, nothing made me feel as well as alcohol. It calmed my anxiety and gave me a sense of self-esteem that I could not otherwise achieve. My interactions with other alcoholics in AA and the hospital outpatient program, and with addicts of all sorts in rehab, told me that they did not take an addictive substance only to indulge themselves in wild pleasures but also to quiet emotional pain that long preceded their addiction.

Unfortunately, the effectiveness of alcohol or any other addictive substance as a remedy for emotional "dis-ease" (to echo AA) sooner or later fails through excess. Tolerance is unstable, and there is no way to calibrate a dose that will remain effective as there is with medications for hypertension, diabetes, or a host of other illnesses. To start a drinking binge was therefore to embark on a roller coaster ride with some level stretches, a few exhilarating moments, and an inevitable, scary crash into hangovers, stupors, gastrointestinal distress, blackouts, and worse.

Over the July 4 holiday, I was in the middle of that process, glumly drinking to keep my anxiety and panic at bay. On Sunday,

July 5, a woman named Claudia, a friend but not a girlfriend, brought me some soup, and a little later Joan stopped by. We had been chatting for about an hour when an acquaintance named Tom, a public relations guy I met through mutual friends, joined us.

I was glad to have their company until Tom asked, "When do you plan on stopping drinking?"

Drink in hand, I said, "Look, guys, I intend to stop at some point soon and go to rehab again or do something else to quit for good. I don't know when or what that will be, but it is not today. And if there is one thing AA and rehab and my doctors all agree on, it is that the decision to stop can only come from the alcoholic. You have to be psychologically ready. It's like deciding to stop smoking. You can't impose it from outside. That's not going to work."

Tom said, "I think you should be hospitalized."

I said, "What is the point? I've been hospitalized before and it accomplishes nothing except to make me uncomfortable. Perhaps I will go to the hospital in a few days, or perhaps I will detox myself here at home."

Tom said, "But look at you. You're drinking and you're in a terrible state."

"Drinking is not against the Constitution. It's something that every citizen has a right to do in his own home. I'm not bothering anybody, and you're welcome not to stay if you don't like it."

He said, "I think you should go to the hospital."

Joan said, "Well, maybe not."

Tom pushed Joan into the other room. I was appalled at that and said, "Please leave. If you want me to call the police, I'll do that. I need to rest."

Tom called EMS, and when they arrived he told them that I needed to be hospitalized for my own protection. I insisted that this was not so, but I had alcohol on my breath and they believed him instead of me. They took me to the emergency room at Lenox Hill Hospital. It was the usual uncomfortable, noisy scene, and in the midst of that I passed out.

Some time later I woke up with an IV in my arm and a security guard sitting watching me. I asked him when the doctors would come, and in a Haitian accent he said, "Not yet. Just rest."

I rested. After a few hours I said, "Okay. My alcohol level has to be back to zero by now, and I'm ready to leave."

"You can't."

"Why not?" I asked.

"Because this is a closed service."

"What? Why am I here?"

"I can't tell you."

I was in the hospital's locked psych ward. Had I done something terrible? When an orderly and a nurse came to check on me, I asked if I could make a phone call. No. No telephone calls during the first few days in the ward.

I was assigned to share a room with an enormous man who in the middle of the night began hallucinating. "I'll kill you! I'll kill you!" he screamed. I did not sleep a wink the rest of the night for fear of being attacked in my sleep.

I asked if someone from AA could visit me. No visitors were allowed during the first few days. Trying to make the best of things, I cooperated with the routine and spent the time chatting with other patients. A nice Park Avenue lady wanted my phone number so she could set me up with her daughter. "You're quite a catch, even if you are having a rough time right now."

After three days, two residents came to see me and said, "You have a problem."

"I know I have a problem. I am an alcoholic. I know."

"There is another problem. We want to protect your license."

"There is nothing wrong with my license."

"It doesn't matter. CPH is in the picture, so you have to go into rehab at Marworth in Pennsylvania. CPH decided."

CPH was the New York Medical Society's Committee for Physician Health. Struggling to take in the news that someone had reported me to CPH, I said, "I've gone to rehab at High Watch Farm, and I'd be happy to go back there."

"CPH wants a more active treatment center."

"How much does it cost? I'm paying out of pocket."

"We don't know exactly. Maybe ten thousand dollars a month."

"I can't pay that. I am going broke as it is. And since I haven't seen patients for over a year, I don't see why this is even necessary."

"But don't you want to protect your license?"

"It's not worth ten thousand dollars a month."

"But your training must have cost you more than a hundred thousand dollars."

"No, in France medical school is free. I didn't pay a dime for that, and I'm not going to pay a dime to protect a license that is useless to me. My New York State license is worthless in France. I'll just go back to France. Besides, like I said, I'm not practicing. I closed my practice over a year ago. What did I do wrong?"

The residents had no answer for that, and they plainly did not like my saying that my New York State medical license was worthless to me. They repeated that I had to make a decision about Marworth.

"Can I think it over a little?" I asked.

"Yes, but please do it quickly," they said. They wanted to free up the bed I was occupying in the ward.

The residents left me feeling bewildered, disheartened. I could now use the telephone. I called my cousin Steve. I loved and trusted him so much that I sometimes felt closer to him than to my immediate family.

"I'm locked up in this place and it is absurd," I said. "They are not doing anything for me. They're detaining me against my will. New York law is very clear: once your blood alcohol level has dropped below a certain point, they have to release you. Get me a lawyer."

He said, "I don't know what is medically right for you, Olivier."

I said, "There is nothing right in locking someone up in a psych ward without a legitimate diagnosis of incapacitating mental illness. Get me out of here, you son of a bitch!"

Naturally the conversation went downhill from there.

I called Joan. I demanded to know what the idea was railroading me into the psych ward. She said that it was not a planned intervention, but that Tom cowed her into going along with things for my own good. To make sure I was not released after detox in the normal way, Tom had lied and said that I had been fired, that I owed money, and that I left rehab against medical advice. He had also told the hospital staff, "If you release this guy and something happens to him, I will call the *New York Post* and blame you."

I called my mother in Paris, and she said, "Let them take care of you."

I said, "Perhaps you would have liked me to say at Auschwitz, 'Let them take care of you.' It's illegal detention. Being locked in a room for the night with a violent schizophrenic is not doing anything for me medically."

Alcoholics inevitably say hurtful things to their friends and family. In the midst of the frightening, confusing experience of being locked up against my will, I felt betrayed by everyone. I was like a wounded animal in a cage, lashing out at anyone who came too near the bars. I was being given 80 milligrams of Valium a day, and I was still panicky.

In the immediate term, it did not even matter if I voluntarily relinquished my license to practice medicine in New York State. A bureaucratic machine had been set in motion, and it was going to grind me through it one way or another.

Desperate to find a way out of the trap that had been set for me, I called André Gadaud at the French embassy in Bern, Switzerland. "It's a neutral country," I thought. "No one can touch me there." In a recent telephone call I had finally told André about my alcoholism, as I had meant to do in person the year before, and he had reacted with great empathy.

I described my predicament and asked André, "If I can make it out of here and onto a plane, will you give me sanctuary at the embassy? I won't tell anyone where I am going, not even my mother."

"No problem," he said. "Come whenever you want and stay as long as you want."

To carry out my escape I needed my credit card and my passport. It was Friday the 10th of July, and on unlucky Monday the 13th a driver from the rehab center at Marworth, near Scranton, was supposed to come fetch me. When I arrived at Marworth,

I intended to say, "Oh, what a shame, I don't have my credit card." At that point I assumed Marworth would send me home to get my credit card. Left to my own devices, I would head straight to JFK and catch the first flight to Zurich. It would be hard not to drink on the journey, but I felt sure I could do it out of sheer desperation.

The hospital wouldn't sign me out except to hand me over to the driver from the rehab center, so Joan and Steve were going to my place on Saturday to pack a few things for me. I told Joan, "Thank you very much for the shit you've gotten me into. In addition to some clothes, I need my credit card, of course, and I need my passport."

"Why do you need your passport?"

"Because I do, and I'm asking you to bring it. You've done enough damage. You've taken me to the ER and let someone lie about me, and here I am on the verge of losing my license. Thanks to you I'll lose everything. Will you bring me my passport?"

"No."

"Do you think that's fair? I am locked up when I have no mental illness, and you are making yourself an accomplice of these people."

"I don't want to take the responsibility of giving you your passport."

"Fine. Then don't ever talk to me again. It's over. You won't hear from me ever. It's finished. If that's your support."

The next afternoon, she brought me a small suitcase. I trembled with anxiety as I looked inside, and then saw with relief both my credit card and my passport. I thanked Joan, who clearly remained worried about what I might do.

Encouraged by a plan I thought worthy of an Alfred Hitchcock thriller, I passed a relatively peaceful night.

On Monday morning the Lenox Hill psych ward signed me out in the charge of the driver who had come to take me to Marworth. The driver was a very nice fellow and a few minutes of conversation made it clear that he was a former alcoholic whose outlook on life was imbued with the spirit of AA.

It was a bright, sunny day, and France had won the World Cup for the first time the day before. I had called my mother after the game, and she held the phone out the window so I could hear the victory celebration in the Paris streets. Still, my mood was bleak. I saw that the van had a CD player, and I thought it might cheer me up to listen to some music. At my request, Joan had packed a few of my favorite classical and nonclassical recordings. I said, "I brought some CDs."

Before I could go any further, the driver said, "You can't listen to music at Marworth. It's against the rules."

"Really? The other rehabs I have been to allowed music."

"That's against Marworth principles. They say it takes away from the focus on your recovery."

That news stunned me. I thought, "I'm forty-five years old and my life is over. My reputation is ruined. I'm a broken physician. My license to practice in New York may or may not survive. It's the end of what could have been a beautiful career. I'm being forced to go to a place where I'll spend a fortune for treatment that is useless, and where I won't even be able to listen to music."

The driver interrupted these thoughts by saying, "We won't be at Marworth for a couple of hours yet. Would you like to listen to something now? I have a few CDs myself."

He had a version of Beethoven's *Emperor* Concerto, and I asked him to play the second movement. When the music started, tears came into my eyes. It felt like the last cigarette before the firing squad took aim and fired.

Marworth was a handsome old estate converted into a treatment facility, and I liked the look of the place as soon as I saw it. I intended to follow my escape plan and flee to neutral territory in Switzerland, but the people at the front desk were very pleasant and even congratulated me on France's winning the World Cup.

"And tomorrow is Bastille Day," I said.

When they asked for my credit card, I handed it to them. I thought I would give the place twenty-four hours, and if it was bad I would find a way to leave. I felt a pang of regret when they made me turn over my CD player and CDs, but then a couple of other physicians who were there for rehab came and spoke to me and showed me around a little, and I felt a little better about staying.

I had a very difficult time calming down and settling in, however, much more so than at my previous rehabs, because Lenox Hill had tapered my Valium to zero before discharging me. The Marworth staff said they did not want to give me Valium, because "it's a mood-altering drug and will keep you in addiction mode." The result was that for the first ten days I felt panicky and confused, so much so that I even briefly insisted that I was not an alcoholic but the victim of mistaken identity.

The placid mask I habitually showed the world did not help me here. I told the staff how I was feeling, and they said, "You look calm. Your symptoms seem mild." They probably thought I was a con artist, when in fact I had insomnia and was so stressed day and night that I thought I was going to have a heart attack.

The day after I arrived, a counselor told me, "CPH wants you to sign a five-year contract agreeing to be monitored by them for abstinence from alcohol and other drugs."

The mention of "other drugs" went in one ear and out the other. I said, "But I'm not practicing medicine now. I stopped practicing a year ago."

The counselor said that did not matter to CPH. If I did not sign the contract, CPH would report me to New York State's Office of Professional Medical Conduct (OPMC), which would then investigate me. Colleagues had told me horror stories of OPMC investigations, saying they made an IRS audit look like a walk in the park, and the counselor agreed with that comparison. Part of me wanted to say, "Fine, let OPMC investigate, and they will discover I have done nothing wrong as a physician."

Like the residents at Lenox Hill Hospital, the counselor at Marworth was astonished that I did not care about the threat of losing my New York State medical license. I said, "The license is a complete nonissue to me. I did not want to come here, but now that I am here, my only concern is my health. I am trying to save my life from alcoholism. They told me in AA that anything I put ahead of my recovery, I will lose, and as far as I'm concerned that includes my license to practice medicine in New York."

The counselor told me I could take a few days to think about the CPH contract. Speaking with other physician rehab patients, all of whom were at Marworth in compliance with CPH or counterpart organizations in other states, I asked, "Why do I have to sign this thing?"

One said, "They hold you by the balls. There is no choice."

Another said, "When CPH tells me to jump, I don't ask why. I ask how high."

That made me feel like I was sinking down to the bottom of the barrel. The feeling grew stronger when I found that the other physician patients had all been caught practicing medicine or driving under the influence of alcohol or another drug of abuse, or committing some other crime, such as stealing painkillers from a hospital pharmacy. I was the only one who had voluntarily stopped practicing medicine as soon as I realized my drinking was out of control; I had never been anything but completely sober when I saw patients in my office or at the hospital; I had never driven drunk or broken any other laws; and I was already going to AA daily and had voluntarily spent three of the previous nine months in rehab when a pack of well-intentioned lies brought me into CPH's orbit. Yet I was treated like a criminal, subjected to the same penalties as the physicians who were guilty of misconduct.

In the end I decided it was better to sign the CPH contract and avoid a state investigation, but not because of the threat of losing my license. What was far worse in my mind was that even though I had done nothing wrong, the investigation might still ruin my reputation. Investigators would interview my neighbors, as well as colleagues, and ask questions like "Does Dr. Ameisen's behavior seem normal?" or "Have you ever seen him walking unsteadily?" It was redolent to me of people informing on their neighbors during the Holocaust and in Vichy France, or in America during the McCarthy era.

Marworth had all the patients who were physicians, nurses, and pharmacists room together. It also kept them in a group for all organized activities. This struck me as ridiculous. Doctors are okay, but I generally socialized with people outside the medical profession.

"I was born with a first and last name, not with a title of M.D." I said. "Put me with the real people. Just put me with the other alcoholics, whether they are janitors or generals."

The counselor explaining the situation said, "You medical professionals have similar issues."

"Alcohol? Addiction? That's similar with everyone else here, it seems to me."

"Yes, but physicians, pharmacists, and nurses have licensing issues in common."

"Nobody's going to talk about that, I'll bet, because it is too embarrassing," I said. Marworth wasn't about to change its rules for me, however, and so I joined its medical addicts rehab club, only physicians, nurses, and pharmacists allowed. The membership averaged about a dozen people while I was there.

Creating a class system within rehab made no sense to me, and I am sure that it hurt some other patients' feelings. I never saw it at any other rehab, and one of the things I love and respect in AA is that everyone is equal. I resented being stuck with the medical professionals in the organized activities at Marworth, and I spent a lot of free time with patients from different walks of life. I formed some good relationships in both groups.

My roommate was a delightful guy named Peter. In rehab lingo, Peter and I were "dinosaurs." That is, we were pure and simple alcoholics, whereas most addicts today use more than one substance, a phenomenon known as cross-addiction or polyaddiction. In AA and at NA meetings in rehab, I often heard people talking about balancing out a "downer" like alcohol, heroin, or barbiturates with an "upper" like cocaine or methamphetamine. Most of the other medical professionals in rehab at Marworth were primarily addicted to prescription painkillers like codeine and anesthetics like fentanyl, with alcohol or some other drug as their secondary addiction.

Practically all alcoholics and addicts are also addicted to nicotine. When I met people in AA and rehab, they were shocked that I didn't smoke. But the addiction treatment community does not consider smoking a cross-addiction, and it is the one addictive behavior that twelve-step programs and rehabs don't prohibit. The smokers at Marworth—again, almost everybody but me—regularly gathered to puff away together.

I certainly had a precedent for becoming a smoker—the only drug used regularly in our household was nicotine. My father began smoking in the forced labor camp to blunt hunger, as he told us, and my mother picked up smoking from him. When I was a little boy, they each smoked two packs or more a day. My father quit when I was six or seven years old. He picked up the habit again when I was eighteen, but after about a year he quit again for good. My mother continued to smoke heavily until her death. My brother, Jean-Claude, and my sister, Eva, began smoking as teenagers at summer camp. Eva quit several years ago, and Jean-Claude still smokes.

One of the clichés of smoking is that it calms the nerves. In fact, this is one of its best-documented features. It can also elevate mood slightly. Studies have shown that smokers modulate their moods subtly throughout the day with nicotine. My mother regularly reached for a cigarette in an anxious or nervous moment.

I stayed away from cigarettes because I took to heart my father's repeated warnings not to start, because it was so hard to quit. He never said anything about drinking, because no one in the family had a drinking problem. When I started drinking, I assumed that this somehow meant I was protected against alcohol dependence.

If my father had warned me against alcohol, I would certainly have tried to steer clear of it, and I doubt I would ever have tried to soothe my anxiety with it. There is no way of knowing what would have happened to me then, but there is also no doubt that my anxiety, which failed to respond to any medication I was prescribed, would have had a devastating effect. It could well have driven me crazy, I believe, or caused me to commit suicide as a way out.

What struck me as ironic was how people who are addicted to one thing often look down on people who are addicted to something else. The heroin addicts think they are at the top of the hierarchy. The cocaine addicts think the same. And they both look down on alcoholics. In the detox ward of a hospital in New York City, a pretty girl who was a street singer told me, "You should try heroin, Olivier. It's so much easier on your body than alcohol. With heroin you fly."

A woman I met in AA spoke wistfully of how nice heroin was. When I said I had never injected myself with anything and never could, she responded with the classic AA rejoinder, "Yet." If you said you never drank in the morning or never fell into some other drinking trap, the old timers said, "Yet."

At Marworth several physician and pharmacist patients agreed that the anesthetic fentanyl was "the Rolls Royce of drugs." One of the deadliest, too.

One physician patient was a codeine addict, and he had contempt for alcoholics. "How can you drink that foul-tasting, foul-smelling stuff?" he said. He was not a bad fellow, in fact I got on very well with him, but he was grumpy and a bit of a snob. He always dressed in designer clothes and he regularly criticized my rumpled shirts and jeans: "You're such a distinguished guy, Olivier. How can you wear that crap?"

I said, "Do you realize where we are? We are in rehab. It's not jail, but it's not very much higher up. We're not exactly going to a black-tie gala."

When I said hello to this guy in the morning, he always replied, "Another day in paradise." And then he complained about how he could be on the golf course or taking a drive in his exotic sports car. He was very proud to be with the physicians, nurses, and pharmacists, rather than the general Marworth population.

On paper, we were an impressive bunch, our résumés studded with credentials from elite universities and teaching hospitals. We had shown plenty of smarts and willpower in achieving these things, and like all addicts we had tried to use our wits to manage our addictions successfully. As one of the group said, "If we put the same dedication and ingenuity into our careers as into obtaining a drink or a fix, and using only so much at a time and no more so that it would not be noticed, we'd all have Nobel Prizes." (Of course, nonphysician addicts and alcoholics will make similar claims.)

The effort is often brilliant, but when it fails it's a disaster. In a group therapy session one day, a pharmacist described an incident in his life and said, "I had some vodka, but only a little bit, so I injected myself with the vodka."

When it comes to self-injection, I am so squeamish that you would think I had no medical training. But my curiosity was aroused and I said, "I know vodka. I've drunk a lot, as I'm sure you have. What's the point of injecting it?"

Pharmacists know the half-life of everything in your bloodstream, how to spare the kidneys by injecting a drug in one way rather than another, and so on. He said, "If you only have a small amount of liquor and you drink it, it will be absorbed in your stomach and then diluted in your entire system, so you will feel no effect. If you inject it, the bolus gives you a concentrated high."

"Oh, thanks, that hadn't occurred to me," I said. Some people, I realized, might be even farther gone in addiction than I was.

It was fascinating to see these smart people with all their calculations ending in disaster. Addicts all invent the wheel, only to lose their balance and crash, as this pharmacist did while stoned out of his mind on a motorcycle. Loss of control is part of the definition of substance dependency, and trying to control an addiction is like trying to drive a vehicle without brakes. No matter how smart you are, addiction pits you against yourself, and you cannot outsmart yourself for long. If it continues, sooner or later the addiction takes control. It frightened me to realize I could not outsmart myself with respect to alcohol and moderate my drinking.

In this respect the medical professionals were no different from anyone else in rehab at Marworth, or from anyone I'd met previously in AA or other rehabs. When I was getting to know my first sponsor in AA, I complained that I didn't see the point of constantly going to AA meetings because I had nothing in common with the construction worker from Brooklyn or the ex-con from the South Bronx. My sponsor said, "Don't look at the messenger, listen to the message" and "Don't judge, identify."

AA is full of wise sayings, and those are two of the wisest. Gradually I learned to listen carefully to what other alcoholics and addicts said. In rehab I attended Narcotics Anonymous meetings as well as AA meetings, and I also came into contact with many people with obsessive-compulsive disorders and binge-eating problems. Whether they were black or white, gay or straight, rich or poor, ex-cop or ex-con, I saw and heard myself in all of them.

As I have already said, the common threads in what I heard made me suspect that shared biological mechanisms must underlie all addictions and compulsions, and that a medical treatment for addiction must be possible. This thought never left my mind during my illness, but it receded into the background as the calming rehab routine took effect and I began to hope, once again, that I would achieve lasting abstinence through heightened self-awareness, improved coping skills, and AA.

I saw lots of willpower and commitment to recovery in my fellow patients at Marworth, whether they were medical professionals or not, and I told myself that I too had enough of these qualities. We all hoped that we could leave our addictions behind, and we were encouraged in that hope by Marworth's reputation. My best friend in the medical addicts rehab club, Daniel, another cardiologist, said, "This is the Harvard of rehab." He was being sarcastic, but underneath that was a kernel of pride and hope that Marworth would help him.

If Marworth was the Harvard of rehab, we all wanted to graduate with honors. Although there was nothing on paper, the scuttlebutt was that Marworth's success rate was among the highest in the country, perhaps 66 percent or even 75 percent.

You can search high and low, but no rehab center will ever state a specific success rate. Nor will they reveal the sad fact that the overwhelming majority of alcoholism rehab patients relapse within four years, even if they have been abstinent the entire time. The relapse percentages for other drugs of abuse are similar.[1]

Rather than admit these depressing statistics, rehab centers speak in vague positives, such as "Our patients have a higher abstinence rate one year after treatment than patients in an objectively matched comparison group." The abstinence rate will almost certainly be based on nothing more than patients' responses to a follow-up telephone call or questionnaire. And addiction patients commonly lie about how they are doing, because they have so much to lose—jobs, relationships, custody of their children—if they are not thought to be doing well and maintaining their abstinence without too much stress.

That rehab centers can make such claims is part and parcel of the fact that there is no proven protocol for addiction treatment. In this context, relapse equals noncompliance on the part of the patient. After I recovered from alcoholism thanks to baclofen, I obtained my medical records from my stay at Marworth. My discharge report says, "[Olivier] has a history of not utilizing twelve step support, as seen by several relapses despite having a sponsor and home group."

This is doublespeak that could have come straight out of George Orwell's *1984*. I went to AA regularly, I had a sponsor, and by all reasonable criteria I diligently utilized twelve-step support. But like the vast majority of AA members, I did not benefit enough from twelve-step support to be able to stop drinking for good.

Outside rehab, I worked all day to abstain from drinking, and each day was as hard as, or harder than, the day before. Addicts struggle to abstain, they painfully accumulate days, weeks, months, and even years of sobriety, but they get no credit for that when craving overcomes them and their abstinence ends.

Based on my own experience and my observation of fellow patients, I offer the following axioms for anyone undergoing, or delivering, treatment for addiction.

- Relapse does not necessarily equal noncompliance.
- Rehab does not equal cure.
- Rehab equals respite.

I was in dire need of a respite when I arrived at Marworth, and much as I resented being taken to Lenox Hill, I am grateful for my friends' intervention, although the lies Tom told about me are another matter. In my intake interview at Marworth, a psychologist told me, "When you were admitted to Lenox Hill, your transaminase [liver enzyme] count was 300. As you know, that's almost ten times normal. At this rate of drinking, you have at best five years of life left." Transaminase levels that high often signal acute alcohol-related hepatitis, which can be a precursor to fatal liver cirrhosis, but Joan, Claudia, and Tom had stopped my binge in the nick of time.

Like AA, a good rehab program teaches many valuable life lessons. One of those I learned at Marworth was to look in the mirror every morning and say something positive about myself.

In an AA meeting, I had heard a man qualifying who said, "You know how, when you're shaving, you try to avoid looking at your eyes in the mirror?" People with addiction don't like themselves, they think they are worthless losers, and they avoid looking in the mirror as much as possible.

A counselor at Marworth spoke about this issue and told us, "Look at yourself in the mirror. Look, and like yourself. Do as they say in AA, 'Fake it till you make it.' You hate what you see in the mirror, but fake that you like it. Smile at yourself and say, 'I'm an attractive person.'"

The counselor looked like Albert Einstein on a bad hair day with no sleep. When he said, "I look at myself in the mirror and I love what I see," we all laughed. But I took his advice, and even though I thought I was ugly, I wound up liking what I saw in the mirror.

Marworth's life lessons also included writing daily gratitude and next-day planning lists. The gratitude list was everything good that happened during the day. The idea was to appreciate simple things that people normally take for granted, like being alive and breathing, eating good food and having a roof over your head, seeing something beautiful in nature, having a pleasant conversation with someone, and so on.

Whereas the longer the gratitude list the better, the planning list was supposed to be short and sweet—and readily achievable. That way we could derive satisfaction from meeting our goals without becoming frustrated and disappointed in ourselves and the world. Anything that got accomplished without being on the list was a bonus.

I loved doing the gratitude and planning lists. My goals for the next day were things like go to an AA meeting, eat three good meals, take a walk, and have a good conversation with a friend. I knew my mother's reaction to this would be, "If that's your ambition, my son, good for you. But it's not very impressive." That was okay. Trying to impress people was no longer a goal.

The counselors at Marworth also tried to get me to do a list of my achievements. They said, "You are wonderful at supporting others and giving them credit for what they have accomplished. You would make a great counselor here. But you need to do that for yourself, too. You don't accept your achievements. They aren't part of you. Ordinarily we don't ask for lists of achievements, because it puffs people up. But you are too humble. We would also like you to talk more about yourself during meetings."

It took me three weeks to begin opening up a little about myself in group sessions. But I could never bring myself to write a list of my achievements when I was ill with alcoholism. I could not believe that anything I had done really deserved to be called an achievement.

While I was at Marworth, I learned that I would have to vacate my apartment on East 63rd Street, where I had lived for ten years. New York Hospital owned the building and wanted to put someone new into the apartment. I said I was sick and couldn't move right away, but the response was that I had to move out of the apartment by the beginning of September.

I told the staff at Marworth that I had to leave rehab for a few days to take care of this problem and then would return. They said, "We don't think you're ready."

"If I don't move out of the apartment, I'll be in deep legal trouble."

"If you leave now, you will be in deep trouble. Because you will drink and you will die."

"When will I be ready to leave? Is it going to be six months or a year from now?"

"It takes as long as it takes. We'll tell you when we think you're ready to go."

An old Irish guy on the staff, an ex-alcoholic with many years of sobriety, told me, "Things will fall into place."

My first reaction to that was, "Keep dreaming." Finally I said to myself, "Olivier, it's out of your hands. You can worry or not worry." I managed not to worry about it obsessively, and things indeed fell into place. Marworth sent a medical certificate to New York Hospital, which bought me a couple of extra weeks. And I asked Joan, who had a large apartment, "Do you think I could stay with you for a while?"

"Only with a ring," she said.

"Are you serious? Do you want me to marry you under duress? I'm in rehab, and I'm not going to marry anyone now."

Joan was only half joking. She had put up with a lot from me. But before I landed in the Lenox Hill Hospital psych ward, we had discussed the fact that our romantic relationship did not have a future, a conversation I only had the courage for after several drinks. Through one of her relatives, she helped me find an apartment to sublet on the Upper West Side.

A year after closing my practice informally, I was still paying rent and a portion of employee compensation and benefits for my medical office space, as well as continuing to carry the lease on a Hewlett-Packard echocardiography machine and very expensive malpractice insurance. That was in addition to my normal living expenses and the huge rehab bill I was running up on my credit card.

Spending so much money on an inactive practice made no sense, but it let me hold onto a portion of my identity as a physician. I wasn't yet ready to lose that. I couldn't yet see that I would remain a physician after the last tangible tie to practicing medicine was gone.

A member of the Marworth staff researched my insurance coverage and told me that although my regular health insurance would not cover any more rehab, my disability insurance probably would. It had never occurred to me that addiction would count as a disability, and I thought back to the insurance salesman's relentless hard sell when I was setting up my private practice. I needed to buy my own health insurance for the first time, after previously being covered under France's universal health care system and Cornell University Medical College's employee benefits.

I bought comprehensive medical insurance, but I told the salesman, "I don't need disability insurance. I don't have any health problems."

He wouldn't take no for an answer and kept coming back to the office to make a fresh pitch. "You're a cardiologist, but you could have a heart attack yourself, Doc," he said. "You could get cancer. You could get hit by a cab right out there on York Avenue."

Finally I bought the insurance, thinking I was throwing away $350 a month on the premium, just to get the guy out of my hair. Not once in any of his sales pitches did he mention addiction as a covered disability. When I became ill I never thought of asking, because I assumed that addiction was not considered a real disease like cancer, and some of the physicians at Marworth bitterly lamented the fact that their disability insurance did not cover addiction. Thanks to my having put all my expenses on automatic bill payment the year before, however, my premiums were fully paid and up-to-date.

After I finally left Marworth on September 16, I got in touch with my insurance company. It took some debating, but the company finally agreed that the disability insurance covered my alcoholism. I was reimbursed for my costs at Marworth and High Watch Farm—and for a time I received money for living expenses, a fraction of what my final salary at Cornell University Medical College had been.

With the disability insurance payments I had a little breathing space financially. In addition, I had Marworth's seal of approval. The Harvard of rehab assured me that after two months of study I had earned graduation and was ready to reenter the world.

Just before I left Marworth, the psychologist gave me great news: my liver enzyme level had normalized. The specter of severe liver disease had preoccupied me throughout my stay. Then my counselor told me to call my case manager at CPH so that she could explain the monitoring system.

"Okay," the case manager said, "a psychiatrist affiliated with CPH is going to page you once in a while, so you have to carry a beeper. At first you'll meet him at his office on the Upper West Side. And then he'll page you around twice a week at random. There will be no set schedule. When he pages you, you have to go downtown and give a urine specimen within a couple of hours. That could be any day of the week."

I said, "Urine? For alcohol? Urine specimens are stupid for alcohol." If you drink, your urine will be clear in a few hours because of how the body metabolizes alcohol.

"Yes, but we have to check for cocaine, heroin, methamphetamine, prescription painkillers, cannabis, benzos, and other commonly abused drugs. Those can be detected in the urine for days or even weeks after you stop using them."

"I've never seen a line of cocaine in my life. I've never taken an illicit drug."

"We still have to check."

"But you tell me CPH is a program of honesty like AA. AA says if you're dishonest, your recovery will fail, and I'm being honest. I tell you I've never seen cocaine or heroin. And the only drug I have ever abused is alcohol. Do you believe me or not?"

"Of course, we believe you. But we still have to check," the case manager said.

"My doctors regularly prescribe benzos for my anxiety and panic. My addiction specialist, Dr. Elizabeth Khuri, is a leading researcher in the field and associate professor of psychiatry at Rockefeller University, and she prescribes them."

"CPH protocol prohibits those drugs. They can be abused, they cause dependency, and you're going to have to function without them. One more thing: you will have to urinate in front of a witness."

"Excuse me?"

"Yes, some people try to do a switch."

I told Joan, "Look where I am now. I can't go away even for a weekend, because I have to be available to give urine within hours of being paged, unless I inform them ahead of time and find an approved lab wherever I am going. I closed my practice to remove the possibility of my drinking affecting someone's care, and now, at the sound of a beep, I have to go pee in front of a witness to check for drugs I have never seen in my life, much less used. On top of that, I am denied normal medication for anxiety. You've witnessed my panic attacks. They say they want me to stay sober and keep my license, but they are stacking the deck against me."

Besides urine monitoring, CPH mandated that I rejoin the alcoholism outpatient program at St. Luke's–Roosevelt, and in addition see a CPH-affiliated psychologist twice a week. "You need to have a private session with me, which will cost one hundred fifty dollars," the psychologist said, "and you need to join a group therapy session, which will cost eighty-five dollars." My health insurance did not cover the $900 to $1,000 a month this would cost.

I continued to consult Liz Khuri at Rockefeller, and she generously did not charge me because I was not working. I asked the CPH psychologist if my weekly appointment with Liz could replace a private session with him, and he fortunately agreed that it could.

One day I had a panic attack in Liz's office. She was very concerned and immediately wrote me a prescription for Valium.

I got the prescription filled, but I didn't touch it. I called the CPH psychologist and asked if I could take the Valium. He said, "Don't take a single pill. If you have it in your urine, you will have to go straight back to rehab."

"But I have severe anxiety and panic attacks."

"Don't take the Valium. The anxiety will subside."

The anxiety subsided, then quickly surged back up. It ebbed and flowed like the tides, but it never went away. And the panic did the same. I took the untouched Valium to the next CPH group therapy session and handed it to the psychologist in front of the whole group, physicians all.

"Congratulations!" he said. "You are doing great."

"I am not doing great by any means; I am struggling desperately to save my life from alcoholism. But let me ask you something. You know my psychiatrist Dr. Elizabeth Khuri's reputation as a physician-scientist working on addiction, don't you?"

"Oh, yes, of course I do. She is very well-known and respected in the field."

"In your professional opinion, is she right or wrong to prescribe Valium, when she sees me having a panic attack right in front of her and knows that I have a history of anxiety and panic that predates my drinking?"

He would not answer. I said, "I know CPH forbids it and that is why I brought you all the pills. But in your own professional judgment, is Dr. Khuri right or wrong?"

After a long pause, he said, "Well, medically she is right."

"So can I take the Valium?"

"No, you have to follow the CPH protocol."

It was only a moral victory. But the looks on my fellow physicians' faces suggested that they appreciated it as much as I did. From conversation I knew they also resented the charade of our forced therapy sessions. It was impossible to speak with complete honesty in these sessions, because the psychologist had informed us that some of their content would be reported to CPH. In such circumstances there could be no real patient confidentiality and no mutual trust, the two preconditions for therapeutic progress to occur.

Programs like CPH—I believe every state has one—are important to protect the public from physicians practicing under the influence of mood-altering substances and to help physicians themselves. But it is strange, indeed, when the program dictates that physicians receive substandard medical treatment, denying them the basic human right to appropriate medication and compassionate care.

Acting with her characteristic concern for the patient, Liz Khuri called CPH in the state capital in Albany, while I was sitting in her office. I listened to her explain why in her medical opinion Valium was an appropriate medication for me. And then I watched her face turn pale as she listened to whoever was on the other end of the line.

She hung up and said, "Olivier, I can't prescribe it to you. I am so sorry."

Being denied a standard medication for severe anxiety, the condition that triggered and fueled my craving for alcohol, was at best counterproductive and at worst callous and cruel. If I had not been subject to monitoring by CPH, Liz Khuri could have treated me like a normal alcoholism patient. I began to think more and more about relocating to France, where I could seek an adequate level of care.

In the meantime I felt like a shadow of myself, dutifully trying, just the way Marworth taught me, to avoid strong emotions that might raise my mood too high or sink it too low. I labored under what one of my psychiatrists later called "the conformist dullness" of those struggling to remain abstinent while their underlying dysphoria remains untreated. Every ounce of my energy went into resisting the craving for alcohol.

One place I sought relief was in music.

I had become great friends with the legendary producer Arif Mardin and his wife, Latife. Arif and I had met in August 1988 at a party given by his Turkish countryman Engin Ansay, a diplomat I knew through Murat Sungar. Arif was like a Marcello Mastroianni character in a Fellini film, someone who is always on, who is always performing, with a splendid flair for the dramatic gesture or remark.

The Mardins frequently invited me to parties and to dinner in their grand apartment on Central Park West. It was a special treat for me that Arif usually asked me to play the piano on those occasions, when the other guests might include one or more of the extraordinary musicians he worked with. I played my own compositions for Arif, and he was so taken with them that he did studio arrangements of several of them over the years, beginning with one, "Una flor en la memoria" (A flower in memory), that I wrote with the Cuban poet and novelist Reinaldo Arenas, as Arenas relates in his autobiography, *Before Night Falls*. Arif told me he had never done this for any other nonprofessional musician.

In the spring of 1990, Arif told me, "I want you to meet Bette Midler. Latife and I are going to invite just you and Bette and her husband to dinner. When the time is right, I'm going to show her the last song of yours that I arranged." As producer and performer respectively, Arif and Bette Midler had recently won the Grammy for Record of the Year for "Wind Beneath My Wings," the theme song from the movie *Beaches*. While we were lingering over dessert and coffee, Arif asked me to play the piano. I always enjoyed playing his Steinway concert grand, and I happily complied.

After I had been at the keyboard for a little while, I wondered if I should play the melody of mine that Arif wanted Bette Midler to hear. Before I could act on the thought, the fear struck me that this would be trespassing on Arif's good graces as a host. Surely if he wanted me to do that, he would have said something about it when he asked me to go to the piano. I tried to tell myself that out of concern for both of his guests' feelings, he would naturally rather play her a tape or show her the song in a private working session, where she did not have to be diplomatic if she was not crazy about it.

The conviction that my compositions were really no good began to fill my mind. In the meantime, my fingers were doing whatever they were doing, drawing on my memory below the level of consciousness. I didn't know what I was playing; then I heard Bette Midler sing, "Non, rien de rien, non, je ne regrette rien" (No, nothing at all, I regret nothing at all), the first line of Edith Piaf's signature song, "Non, Je Ne Regrette Rien."

I looked up from the piano at Bette Midler, a tiny woman not much bigger than Edith Piaf herself, who had seemed like a quiet little mouse during dinner. She had pushed back her chair and stood up to sing, and she was transformed, a titanic figure who had suffered all the sorrows of life and remained strong at heart.

That took my whole mind deeply into the music as Bette Midler continued to sing. When we finished the song, I stopped playing. After that spontaneous duet, one of the greatest compliments I have ever received as a musician, silence was the best encore I could offer her.

Arif's friendship was a great support. He never judged or criticized me for drinking, only encouraged me to do everything I could to stop. In New York the bars close at four a.m. If you are an alcoholic and you have not drunk enough by last call to be able to go to bed and sleep, and if like me you cannot stand drinking beer, which can be bought in all-night markets, and you do not have any liquor at home, you are in trouble. One night that happened to me, and I decided to go see Arif. I went to his building on Central Park West and told the doorman, "I'm going to the Mardins'."

The doorman recognized me from previous visits at less ungodly hours and said, "Are you sure, at this hour?"

"Yes, yes," I said.

He called Arif on the intercom, and then said I could go up.

Arif's drinks were famous among his friends as Mardinis. He came to the door in his robe, and I said, "I need vodka."

He brought me a glass of vodka, and I drank it gratefully. Arif said, "More?"

"Yes, please."

He brought me another glass, I drank it, and he said kindly, "Now it's time to leave." It was an embarrassing moment, but Arif handled it beautifully, and I was then able to go home and sleep. He knew I was too drunk to listen to anything he might say about getting sober.

I was tremendously lucky to have Arif as a friend during those troubled days. Lucky, too, to be friends with Maurice Blin. I met Maurice around the same time I met Arif. Maurice was seventy-two and I was thirty-five, but he became my best and closest friend. He and his wife, Melita, frequently invited me to their homes in New York and Southampton. He had a great zest for life. He played the cello, if modestly, and it always delighted me to play their beautiful Steinway for Melita and him. When he asked people to dinner, he cooked for them himself with talent and love. Despite the difference in our ages, he was like a charismatic older brother. One of his sons told me good-humoredly, "People say he talks much more of you than of his own children."

After my drinking became a problem, Maurice was convinced that all I needed to do was give up hard liquor for good Burgundy and I would be able to drink in moderation. He even gave me a book on the wine-drinking cure for alcoholism. I knew this wouldn't work and didn't try. In AA they call this "trading seats on the *Titanic*." Maurice never lost hope for my recovery, however, and always said, "Try again. Try again."

While I was locked up in the psych ward at Lenox Hill, Maurice's health began to fail. Until then he'd been remarkably active, riding his bike or swimming every day. But now he had cancer, and he left heartbreaking messages on my answering machine asking me to visit him and saying, "Why are you dumping me when I most need you?"

When I was taken to Marworth, I figured that Maurice would die before I could return to see him. He was very weak, and over the next few months he became much weaker and was sometimes incoherent. But I was able to visit him a few times in Southampton and more regularly when he was moved into Cabrini Hospital in New York City, near Gramercy Park.

In December Maurice died, and a few days before Christmas I went to the funeral. It was an enormous loss and I was sad, but not letting myself feel all the sadness. I had reacted the same way when my father died of cancer in November 1991. It was seventeen months before I could cry in mourning for my father, while I was hiking in the Alps near a spot where he had taken my brother and sister and me when we were small.

As New Year's Eve approached, Joan suggested that we make a reservation at a restaurant to celebrate both the New Year and my not drinking since leaving Marworth. I had 115 days of sobriety, the longest I had managed. I told Joan, "AA and rehab both say not to celebrate too much. I didn't celebrate Hanukkah, I didn't celebrate Christmas, and I'm not celebrating New Year's. One day at a time is the watchword, and one day should be like every other day. I'll just live every day the same, holiday or no holiday. Patrick, my friend from Marworth, is coming to visit, and we will just stay in and wish each other happy New Year here and that will be it. I am feeling enough pressure about Patrick's visit already. I don't want to mess up and drink while he is here. That would be a disaster for both of us."

Joan, a nondrinker herself, was unhappy with this. "We should go out and celebrate like the rest of the world," she said.

"The rest of the world drinks."

"That's not what I meant."

In addition to this pressure and my sadness over Maurice's death, although I had pushed the latter below the level of conscious awareness, there was another stress on me. My mother had arranged a ceremony on January 27 for me to receive the Legion of Honor that President Chirac had awarded when I was in rehab at High Watch Farm. A list of recipients is announced three times a year, at Easter, on Bastille Day, and at Christmas, and every individual usually arranges his or her own ceremony, the only requirements being that the ceremony must be registered at the Grand Chancellery of the Legion of Honor and that someone who is already a member must pronounce the words of investiture and pin on the official cross and ribbon.

Feeling that I did not deserve the award, I dreaded the ceremony. I was trembling with anxiety about that and everything else in my life. And I began experiencing increasingly frequent episodes of raw panic. Hoping desperately that I might be able to get away with a brief relapse over the holidays without CPH finding out, and before Patrick arrived the next day, on December 30 I went to the liquor store, bought a bottle, and began drinking.

CPH did not catch it for a few days. I missed a group therapy session, and I called someone about it drunk, either a CPH person or another member of the group who reported me. That was inevitable. What was harder to accept was the look of horror on Patrick's face when he walked in the door on New Year's Eve and saw me drinking. He almost ran back out, as if I were contagious.

Not that I blame him. He had to struggle against addiction for his life just as I did for mine.

I landed at the Brattleboro Retreat, on the edge of a small town in Vermont's low mountains. A young friend from Paris, Antoine, flew to New York, loaded me into a car service, and took me the 190 miles north.

I was in bad shape.

In Vermont they have five seasons: spring, summer, fall, winter, and mud season. By early April, when the paths in the hills around town were still muddy from melting snow, the Retreat staff said, "Olivier, you are doing really well, magnificently, in fact. You're ready to go home; you're going to do fine."

I said, "You know, guys, everybody tells me that, and then I don't do so well."

The staff assured me that this time would be different.

Brattleboro is on the railroad line from Vermont to New York. I boarded the train by myself. A few hours after I arrived in

Penn Station, I was drinking again. Ten days later, Antoine brought me back. The Retreat staff greeted me with what I thought was evident disappointment and even disapproval. "We thought you were going to be a winner," their looks said, "but you turned out to be a loser."

There was one member of the staff, though, who didn't seem to see me that way. Alan Cohn was a tall, shy man with a Ph.D. in psychology, who led classes on positive affirmation and cognitive behavioral therapy. He coached us not to worry about other people's judgments and to accept ourselves, even to the point of making fools of ourselves in public.

"When you get up in the morning, put on socks of different colors," Alan said. "If people laugh, you have deliberately triggered it and you know why they are laughing."

The idea was that if we did such things, we would see that the worst that could happen was usually not so bad, and we would not let shame and guilt rule our lives. What made us anxious and depressed and likely to drink, Alan said, was "shithood." Alan defined lots of things memorably in terms of shithood. "Toxic shame is embarrassment plus shithood," he told us. "Guilt is remorse plus shithood. Embarrassment and remorse are normal healthy emotions. Toxic shame and guilt are counterproductive shithood."

It was simple, straightforward wisdom, and I treasured every word. When I'd been introduced to CBT back in New York, it had struck me as pretty much worthless. But Alan brought it all to life for me. He made CBT as simple as ABCD. It is all about correcting the "cognitive distortions" that you have internalized since you were a young child. When you experience unwanted feelings or behaviors,

- A is the Activating event that triggered them;
- B is the negative Belief system you have about the event and yourself;
- C, the Consequence of A and B, produces the unwanted feelings or behaviors; and
- D, how you Dispute the belief system, is how you break the pattern and regain stability.

As for positive affirmation, Alan told us, "You don't have to believe that positive affirmation works. Clinical studies have shown that if you do it enough, it will take effect. You just have to use the right technique. You can't put your new belief system in negative terms, like 'I'm not stupid, I'm not ugly, I'm not unlikeable.' You have to do it in positive terms.

"If you think something negative about yourself, like 'I am stupid,' write the opposite, 'I am intelligent,' on a piece of paper. Make a list of two or three negative self-perceptions, and write down the opposite. Memorize the positive statements and repeat them to yourself in your head ten or fifteen times throughout the day. Say the words with conviction, even if you don't believe them. If you do this for fifteen days in a row, the positive perceptions will become true. You will self-appropriate them."

Many people greeted Alan Cohn's advice with skepticism. Listening to him, I thought, "This is what I've been looking for. This is what I need not to drink anymore. There is finally light at the end of the tunnel." I read a little about CBT and practiced positive affirmations almost obsessively. Instead of ten or fifteen times a day, I said the positive affirmations dozens of times. I repeated them in my thoughts constantly. When I was not in the

Retreat's programs or at AA meetings, I hiked for hours in the hills around Brattleboro, soaking up the sensations of spring: the blossoms coming out everywhere around, the myriad birds and their songs, the lengthening days and the warming breezes. Following Alan Cohn's instructions, I repeated over and over, "I am a good person. I am charming. I am bright. I am likeable."

Being close to nature calmed and soothed me, as did the rehab routine. And just as Alan Cohn promised, my attitude about myself gradually changed and became much more positive. But I had no idea how I was going to function in the normal world without a cure for my alcoholism. Perhaps things would be better in Paris, as my mother kept insisting. I made plans to relocate to the city of my birth.

At least the move, which CPH enthusiastically endorsed, would end its monitoring and restrictions on my care. It would be a relief to return to France and be treated like a normal patient.

5. Falling Down

IN MY SIXTEEN YEARS in the United States, I had remained a proud Frenchman. But I had also made my home in New York, and returning to Paris as an alcoholic felt like a regression. I mourned the loss of the life I had built for myself as a person and a physician, and worried about what lay ahead.

I was moving in with my mother, which was not a terrible thing. In her seventies, my mother remained an active, fun-loving, social person, fully engaged with the world. My girlfriends all loved her; many of them sought her out for advice long after their relationships with me had ended. Eva's friends sought her out, too. She was a brilliant conversationalist on matters high and low, with hard-won wisdom on the struggles of life. I looked forward to spending time with her and finding shelter in her well-ordered sphere.

Nevertheless, there was a dark spot on the horizon: sooner or later anxiety, and craving for alcohol to soothe it, would force me to drink in front of her. I dreaded what that would be like for both of us.

With Antoine accompanying me one more time, I boarded the seven-hour flight to Paris on the night of June 3, 1999. As the plane took off, I felt a mingled sense of elation and foreboding. I tried to focus on the positives and be hopeful. Certainly I could not ask for better help from my friends than I had received during my illness. It filled me with gratitude (if also with an uneasy sense of unworthiness). But as the minutes ticked away, the grimmer feelings ate away at the happier ones. My calf muscles twitched, tension gnawed at my gut, my chest tightened, and anxiety about what my mother would think insistently triggered craving for alcohol. By the time the flight attendants trundled the drinks cart along the aisle, I had a thirst I could not control.

"If you love your family, why are you doing this?" my mother asked when I came in with a bottle late one afternoon.

"I am an alcoholic. I drink. That's what alcoholics do. I'm not breaking any laws," I said.

"You are a gifted musician, you are a fine doctor, you are a wonderful person," she said. She lit a cigarette, inhaled sharply, and returned to one of her favorite themes. "Why don't you get married and have a family and think about someone besides yourself for a change?"

"I am not going to inflict this on a wife and children. I've done enough damage to my girlfriends."

"If you have a wife supporting you emotionally, things will be different. And if you have children, the responsibility of supporting them will help you not drink."

"You went to AA meetings with me in New York and heard the horror stories of how alcoholics lose their spouses and children. If you need to be reminded, come with me to more meetings, and you will hear it all again."

My mother looked out the window onto the U-shaped terrace where Jean-Claude, Eva, and I had scampered as children. I poured a drink, feeling like a worthless, horrible person.

"Jews aren't *schickors*," she muttered, using the Yiddish word for drinkers.

"I've met quite a few in AA. And when it comes to coke addicts in New York City, the Jews hold their own with the South Bronx."

My mother waved her hand dismissively and stomped out of the living room. I had been home only a few weeks, and our conversations were becoming bitterly repetitive.

When my cousin Steve called from New York to see how I was adjusting to life back in Paris, he chimed in as well. "You have everything to be happy for, Olivier," he said. "Your father, thank God, died before you became an alcoholic. But look at what you are doing to your mother. She survived Auschwitz; she and your father built a beautiful life for your family from the ashes of the war. If you die from alcohol, Hitler will get the last word. Your drinking is torturing her."

The testimony I'd heard in AA and rehab made it plain that all addicts hear this kind of talk from their families and friends. It is well-intentioned, and I do not want to minimize the pain that addiction inflicts on a whole family. But saying, "If you really love me, you'll change," is emotional blackmail that misunderstands the addict's dilemma. It implies that use of an addictive substance is under the addict's control; that it is a matter of deciding to stop being "selfish" and "self-indulgent," and it isn't. Alcoholics and other addicts live in a biological prison from which there is no escape. As Pierre Fouquet, the founder of modern French research into what he dubbed "alcohology," put it, the addicted patient "has lost the freedom to abstain."

Emotional blackmail and shock therapy might be acceptable if they were productive. Instead, such language amounts to kicking someone who is down, as if more kicks will make the person get up and walk. Suppose he or she can't?

Growing up, I was always anxious about pleasing my parents. They had suffered so much, they deserved to be happy. They *had* to be happy. I could not bear the thought that I might hurt them. When we met my classmates on the street, I felt guilty about expressing my pleasure in seeing them—as if that pleasure, that excitement, were somehow a betrayal of my parents, and especially my mother.

I took this even further as a grown man. My mother encouraged me to marry and have children, but that, too, somehow felt like a betrayal. To paraphrase the writer Romain Gary, compared to my mother, all the women in my life have been *buffet froid*, roughly, a "cold feast." That is not fair, I know, to my girlfriends, who have been a remarkable group of women—smart and generous—but I imagine every son with a charismatic mother can relate to it.

As for my father, my shining, handsome father, no matter how successful I might have become, I could never hope to match up to him. He was an accomplished musician and a highly cultivated intellectual, and as for success in the world, he had proven his mettle in war and peace by serving with distinction in the French army and making signal contributions to French industry and foreign trade not only as managing director of Helena Rubinstein but in the same role, some years after his retirement, at the great couture fashion house Balenciaga, which he helped revive from difficult times. Above all, when he died in 1991, there was a chorus of praise for him as a "tzaddik," a righteous man.

Caught in the grip of relentless anxiety and the distorted perceptions it created and reinforced, I strove mightily not to cause my mother more pain. And I failed. During my binges, I could grow self-righteous and paranoid. I spat verbal abuse at my mother—at my brother and sister and dear friends, too. When my mother urged me not to drink, I said things like, "You are intolerant. You are like a Nazi."

In such moments she customarily spoke to me with forbearance, tenderness, and passionate concern for my well-being. But she struggled, and her occasional outbursts of exasperation and anger were part of the toll that addiction takes on everyone who loves a person who suffers from the disease.

As June advanced, she begged me to see a psychiatrist she knew.

I was not eager to see him. "This guy does not specialize in alcoholism or addiction treatment," I told her. "I have seen the best experts and gone to the best rehab centers. But right now there is no effective treatment for alcoholism. What is the point of going to a psychiatrist's office so that he can urge me to stop drinking? You do that very well on your own."

"Maybe he can help you."

After several such discussions, she finally wore me down.

She made the appointment and went with me. I was half drunk when we arrived, but there was a long wait and I grew impatient. I turned to my mother and said, "Look, I've had it," and walked out. She and a nurse ran after me and brought me back, and the psychiatrist gave me a sedative. A few hours later, I woke up in a Paris hospital where I had done one of my internships.

I said I wanted to go home. "You can't," said the hospital staff. "This is the psych ward, and you are here HDT."

"What are you talking about?" HDT was *hospitalisation à la demande d'un tiers* (hospitalization at the request of a third party), which requires the signatures of a family member and two physicians and means that one is considered dangerous to oneself or others. Less than a year after being locked up in a psych ward in New York thanks to my friends, I was meeting the same fate in Paris thanks to my family. The experience induced a sense of despair and of a complete loss of trust between the family and me.

After a couple of days, I wasn't allowed to leave, but I could make phone calls. If the full HDT procedures were followed, I would be there for quite a while. In addition to the indignity of being locked up against my will, that was going to cost me a lot of money, because I hadn't been back in France long enough to qualify for universal health care coverage.

I called my mother, and she came to the hospital with my brother and sister. We had a conference with a woman psychiatrist, the vice-chairman of the hospital's department of psychiatry.

"Look at what you've become," the doctor said to me.

"What do you mean?"

"You're not even making a living."

"That may be. But my income in the U.S. was probably much more than your hospital salary, and I could always go back," I said.

"That's true," my mother said, before the psychiatrist could reply. My mother might criticize me in private, but she would defend me to her last breath against the rest of the world.

The conference with the psychiatrist was futile. She said that I had been admitted to the hospital according to a strict legal procedure that had to take its normal course, and my family concurred.

My family went home, and it seemed that I was stuck. But shortly afterward there was a little hubbub in the ward because an official from the Ministry of Justice was making a semi-annual visit to listen to patients' concerns. At first I thought, "What's the point?" But my second thought was, "What do I have to lose?"

A number of other patients were ahead of me. When my turn came, I saw that the official was a woman in her fifties with an austere yet kind look. I told her, "The situation is absurd. I am a diagnosed alcoholic. I'm not in denial of the fact. I have been to the best places in the world for alcoholism treatment. And as a physician I can tell you that the day I am released from here, I'll go and drink. That is the nature of the disease. You can keep me here six months if you want, but who gains from that?"

"So you're locked up in the psych ward here simply because you are an alcoholic?"

"Yes."

"This is Kafkaesque," she said.

"I think so, too."

"I'm going to order that you be released," she said. "Tomorrow morning you will be free to go."

"What if they forget or don't release me?"

"Either you will leave the hospital tomorrow morning, or the chief of the department will."

Nightmares of being permanently locked up persisted throughout the rest of my alcoholism.

The last night before my release, as I waited nervously, I met a beautiful young woman patient of twenty-three. She had blond hair and blue eyes, and a constellation of diagnoses including depression and binge-eating. At the end of an hours-long conversation, we kissed each other good night.

The next morning, when my mother, Jean-Claude, and Eva arrived to pick me up and drive me home, the beautiful young woman saw me to the door and we kissed again. My mother asked who she was and why she was in the psych ward.

"She's very attractive," my mother said. "But couldn't you find someone without clinical depression?"

"I find the people you lock me up with," I said. "She comes from a good family. Her father is a physician and her mother is a nurse."

My fury at my family—especially my brother and sister—caused a rift between us that would last a painfully long time. In recent talks with Jean-Claude and Eva, I've learned that the hospitalization had not been planned. It had been spontaneously organized by my mother in desperation over my walking out of the psychiatrist's office. And in fact my brother had opposed it, only going along with it because my mother begged him to do so.

I also learned that all during my illness, the family struggled with whether or how to intervene in my drinking. They'd been bewildered by the conflicting advice from addiction treatment specialists. Most said, "Don't intervene. The alcoholic or addict has to hit bottom and change on his or her own initiative. There is nothing you can do." Whereas others said, "By all means, intervene if the opportunity presents itself. You never know what may help."

In truth there was nothing that my mother, Jean-Claude, and Eva could have done to cure my severe alcoholism. What I needed from them, and what the families of all addicts find it hard to give in a way that the addict can appreciate, was love and compassion.

From my reaction to being locked up in the psych ward and my continued drinking, it may have seemed to my family that I had stopped trying to fight my alcoholism. That was not at all the case. I went to AA meetings regularly, usually at least once a day if not more often. I got a Paris AA sponsor, a very kind, patient man who spoke to me for hours at a time. And I looked for help everywhere.

I went to see the world-renowned cardiologist Philippe Coumel, who had supervised my M.D. thesis. I told him, "I am so ashamed of my drinking. I shouldn't bother you by calling or visiting."

He replied, "As a physician, how can you be embarrassed about having a disease?"

In the midst of a binge, I could repay such kind, wise counsel with the same abuse I sometimes hurled at my family. I once called Coumel up at four in the morning, waking him and his wife, and railed at him for letting me down and dropping me as a friend because of my drinking. I blacked out and had no memory of what I had done. But the next day he wrote me a letter in which he said, "I never let you down, and I will never drop you as a friend. More important, I cannot believe that a man of your intelligence cannot find the solution."

Coumel's generous words kindled a spark of hope in me. But I thought, "This disease has killed some of the strongest-willed and most intelligent people on the planet and it is defying the smartest researchers and practitioners in the field. How am I going to find the answer?"

My mother's health began to decline. Decades of heavy smoking had taken their toll, and she suffered from chronic obstructive pulmonary disease and chronic bronchitis. At the end of the year, she began using a small oxygen tank at night—she took off the mask to smoke in bed—and intermittently during the day.

Still, my mother did not let her illness stop her from carrying on her active social life or helping Eva with her young son, Emmanuel. She also insisted on arranging a Legion of Honor ceremony for me. Mindful of having had to cancel the last time, this time she invited a smaller number of guests, mainly people who lived in or not too far from Paris. Otherwise the plans were all the same, including a videographer to record the event. Unfortunately she could not attend the ceremony on January 26, 2000;

she was briefly in the hospital with respiratory problems. And my brother and sister chose not to attend.

When my mother returned home from the hospital, I picked up the tape of the Legion of Honor ceremony from the videographer to show to her. I prayed it wouldn't be too embarrassing—or too damning. Would the toll of my drinking show?

We went into the living room and I turned on the television and VCR, while she settled herself on the sofa and lit a cigarette. As I sat down beside her, she raised her head and gave me a look of loving concern that simultaneously soothed me and filled me with guilt for the sorrow my drinking had brought into her life. I pressed play on the remote control, and her gaze shifted to the television screen.

The show began outside the Hotel Lutetia on Boulevard Raspail, a Belle Époque gem with its façade lit up cheerfully on a cold, clear night. I had supplied the videographer with a tape of some of my music, and here at the beginning of the soundtrack was a song I had written the previous spring at rehab in Vermont. It was called "My Gift."

A quick cut (the videographer had done a marvelous job) shifted the scene into the magnificent lobby and a brief montage of me greeting varied guests. I had given my mother no help with the arrangements beforehand, but I at least had managed to get there early enough to welcome the first guests as they arrived. Accompanying me for moral support was my new girlfriend, Danielle, who for good measure had brought her little dog, a great favorite of mine. I had twenty-four hours of abstinence under my belt, along with Valium to prevent acute withdrawal, and three double espressos.

I was greatly relieved at my appearance on the video. There I stood, well groomed in an elegant suit, my eyes bright and open, a cheerful smile on my face, no hint of the turmoil within.

I watched ninety-two-year-old Jean Bernard, a world pioneer in oncology and hematology—and our family's first pediatrician—approach me with a spring still in his step at his advanced age. It was moving to see him smiling like a proud uncle. But I also felt slightly uneasy (as I had that night), because I surely didn't deserve such kindness; it could only be a holdover from his long friendship with my family.

There were Philippe Coumel, who was then chief of cardiology at Hôpital Lariboisière; Jean Dausset, winner of the 1980 Nobel Prize in medicine for his research in immunology, and his wife, Rosita, who'd been close friends for more than ten years; Bruno Durieux, former minister of health under Mitterrand; and former prime minister Raymond Barre, then mayor of Lyon, France's second-largest city.

The videographer's microphone picked up Raymond Barre's "*Bonsoir, cher ami*," as he came up to me, smiling widely and kissing me on both cheeks. Again I felt a disconnect watching the tape, and sitting beside my mother the pang was even sharper. I looked at Raymond Barre on the screen and thought, "That is not the practiced smile of a politician. That is a smile of real affection. How could I merit that?"

I studied myself and thought, "It's amazing. I seem normal. My voice is steady. They are fooled for the moment and can't see what a wreck I am."

I glanced at my mother and saw her joy. She leaned toward the screen as if to enter the scene through her gaze.

I turned back to the television. The video had moved upstairs to the Boucicaut Room, named for a marshal of France and one of the greatest knights of the Renaissance era. Ten years earlier, my father had received his Legion of Honor from Raymond Barre in the same room.

The separation I felt between myself and my video image widened as the video showed Raymond Barre telling the assembled guests that he had been delighted to join Nobel laureate Jean Dausset in compiling my preparatory dossier for the Legion of Honor and was especially pleased to be able to bestow the award personally. Was he really talking about me when he began reciting the accomplishments that "amply merited" the award? For every supposed victory Barre recited, I thought of an alcohol-related defeat that landed me in a hospital emergency room, a detox or psych ward, a rehab center.

Barre concluded by saying that I would now "go on to do new medical research."

I turned to my mother and cracked, "Research for the next bottle."

"Stop it!" she said.

On the video, Raymond Barre beckoned me forward and pinned on my lapel a Legion of Honor cross from President Chirac's personal reserve of crosses, saying, "In the name of the President of the Republic and by the powers vested in me, I make you Chevalier of the Legion of Honor."

He kissed me on both cheeks, the guests applauded, and my mother clapped her hands along with them. On the video one of the guests called out, "Your turn, Olivier."

Raymond Barre kindly said, "No reply is necessary."

I had not prepared any remarks, but I managed to smile and say that I was not at all sure that I deserved the evening's award.

Thanking the guests for coming on behalf of myself and my family, and acknowledging many questions earlier in the evening, I explained that my brother and sister were absent because of my mother's illness. Those remarks pleased my mother, as I could tell from the expression on her face.

The video ran on with a brief additional montage of departing guests. There I was with Jean Bernard, asking him how he was getting home in the bitter cold and hearing him say, "I am walking, of course. It is only a few steps." There was Jean Dausset, expressing his disappointment that there was not a piano for me to play or at least a tape of my songs. And there was Raymond Barre saying, "Come visit me in Lyon, where we can have more time together. Congratulations once again, my dear friend, and good night."

Another exterior shot of the hotel with its lights ablaze followed, accompanied on the soundtrack by Arif Mardin's arrangement of "Your Heart's Desire," which I composed after finishing rehab at Marworth. It moved me to think of all the effort and expense Arif had gone to in arranging and producing a demo track of the song, and it made me feel all the more acutely the loss of my career and the separation from my friends in New York. Then the tape ran out and the television screen went blank.

My mother's seventy-ninth birthday was coming in March. "You have given me a wonderful early birthday present, Olivier!" she exclaimed. I wished I could give her the present she really wanted.

On the night of the Legion of Honor ceremony I had managed not to drink despite the champagne served to the guests, only returning to the liquor bottle the next night. Now I felt the craving for alcohol well up inside me as it did every afternoon and evening, a flood tide of increasing physical tension, emotional anxiety, and mental preoccupation. I had recently moved back into my old apartment. I told my mother I had to leave and went to fetch my coat from the closet.

"May I keep the video?" my mother asked.

"Of course," I said. "I brought it for you." I had no interest in seeing it again. I felt like I had just watched myself playing a part in a fictional movie. The man in the video wasn't a real person. He was a mask I showed the world to hide my inadequacy. If people like Raymond Barre truly thought otherwise, they were naive or deluded.

I began to fall.

Two or three times in the first months of 2000, my mother had to be briefly hospitalized. During one of these stays, I went to her apartment with Danielle to fetch something I had left there. I was drunk, and I stumbled and fell backward into a glass display cabinet that held a Venetian glass vase that my parents bought when I was a child and that my mother loved. It was the vase she always put flowers in.

I cried out, "The vase, the vase!"

Danielle cried, "Your back!"

The vase was okay. My back was a mess, a sea of glass shards embedded in it. At the ER, they picked out the shards and sewed me up. A few days later, the wounds became infected and I had to return.

In April I fell and broke my left wrist while Rollerblading hungover, my second or third attempt at the sport. It needed surgery right away, but I waited until I had sobered up and Danielle told me there was no alcohol on my breath. I wanted to be sure the hospital treated me like a normal patient. It had long since become clear to me that alcoholics and addicts could not count on the usual amount of compassion and concern when they needed medical care.

From the moment I fell, I feared that I would never be able to play the piano properly again. My mother shared my distress. It was one thing my drinking had not affected. I thought, "The piano is all I have left. Now God is taking that from me, too."

Hoping to recover as much of the flexibility and strength in my wrist as possible, I consulted France's preeminent hand surgeon, Professor J.-P. Lemerle, who warned me that after fractures like mine patients did not recover full range of motion. Nonetheless, I committed myself to a strenuous regimen with a physical therapist on Professor Lemerle's team. I worked like crazy on it, blocking out the pain as I did. Again to avoid being treated differently from a normal patient, I did not tell Professor Lemerle or the physical therapist that I was an alcoholic. That required absurd pretexts when I had to cancel appointments because I was drunk. But I only missed a few appointments, and at the end of two months of diligent effort the therapist declared that I had recovered completely.

My mother's and my happiness about this was short-lived. A couple of days later, I woke up in the morning hungover, stumbled into the bathroom, and fell heavily on my left shoulder. I got up and felt all right at first, thanks to the anesthetic effect of the alcohol in my bloodstream. A few hours later, I looked at my shoulder in the mirror and saw an ugly bruise spreading, but I thought that was the extent of the damage.

As the morning passed and my shoulder became more and more painful, I began to suspect that I had a fracture. But I did not want to go to the emergency room with alcohol on my breath. So I waited more hours, and then clumsily cleaned myself up and dressed. I wore the red ribbon of the Legion of Honor on my jacket lapel, hoping it would keep doctors and nurses from dismissing me as a low-life drunk.

At Hôpital Cochin, where I had trained as a medical student, the ER staff told me I had a bad fracture and likely would not regain full mobility in my shoulder. Playing the piano engages muscle groups throughout the body, and I had rehabilitated my wrist only to incur an equally problematic injury. I determined to once again try my best to recover.

I went to see Professor Michel Revel, the chief of functional rheumatology at Hôpital Cochin. Professor Revel was very doubtful that I could regain full range of motion, but he proposed an unusual program of pool therapy. The buoyancy of my body in the water would take strain off my shoulder and allow it to be manipulated and exercised much more vigorously than in normal physical therapy. It was my best shot and I took it.

Once more, I managed to keep most of my physical therapy appointments, and once more, I beat the odds and recovered completely.

My mother could not enjoy the victory with me. She passed away on July 22, 2000.

It was almost unbearable to have to face the fact that I had failed to end my alcoholism while she was still alive. In my grief, I traveled. I visited friends on Lake Geneva, in the South of France, in the Swiss Alps. There was no end to my emotional confusion, and I struggled to stay clearheaded. My thoughts centered on the medical cure for alcoholism that I felt must be possible, but that I was convinced would be found ten minutes after I died from drink. Hiking for hours at a time in the mountains, keeping a fast pace to burn off nervous energy and restore the muscle tone I lost during binges, helped me to stay abstinent.

For a while. I bought my food in a little Swiss market. There, a display of vodka bottles called to me, day after day, like the sirens called to Odysseus. Unlike Odysseus, I had no shipmates with beeswax in their ears to tie me to the mast and prevent me from answering the sirens' call. I eventually succumbed.

A few days later, I struck up an acquaintance with a couple of tourists, and we talked late into the night. I was drinking, and I kept drinking after my newfound friends and I parted. The next thing I knew I was in the emergency room of a small hospital about ten miles away from where I was staying. I had been found drunk on the sidewalk and had a broken nose.

After I returned to Paris, it took me a few days to stop the binge. Then I went to see Dr. Jean-Paul Descombey, the former chief of psychiatry at Hôpital Ste.-Anne and one of France's most eminent specialists on alcoholism, whom I had been consulting for several months. "Should I go into a rehab clinic?" I asked.

Descombey said, "That doesn't really seem to be the answer for you, does it?"

"No, but what else can I do? I think maybe I should live in rehab."

"That is not feasible," Descombey said. "But the way you recover from your binges is extraordinary. You're back on your feet within twenty-four to forty-eight hours, and then only a few days later you just fall again into alcohol. Your cycle is getting shorter and shorter. I am afraid you will not live."

In my cardiology practice, I often found that a male patient's wife or girlfriend was a useful source of information on which to base a diagnosis. The women noticed behaviors and recalled experiences that the men were too embarrassed to mention or had repressed.

During my alcoholism, I told every physician and therapist I saw that my fundamental problem was anxiety, which expressed itself in chronic muscular tension, and which, intensifying to a panic state, triggered the overwhelming need to drink for relief. None of the doctors who treated me for addiction took this seriously.

But my old girlfriend Joan remembered it well, perhaps because she heard me talk about it many more times than any physician did. One day in November 2000, while riding on the subway, she picked up an abandoned copy of *The New York Times*. There she read an article about a University of Pennsylvania researcher who was studying the effect of a muscle relaxant called baclofen on a drug addict's craving for cocaine. She tore the article out of the paper and mailed it to me in Paris.

When it arrived, I was in the middle of a huge binge. I glanced at it and tossed it aside. A few days later I vaguely recalled it and went looking for it, but I couldn't find it. I assume I spilled liquor on it, and the cleaning lady threw it away.

My life continued as before. My drinking meant I could not avoid hospitals altogether, but whenever possible I detoxed myself on my own as I usually did in New York. However, in December

I went for detox into a hospital where I had done some of my medical studies, and where an old friend from those days, Élodie, was now the head nurse. And then in June 2001 I had another bad fall.

I may have fallen on the street or at home. I don't know which, because it happened in a blackout, but if it was on the street, I managed to get home and go to bed. Despite the alcohol in my bloodstream, I woke up with pain in the left side of my chest. The pain became acute, and then extreme, but I thought it would pass. By now I had become used to waking up with bruises and aches from falls during binges, and anesthetizing the pain by drinking more alcohol. I tried the same tactic for the chest pain.

Two days later, in even more intense pain, I called my friend Élodie at her hospital. Élodie spoke to the head of the department of medicine, also a friend from medical training, and he made a special one-time arrangement for EMS to take me there, in Paris's suburbs, rather than to a closer hospital in the city.

I arrived unconscious. When I woke at 5:30 the next morning, the nurse on the floor told me that they had considered putting me in intensive care and intubating me to make sure I got enough oxygen in my lungs. But they decided I could breathe on my own and put me in a regular room. The nurse also told me that I had three fractured ribs. These had perforated the pleura, the envelope around the lungs, giving me pneumothorax, air around the lungs, a condition that can collapse one or both lungs. There was also blood in the chest cavity, a serious complication known as a hemopneumothorax.

In medical school they teach students that fractured ribs are among the most painful of all injuries. As an intern I saw the distress of patients with even one broken rib. The only way to reduce the pain even for a few seconds, without medication, is to hold your breath. Moreover, I began hiccupping, which made the pain atrocious. I tried holding my breath and drinking water to stop the hiccups, but neither tactic helped.

I asked the nurse if I could have metoclopramide to control the hiccups and something for pain. She said, "There is nothing on your chart. Can you hold out with some Tylenol until the doctor makes rounds later this morning?"

I asked her to call the intern on duty, but she did not want to wake him. She gave me Tylenol, which had zero effect, and I waited. The hiccups hammered my broken ribs for a long time before eventually subsiding on their own, but I continued to have intense pain.

Four hours later, after this nurse had gone off duty and been replaced by a new nurse, an attending physician came on rounds with a group of interns. I recognized his name as someone who knew my sister, and we spoke briefly about Eva. I told him the Tylenol was not moderating the pain.

The attending physician said, "Of course, it's insufficient. We'll give you Tylenol with codeine—" He stopped himself. "Well, in your case, we'd better not."

"Why not?"

"Because you could become dependent on it."

"I realize that alcoholics have an increased risk of becoming dependent on painkillers. Even alcoholics do not become addicted to painkillers when they take them for actual pain, however, but when they take them in anticipation of pain." I did not add that this was basic pain medicine and something all doctors should know, not just pain medicine specialists. Patients who are on a self-controlled morphine pump do not become addicted to morphine.

The attending physician said, "I'd rather be on the safe side. You'll just have to suffer a bit on Tylenol, and wait for the pain to go."

"Suffer a bit? With three broken ribs and hemopneumothorax?"

The attending physician would not be persuaded, and he left the room with the interns. The nurse who had come on duty that morning followed him out. When she returned ten minutes later, she had six tablets of Tylenol with codeine. She gave them to me and said, "Take two at a time every eight hours."

I took two because the pain was then very bad, and within fifteen minutes they produced complete pain relief. Eight hours later the pain had once again become severe. This time, afraid that I would not be given more the next day, I took only one pill, and it worked. In the middle of the night, I again took one pill to help me sleep. Although the pain was still bad, it lessened to the point where I could just barely tolerate it. The next day I was given more Tylenol with codeine, but I continued to take the absolute minimum I needed to rest.

The nurse told me that she had forced the attending physician to prescribe the six tablets by saying she would report him for cruelty. That was a brave and compassionate act. She said her father had died of alcoholism, and that he had sometimes been treated callously by physicians who knew that an alcoholic's complaint would likely be dismissed as delusional. She also said the attending physician had expressed anger at me for being an alcoholic doctor and said that my asking for pain medication was a sign of weakness.

As for the hemopneumothorax, two attempts were made to evacuate the blood from my chest cavity with a needle. It is a slightly risky procedure, because the needle can introduce more air and increase the pneumothorax. The first time, they got nothing; twenty-four hours later, after more X-rays to check that the pneumothorax had not been increased, they drew off a small amount. As the pneumothorax did not impair my breathing, it was decided not to do anything more and to let the lesions in my pleura heal on their own.

This hospital had an excellent alcoholism treatment center. While I was there, I talked to one of the physicians in that department, Dr. S., and she agreed to see me as a patient. She also arranged for me to have a body computed tomography (CT) scan to check for any further internal injuries and, at my request, a sonogram to check for liver cirrhosis, which would be a death sentence. I was terrified of having contracted cirrhosis, but I had never asked for a sonogram before because I didn't want to know.

In the United States sonograms are usually performed by medical technicians, whereas in France they are performed by physicians. During the sonogram, I asked the physician doing it if she saw any signs of cirrhosis. Although she was naturally supposed to report only to the physician who ordered the test and not the patient, she told me, doctor to doctor, that she saw fatty liver tissue, but no cirrhosis. It was a huge relief to hear this.

Being accepted as a patient by a new alcoholism specialist and having another medical lifeline eased my mind a little. But within fifteen months I had broken my wrist, shoulder, nose, and three ribs, the last with potentially life-threatening complications. Surely it was only a matter of time before I broke my back or my neck and wound up paraplegic or quadriplegic. Who would give me a drink to quiet my alcohol craving then, or help me pass out of this world and end my alcoholism that way?

It wasn't until November of that year that I dimly recalled the *New York Times* article Joan had sent me twelve months earlier. I called Joan and asked her to track it down and send it to me again, which she did.

This time, I was not intoxicated when it arrived, and I read with fascination about how positron emission tomography (PET) scans conducted by the psychologist Dr. Anna Rose Childress, an addiction researcher at the University of Pennsylvania's Treatment Research Center, showed a remarkable quieting of brain activity in a cocaine addict who was taking baclofen, a muscle relaxant, to control spasms. The addict said that this medication reduced his craving substantially. I did not want to get my hopes up too much, but I did have to wonder: Could baclofen help me stop drinking?

6. *Against Medical Advice, or,*
The Life of Afterward

READING—WITH A CLEAR HEAD, between binges—the *New York Times* article about baclofen's effect on an addicted patient, I was encouraged by three things.

First, baclofen reduced craving as experienced by the patient in the experiment—a cocaine addict and paraplegic—and did so not only for cocaine but also for alcohol and nicotine.

Second, baclofen changed the patterns of neurotransmission in the patient's brain visible on PET scans, quieting activity in the amygdala. Studies associate the amygdala with memories of pleasurable events, and with experiences of craving for, or anticipation of, a variety of addictive substances and compulsive behaviors.

Third, baclofen resolved the patient's muscular spasms, the purpose for which the medicine was originally prescribed.

The reporter, Linda Carroll, vividly conveyed all this, dramatically and scientifically, in her article. For me, the idea that a drug could quiet both a patient's muscular spasms and addictive cravings was tantalizing. Perhaps baclofen could relax my chronic muscular and nervous tension, keep it from intensifying into chronic anxiety and panic, and thereby short-circuit the craving for alcohol to resolve that extreme distress.

Relaxation exercises feature prominently in many addiction treatment programs, on the principle that if the body relaxes, the mind will follow. That made sense to me both from my own experience and my observations of others. Although the phenomenon has not been written up in the medical literature, alcoholics and addicts seem to share a high degree of physical agitation. Attend an open AA or NA meeting, and you will see a good deal of leg pumping, toe tapping, fidgeting, and so forth. The question is: Does the agitation result from addictive behavior, precede it, or both? I constantly heard from others in AA that they never felt well, relaxed, easy in their own skins, until they started drinking. I felt the same way, and my suspicion is that chronic physical uneasiness triggers addictive behavior and then is exacerbated by this self-medication gone wrong.

In rehab and outpatient programs, I did relaxation exercises faithfully. I took frequent yoga classes, and practiced self-hypnosis techniques, too, but I could never achieve full relaxation. In group exercises, other people sometimes became so relaxed that they actually fell asleep, and many people reported that they remained physically relaxed for up to a day or more after a set of relaxation exercises or a yoga class. For me, the muscular and nervous tension began to return after twenty to thirty minutes.

Commonly prescribed antianxiety medications like Valium and other benzos belong to the larger category of so-called sedative-hypnotics, and as the label suggests, they do affect muscular and nervous tension. For example, Valium is often given to relieve severe back spasms. But benzos also induce dependency and have serious side effects, including impaired memory and cognitive function. I never liked the experience of taking these medications—they made me feel loopy or groggy. If baclofen lacked such drawbacks—and no unpleasant side effects were mentioned in the *New York Times* article—it might very well help me.

It was interesting that the experiment on baclofen to reduce craving had its impetus partly in the patient's self-observations. Prescribed 60 milligrams of baclofen a day to calm the muscular spasms associated with his paraplegia, Edward Coleman found it wasn't enough and tried 80 milligrams. That quieted the spasms, but also had two side effects, one negative and one positive, at least from his perspective. The negative side effect was that "it would block his high if he took the baclofen too close to the time he took cocaine." The positive side effect was that "the medication could reduce his craving when cocaine was unavailable." Professor Childress, who had conducted an earlier, pilot study of the effect of baclofen on cravings and planned a longer study, generously acknowledged Edward Coleman's insights, saying, "In a way, he's done my experiment for me."[1]

Over the next few days, my mind buzzed with excitement about baclofen—and with dread. What if this was just another dead end in my quest for a cure? Two questions haunted me: Was baclofen available in France, and was it safe? I wanted to call Childress and ask her, but feared I wouldn't be taken seriously if I called on my own behalf.

Emotional agitation from all these questions and worries spilled over into anxiety, and one evening I drank fairly heavily. The next day I gathered my courage, and allowing for the time difference between Paris and Philadelphia, called Childress hung-over. I identified myself as a cardiologist with an alcoholic patient, said I had come across the year-old *New York Times* article, and asked, "Does it make sense to use baclofen for alcoholism?"

Childress said, "I believe there is a fellow in Rome, Dolo-something, I am not sure of the name, who is looking at baclofen for alcoholism."

I asked about the dose of baclofen her study used: Had she considered trying a higher dose to see if it had a greater effect on addictive craving? She said that this was certainly a subject for further investigation, but that she did not know enough about baclofen at that point to speculate on the likely effect of a higher dose. All she could tell me was that Edward Coleman reported no unpleasant side effects from taking 60 to 80 milligrams of baclofen a day for his muscle spasms.

It was a very encouraging conversation, and Professor Childress kindly invited me to keep in touch. But my two burning questions remained unanswered: Was baclofen available in France, and was it safe?

I asked my alcohol treatment specialist and the psychiatrist I was seeing for cognitive behavioral therapy about baclofen. They knew nothing about it and were not interested in discussing an unproven medication.

I was clearly alone with the problem of how to learn more about the drug. As an associate professor at Cornell University Medical College and an associate attending physician at New York Hospital, I had been part of a research team and a community of physician-scientists, but I was living thousands of miles away and had no contact with the institutions or my colleagues there.

Addiction isolates everyone who suffers from it, and I felt very much alone in the world in general. I had come to rely on seeing Jean-Claude and Eva every Sunday at lunch with our mother, and we got along so well on these occasions that I thought the rift between us was healed. Yet after our mother died, I showed up at the Chinese restaurant on Sunday as usual for several weeks, and I was shocked and hurt that they never came. It felt impossible to call them. I thought they had had enough of me, and was simultaneously convinced that they were right to feel that way—and that it was unjust of them to abandon me. For their part, as I only learned after I became well, they were frustrated and baffled at how to help me, especially when doctors told them, "Leave Olivier alone and let him hit bottom. He hasn't lost enough to stop drinking yet."

People in AA often told me the same thing. Yet how much more was there to lose? If only quitting drinking were possible on the basis of willpower, twelve-step support, rehab, cognitive behavioral therapy, and the usual medications. For me, as for most alcoholics, it was not, and the idea that I needed to lose more before I could face up to reality and pull myself together was a cruel joke.

I thought about talking to Philippe Coumel about baclofen. Philippe was a great friend to me during this period, often inviting me to lunch, engaging in long, thoughtful conversations about a range of topics, including my illness. But I had too often excitedly told him about grand hopes for alcoholism treatment, only to lapse back into bingeing. It was too soon to mention baclofen; I needed to learn more about the drug first.

Fortunately I had recently made a friend who indirectly put me on the path to some answers, an American expat named Alexander, a very Brando-in-*Last-Tango-in-Paris*-looking guy, an ex-journalist who taught English language classes. Alexander and I used to see each other for espressos every afternoon at the same bistro, when I was between binges, and we talked a lot about politics. Our views diverged widely, but we gave each other full credit for good arguments and developed a warm rapport. For a long time I avoided telling Alexander about my drinking, for fear he'd drop me as a friend. And like Brando's character in *Last Tango*, Alexander never pried when I showed up after a binge. But eventually he pressed me to have dinner with him and his girlfriend, and I had to explain that I was too embarrassed about my alcoholism to meet new people and socialize with them. He understood: he had struggled with drug use himself. Still, I held back from meeting his girlfriend or seeing him anywhere except for coffee in the afternoons.

In our conversations, Alexander often mentioned things connected with the Internet and e-mail, and it dawned on me that because of my drinking I had been missing out on the great technological and societal revolution of our time. Oh, I had used computers a bit in New York, but so much had changed since then. Search engines could now connect you to information anywhere in the world; Google was four years old. If I was going to learn about baclofen, it was by searching the Internet.

In early February 2002, I bought a PC and printer, and while it took a bit to set up the computer and get connected (I am not technical-minded), I was soon able to join the rest of the world. Panic was my most crippling symptom, so I began by typing in the words "baclofen panic."

The first hit was a link to the abstract of a 1989 paper in *The American Journal of Psychiatry* by the University of Arizona researcher M. F. Breslow et al. The paper was titled "Role of gamma-aminobutyric acid in antipanic drug efficacy," and the few lines describing it on Google's webpage said that baclofen was "significantly more effective than placebo" in reducing panic attacks. That astonished and tantalized me.

I clicked on the link and read the 103-word abstract:

All effective pharmacologic agents used to treat panic disorder augment gamma-aminobutyric acid (GABA) transmission . . . To test the hypothesis that GABA activity is a component of antipanic drug efficacy, the authors treated nine medication-free panic disorder subjects with oral baclofen (30 mg/day for 4 weeks) in a double-blind, placebo-controlled crossover trial. Baclofen, a selective GABA agonist, was significantly more effective than placebo in reducing the number of panic attacks and scores on the Hamilton anxiety scale . . .

Panic affects gamma-aminobutyric acid (GABA) transmission in the brain and baclofen is a GABA agonist . . . —I made a note of this for future investigation. For the moment, I was absorbed by the finding that it only took 30 milligrams of baclofen to measurably reduce the experience of anxiety and panic. That was half, or less than half, the amount that Edward Coleman, the patient in Professor Childress's experiment, used on a daily basis for his muscle spasms.

If baclofen was good for panic, I wondered why none of my physicians had ever prescribed it and whether it had a serious drawback. Of course, as a cardiologist I knew that physicians' prescribing habits are formed not on the basis of all potentially applicable medications, but by their training and the marketing of pharmaceutical companies. I don't say this to pass moral judgment. It is a fact of modern medical practice created by increasing specialization and by innovation in the pharmaceutical industry, both of which have been of great benefit to patients. No physician can keep up on developments throughout medicine's many specialized fields or on all available medications.

When I joined the cardiology division at New York Hospital–Cornell as a research fellow, I was surprised to find that American physicians did not commonly take advantage of a unique property of nadolol, a beta-blocker I had been trained to use in France. In 1984 Philippe Coumel et al. reported in *American Heart Journal* that nadolol slows the heart rate around five beats below other beta-blockers. In other words, if a competing beta-blocker brought the heart rate down to 63 beats per minute, nadolol would lower it to 58 beats per minute because of its more powerful effect on the sympathetic nervous system.

Some children have an arrhythmia and go into fainting spells (syncope) that are related to effort or emotion. This is due to severe ventricular tachycardia that is mediated by catecholamines. If the diagnosis is delayed, the outcome is poor. Whereas other beta-blockers may fail to prevent the phenomenon even if they are used at maximal dosage, nadolol will often do so completely.

In New York, I transposed this to some adult patients, including quite a few who came to see me for a second opinion because their cardiologists had told them that bypass surgery was their last resort against crippling daily chest pain that did not respond to other beta-blockers at the highest dose. When I thought patients could benefit from nadolol, I explained how

I knew about it and even told them, "This effect of the medication is virtually unknown here, so if you have a problem, you'll have a good basis for suing me." Fortunately, the patients I gave nadolol did well on it, and it helped many of them avoid invasive surgery.

Amiodarone was another heart medication I learned to use in France. When I came to New York Hospital–Cornell in 1983 and suggested amiodarone for patients, colleagues said, "No way," and referred to American studies showing that amiodarone frequently induced severe pulmonary fibrosis. I looked up the data, and saw that the studies had been of massive doses far in excess of what was needed. It was as if I did a study where I gave people megadoses of aspirin and then said, "Aspirin is toxic. It causes internal bleeding." I kept telling colleagues, "Amiodarone is safe, and it is the best medication in many cases—if you use it at the right dose for the right indication." It took more than ten years for American cardiologists to begin accepting amiodarone. In the meantime, I treated a number of patients, again including quite a few who came to me for second opinions, with low-dose amiodarone. I advised them, "I'm prescribing this off-label, as I've explained. You'll have a win-win situation, if you decide to sue me." Fortunately, the patients did well on low-dose amiodarone, and they were grateful to be spared pacemakers as a result.

After reading the abstract of the paper by Breslow et al., I scanned the other Google hits for "baclofen panic" and clicked through a few of the links, but found nothing as interesting. A bit later I decided to Google the keywords "baclofen anxiety," and again I immediately struck what seemed like gold. It was a link to an abstract of a 1993 paper in the journal *Drug and Alcohol Dependence* by the Russian researcher E. M. Krupitsky et al., entitled "Baclofen administration for the treatment of affective disorders in alcoholic patients."

I eagerly clicked the link and read the brief abstract. It said that ninety alcoholic patients with anxiety and/or depression had been divided into four groups receiving either baclofen, a benzo, an antidepressant, or a placebo. Baclofen, the benzo, and the antidepressant were all equally more effective than placebo at relieving anxiety and depression, but baclofen "[did] not have the side-effects and complications" of the benzo and the antidepressant. Unfortunately, the abstract did not say how much baclofen was used, but I was excited to read that it had been shown to be effective against anxiety in a randomized clinical trial.

Finally I put the keywords "baclofen alcohol" into the Google search engine. The first hit brought up the Italian researcher whose name Anna Rose Childress couldn't quite remember. It had to be. "Dolo-something," she had said, and here was a link to the abstract of a 2000 paper, "Ability of baclofen in reducing alcohol craving and intake," by G. Addolorato et al., in the journal *Alcoholism: Clinical and Experimental Research*:

BACKGROUND: Accumulating evidence shows the efficacy of . . . baclofen in reducing alcohol intake in rats, but no studies have been performed in alcoholics. In the present preliminary study we investigated the effect of short-term baclofen administration on craving for alcohol, ethanol intake, and abstinence from alcohol in alcoholic individuals.

METHODS: Ten male current alcoholic individuals were admitted to the study. Baclofen was orally administered for 4 weeks, at a dose of 15 mg/day . . . for the first 3 days, with the dose increased to 30 mg/day for the remaining 27 days. Each subject was checked as an outpatient every week for the 4 weeks; at each visit . . . craving level was evaluated by the Alcohol Craving Scale (ACS), and abstinence from alcohol was assessed based on the individual's self evaluation, family member interview, and the main biological markers of alcohol abuse . . .

RESULTS: Nine subjects completed the study; of these, two subjects continued to drink alcohol although they substantially reduced their daily drinks in the first week of treatment, whereas seven maintained abstinence throughout the experimental period. Craving was significantly reduced from the first week of the drug administration . . . and remained so throughout the entire treatment period. Participants also reported that obsessional thinking about alcohol disappeared . . . Tolerability was fair in all participants; headache, vertigo, nausea, constipation, diarrhea, abdominal pain, hypotension, increased sleepiness, and tiredness were present as side effects in the first stage of the treatment. No participants showed craving for the drug.

CONCLUSIONS: With the limitations of the low number of individuals evaluated and the open design, this preliminary clinical study supports the preclinical evidence on the effect of baclofen in reducing alcohol intake. The anticraving properties of the drug suggest a possible role of baclofen in the treatment of individuals with alcohol problems.

My head spun with all the intriguing information crammed into this abstract, from the "accumulating evidence" for baclofen reducing alcohol intake in animal studies to the new finding that baclofen "significantly reduced" alcohol intake and craving in alcoholic human beings. That side effects were modest, occurring only in the first three days of treatment, and that baclofen itself was apparently not addictive and induced no craving of its own, also fascinated me. And so, once more, did the dosage of 30 milligrams—half the amount Professor Childress had used in her study at the University of Pennsylvania.

Determined to read the whole article, I visited the medical library at Hôpital Cochin for the first time since my days as a medical student. I was wearing a tweed jacket that had belonged to my father, and in the hope that it would keep people from somehow intuiting that I was an alcoholic and dismissing me on that basis, I once more had the red ribbon of the Legion of Honor pinned to my lapel. The system for looking up medical journals had changed thanks to computerization, but with a librarian's assistance I found the article and photocopied it.

After reading it, I was all the more eager to try baclofen—if I could be assured of its safety. For that I felt I could not rely on abstracts. I needed to talk to someone who actually prescribed baclofen to patients.

The article gave the full name of the lead researcher, Giovanni Addolorato, and supplied his affiliation with the Institute of Internal Medicine at the Catholic University of the Sacred Heart in Rome. On a number of occasions—sober, drunk, and hungover—I tried to reach Dr. Addolorato by telephone, but never succeeded.

I took the article to my alcoholism specialist and my CBT

practitioner. But they both dismissed the paper without looking at it. "It's one small study of an unproven medication," they said, and neither wanted to consider prescribing an unfamiliar drug.

I was beside myself with frustration. My life was hanging in the balance, and neither had a sound medical reason for refusing to prescribe a drug that just might help me stop drinking. I thought, "If I'm going to take baclofen, I'll have to self-prescribe."

My only concern was that I still had been unable to determine how safe the drug was. Then I remembered that Linda Carroll's article described baclofen as "an older medication, used for years to treat muscle spasms." It occurred to me that this meant baclofen was probably used to some extent in neurology, and that my colleague and friend John Schaefer, whom I trusted implicitly, was a top neurologist with long experience in the field. If anyone could tell me about baclofen's safety, it would be John.

But I didn't want John to know the real reason I was interested in baclofen. Even if I didn't mention my drinking, I feared he would say, "Ah, baclofen, you are asking about that for alcoholism. But, Olivier, you must not try to be your own doctor for that kind of illness."

So when I called John in New York, I said, "Do you remember the benign idiopathic fasciculations in my calf muscles?"

"Sure," he said.

"What about baclofen for that?"

"Not a bad idea, my boy," he said in his thick Australian accent. "Not a bad idea at all. It's not addictive, it's a good, safe medication. But you have to take it gradually. And if you decide to stop taking it, you have to taper off gradually, just as you would have one of your cardiology patients taper off a medication for hypertension."

"Any contraindications?" I asked.

"Not for you."

"I had seizures when I was admitted to the hospital in your division."

"Yes, but you're not epileptic. Those were withdrawal seizures. They're not a contraindication whatsoever. You start with 5 milligrams three times a day, and then go up to 10 milligrams three times a day, and so on. At each dosage level, you may experience some somnolence, but that will pass after twenty-four to forty-eight hours, and you can then go up in the dosage again."

"Up to where?"

"To where it works."

"But what about . . . ?"

"Olivier, it's a very safe drug. Don't worry."

In France identity cards issued by the Conseil National de l'Ordre des Médecins (National Council of the Order of Physicians) give physicians the legal right to purchase medications for themselves or others without a prescription.

But was baclofen available in France? I still didn't know. The first two pharmacies I tried had never heard of it. The third told me the same thing, but I showed the pharmacist my medical card, and asked to see the French equivalent of the *Physicians' Desk Reference*, listing all available prescription drugs. To my relief, in the generics section I found "Baclofen Irex," manufactured by Sanofi. Later I learned that baclofen was available from several manufacturers and in France was best, if still relatively little, known as Lioresal, the brand name under which it was originally patented and marketed by Ciba-Geigy (now Novartis). In the

United States, it is available under the brand name Lioresal and, from a different manufacturer, the brand name Kemstro.

The pharmacy was happy to order the drug for me. The next day I picked up a small package of 10-milligram tablets of baclofen, but I hesitated to take it. For several days I carried the package around with me unopened. John Schaefer had vouched for its safety. But I had not been completely honest with him about why I wanted to try it, and insofar as my French doctors were concerned I would be taking it AMA, "against medical advice."

Until this point I had steadfastly tried to be a good patient and had avoided being my own physician, but it seemed to me that in order to save my life from alcoholism, I had no choice but to risk walking out onto a tightrope without the normal safety net of another physician's supervision.

On March 22, 2002, following John Schaefer's recommendations, I began taking baclofen in three doses of 5 milligrams each, breaking the tablets in half to do so. Right away I experienced muscular relaxation that I thought was magic, and that night I slept like a baby. I never expected such a dramatic effect, and would not have believed it beforehand.

The next morning I had an appointment with my CBT practitioner. He didn't seem to notice anything different about me, but I felt calmer than usual.

On the way home from the CBT session, I stopped, as I always did after my sessions, in the big FNAC store in Montparnasse. I loved going in there, browsing the huge CD and DVD selections. I always found something—many things—I longed for. Reissued landmark recordings of the classical and romantic repertory by artists like Josef Hofmann and Arturo Toscanini; the modern composers Ligeti, Berio, Morricone, and Dutilleux; Art Tatum, Aretha Franklin, Natalie Cole, Norah Jones—it ran the gamut.

Forty-five minutes later, as I was leaving the store, I stopped short. "Uh-oh," I thought, "where is my stuff? I must have left the bag at the cashier." I was charging back, through the crowd of shoppers, when I realized: I had not bought anything.

Until that moment, I had never recognized that I had long had bouts of compulsive shopping. I'd go into Bloomingdale's for socks and emerge with a bag full of shirts. (I still have some, unopened, in the original plastic wrapping.) It was the same with other sorts of purchases, but especially CDs. While browsing in a store, I never stopped to think that I already had several fine recordings of a particular symphony, say. If I saw that symphony, and wanted it, at that moment I would reach out and take it. I bought what I craved, and I usually craved a half dozen or so CDs each time I stopped in.

And now, for the first time in longer than I could remember, and without consciously doing it, I was exercising judgment and restraint, and I was walking out of the store without having made a single purchase.

Over the next couple of months, I steadily increased my baclofen dose until I was taking 180 milligrams a day.

The short-term results of baclofen for me were remarkable. It relaxed my muscles completely, something I had never experienced before. It gave me a peaceful sleep that, again, I had never experienced before; I woke up refreshed and alert, without the lingering side effects of normal sleeping tablets. It controlled my anxiety better than any of the standard antianxiety medications. It reduced my craving for alcohol and enabled me to remain abstinent for longer periods between binges. It limited the extent of my binges. And it speeded recovery after binges and moderated withdrawal from alcohol efficiently without dependency-inducing benzos and their debilitating side effects.

Baclofen did make me sleepy each time I increased the dose. But it was a pleasant sleepiness that made me feel naturally relaxed and left my mind clear. It was nothing like the dull, foggy cognitive state that Valium and other benzos induced. And just as John Schaefer said it would, the sleepiness went away after a day or two. And I experienced none of the other potential side effects, such as stomach upset, vertigo, and headache, that Addolorato and his colleagues reported as temporary problems in their study.

The long-term safety of baclofen continued to worry me, however. At 180 milligrams a day, I was in unknown territory, taking six times the dose used in brief experiments with alcoholics. The greatest potential risk seemed to be the possibility that baclofen would relax my muscles so much that it would suppress respiration, with the result that I might suffocate in my sleep.

Calling John Schaefer again did not seem like an option. I was not eager to reveal that I had withheld information from him, and to consider doing it again, well, I couldn't do that. And what if John told me baclofen was not an appropriate medication for alcoholism? Given baclofen's improvement of my sense of well-being and self-esteem, in addition to its other benefits, I was understandably reluctant to give it up.

It occurred to me that maybe I could discuss the matter with someone at the Pitié-Salpêtrière hospital in Paris. Salpêtrière has been France's leading hospital for neurology since the late nineteenth century, when Sigmund Freud studied there under Jean-Martin Charcot, "the Napoléon of the neuroses," who was the first to identify and describe multiple sclerosis and amyotrophic lateral sclerosis, among other diseases. I called the neurology department, identified myself as a cardiologist, and asked to speak to a neurologist. It was a difficult exercise, because I was not asking for anyone by name, and it took several calls and lots of waiting on the line before I was finally put through to one of Salpêtrière's staff neurologists.

I said, "My name is Dr. Ameisen. I am a cardiologist. I have a patient who's just come from the States. He's forty-eight years old, and he's on 180 milligrams per day of baclofen as prescribed by his neurologist there for some muscular problems. What can you advise me? Isn't that quite a high dose?"

"Oh, yes, that's much too high."

"Okay, but my patient's been taking this for two years," I said. I had been taking baclofen for two months, but I figured I might as well give the neurologist a longer time frame and see if that drew any special response. "He's not sleepy, he's happy, he's doing fine, he's in good shape. Should I reduce the dose?"

"I've never heard of anyone taking so much."

"Do you know of any downside?"

"Does he have muscle weakness?" the neurologist said.

"No, not at all. He is jogging, he's active," I said, describing my own exercise routine between binges.

"I don't know. If he is doing okay, maybe don't change it. But I have never seen something like that."

It was far from the all-clear that I had hoped to hear. And the neurologist hadn't given me a safety margin for increasing my dose above 180 milligrams a day. But at least he had no danger sign to warn me to watch for in my imaginary patient from America. For the present, I decided to keep my dose at 180 milligrams a day because of the clear health benefit it was giving me, and between binges to continue searching online for information about baclofen and its use in addiction research.

For safety's sake, I wrote in red on the back of my French national identity card that I was taking 180 milligrams of baclofen a day for muscular dystonia and the dose should not be cut off abruptly to prevent a risk of withdrawal. If I fell again during a binge and became unconscious or unable to communicate for a time, or if I had any other medical emergency that left me unable to communicate, medical personnel would at least know to keep giving me baclofen or taper me off it gradually.

For the same reason, it was also important that my doctors know that I was taking baclofen. I spoke to my alcohol specialist and CBT therapist, and told them truthfully, if incompletely, that my neurologist in New York had recommended baclofen for the fasciculations in my calf muscles. They saw from the *Physicians' Desk Reference* that resolving muscular tension was baclofen's standard use, and were happy to prescribe it on that basis. Although baclofen was relatively inexpensive, this meant that I could be reimbursed for its cost rather than paying for it out of pocket. But the main benefit was that if I wound up in the ER, I could show a doctor's prescription for it.

My online searches for information on baclofen soon widened to include addiction research in general. Fabienne, Jean-Claude's wife, gave me an important tip. In addition to her own work as a Chinese teacher, Fabienne helped Jean-Claude prepare his scientific papers on immunology. She told me that Google was a great general-purpose search engine, but that for medical papers I should try PubMed, a website at the National Institutes of Health in the United States. "With PubMed," Fabienne said, "you can search and read abstracts from every medical journal in the world for free."

As I looked at an abstract, I often wished that I could read the full article, but online subscriptions to medical journals were and are prohibitively expensive. At $30 or more apiece, so were individual articles. Finally, even large medical libraries do not have all the specialized journals, and running from library to library every time I saw an interesting abstract online was not practical. The truth is, I was still a clinical associate professor of medicine at Cornell University's Weill Medical College, and as such, I could have been accessing full articles online through the university's library system, no matter where (or how) in the world I was. But that didn't occur to me during my illness, and if it had, I would not have dared to phone Cornell for guidance lest the person at the other end of the line realize I was an alcoholic. In hindsight, it wasn't bad being restricted to reading abstracts. The gist of every article was there, which meant I could read a dozen or more abstracts in less time than it took to read a single scholarly paper in its entirety. I could also more easily see the forest from the trees and retain the most important points, rather than find myself lost in the details.

In the midst of a binge, I could barely focus on the computer screen, much less comprehend an abstract of a scientific paper. I also tried to stay away from the computer when I was drinking, lest I spill liquor into it, and immediately following a binge I needed a few days to recover some clarity of mind. But then I could search online with Google and PubMed for information on baclofen and addiction for several days or more, at least in the morning. In the afternoon, even between binges and with the moderating effect of baclofen, craving proved too distracting for me to concentrate on my search through dozens, hundreds, and ultimately tens of thousands of abstracts.

It was like becoming a student all over again, and took me into fields I had not touched since medical school or my internships, especially chemistry, neurology, and neuroanatomy. The intellectual quest exhilarated me. But I was also often frustrated at how ill I still was. Even at 180 milligrams of baclofen a day, I remained in a moderated binge cycle. Blackouts, accidents, the potential for lethal blood alcohol levels and incurable cirrhosis, among other problems—all the deadly risks of alcoholism remained. It would not matter that I had fewer heavy drinking days per month on baclofen if I stumbled into the street drunk and got run over by a car.

Baclofen seemed to be giving me a hint of a cure rather than a cure itself. There were still dark nights of the soul in which I prayed, "God, if you exist, let me not wake up tomorrow." The next morning I sometimes thought, "Shit, I'm still here," and cursed God bitterly. Addiction is truly a living nightmare in which you wake up *to* the horror, not *from* it.

Sometimes during abstinent periods, I would wake with the taste of liquor in my mouth and berate myself ("When did I relapse? How much did I drink?"), only to realize that I was experiencing what is called an "alcohol dream" or a "drunk dream." The taste of liquor is so strong that you can't help looking around for the bottle you think you drank from. A drunk dream is a very scary, destabilizing experience, and can trigger a relapse even after years of abstinence. In AA and rehab they put a positive spin on drunk dreams and say they represent a sign of progress in sobriety. But it is a strange sort of progress that thrusts the patient into such a miserable state. During my alcoholism, I had drunk dreams as often as once a month, and 180 milligrams of baclofen a day did nothing to stop them.

There was one very positive and significant experience I shared with patients taking much lower doses of baclofen: like them, I had no craving for baclofen. It is essential that an addiction treatment not be addictive itself. So far, baclofen fulfilled that criterion.

Slowly, cautiously, I made forays out in the world, proving to myself that now and then I could still show my face somewhere besides a liquor store or the little orbit of physicians and friends that I circled through during my periods of abstinence. Before my drinking began, I had been an avid skier who fearlessly went down the steepest, iciest slopes without ever hurting myself. (Jean-Claude, Eva, and I had all learned to ski as very young children simply by following our father and imitating his naturally athletic technique. Jean-Claude was so talented that at the age of ten or so a French national ski team coach spotted him and said he should train for competition.) Now, for the first time in so many years, I was able to conquer my fears, and spend a few days on the slopes in the French Alps. I enjoyed it more than I can say (and I managed not to break anything). It felt wonderful to regain a small piece of what I had lost to alcoholism.

I broke up with one woman, took up with another, fell intensely in love with a third. I went on a bona fide holiday: to Eilat, the Israeli resort on the Red Sea, for a week. It was my first plane trip since returning to Paris three years before. I was afraid I would drink on the flights to Israel and back home, but I managed not to do so.

I tentatively made new friendships and reestablished old ones. In the fall of 2002, I was walking on the street one day when I ran into an old friend of Eva's named Rebecca. I hadn't seen her for more than twenty years, but we recognized each other instantly. Rebecca was with one of her two daughters, and she told me she also had a son. She said I must come for dinner to meet all the children and her husband.

We exchanged telephone numbers, and in a phone conversation a few days later I told Rebecca about my alcoholism. "I know it's not the standard you expect from my family," I said. She was very accepting of my disclosure, however, and she renewed her invitation to dinner with her family. Before long, she had become my closest confidante. Much later, she told me that until she actually saw me drunk during a binge she could not believe that I really had a serious drinking problem, because, as she said, "You were always so well-groomed and together. You never seemed in distress. I thought your talk of alcoholism was a romantic pose."

If only my alcoholism had been a pose I could throw off when I got tired of it. Before long, Rebecca not only saw me drunk, but passed out in my apartment, covered in my own vomit or surrounded by broken glass. She cleaned up me and the apartment on many occasions.

Early in 2003, with a few days of abstinence under my belt, I took the Metro to visit my alcoholism specialist in the western suburbs of Paris. It was a normal appointment with no new discussion or decision about my treatment. As I was leaving the specialist's office, which I'd visited regularly for many months, it occurred to me to say, "I know there is a park not too far from here. Could you give me walking directions?" Fifteen minutes later, I was in Parc de St.-Cloud, which commands a magnificent view overlooking Paris to the east.

Parc de St.-Cloud is a French national park, the site of the Château de St.-Cloud, built in the late sixteenth century. Louis XVI bought the château for Marie Antoinette to use as her private retreat, and it was there that Napoléon took the title of Emperor of the French in 1804, followed in 1852 by his nephew Napoléon III. The château was destroyed in the Franco-Prussian War of 1870, but other historic buildings remain amid the park's 185 acres of gardens and woods.

Personal history drew me to the park, however. It was my favorite destination for Sunday outings with my family during my childhood, farther from home and with a greater sense of adventure for me than any other park we visited in or around Paris. The park was also at the beginning of the highway from Paris to Normandy, and as such my private landmark signifying the start of summer vacations and glorious days at the seaside.

Walking in the park for the first time since I was a boy, I felt as if I were experiencing a premonition of the clarity and calm of an existence without anxiety, panic, or alcohol. "It's like I am stepping into the Life of Afterward," I thought to myself. An Alice in Wonderland sensation remained with me strongly for the rest of the day and lingered for a couple of days thereafter.

It was not a feeling of going back to my pre-alcoholic state, which would simply mean returning to a state of chronic anxiety and vulnerability to addiction. Rather it was a feeling of bypassing my illness entirely as if it never happened, of crossing a threshold between my earliest childhood and my future.

Around this time it occurred to me that I should expand my online searches to include animal trials with baclofen. One morning in the middle of February, I did keyword searches with different combinations of the words *baclofen*, *panic*, *rats*, *alcohol*, *cocaine*, *heroin*. Up popped a link to an abstract of a 1997 article in the journal *Psychopharmacology* entitled "Baclofen suppression of cocaine self-administration," by D. C. Roberts and M. M. Andrews of the Institute of Neuroscience at Carleton University in Ottawa, Canada. The abstract said that in an experiment with rats that had been addicted to cocaine and could self-administer it by pressing a lever, a baclofen dose of 1.25 to 5 milligrams per kilogram of body weight "was shown to suppress cocaine intake for at least 4 [hours]" and that "previous results have indicated that baclofen appears to reduce specifically the [addicted rats'] motivation to respond for cocaine."[2]

The use of *suppression* and *suppress* fascinated me. I wondered if baclofen might make it possible to suppress craving for an addictive substance altogether, rather than merely reduce it. The abstract's subsequent reference to baclofen's appearing only "to reduce . . . motivation to respond for cocaine" tempered my excitement, however. Although a reduced motivation to consume alcohol would certainly be positive and desirable, the word *suppression* seemed to promise more than that.

I was also intrigued by the abstract's mention of a dosage range of from 1.25 to 5 milligrams per kilogram of body weight. This indicated that baclofen's effects were strongly dose-dependent. I was encouraged by this because it suggested that a higher dose of baclofen than 180 milligrams a day might enable me to achieve the lasting abstinence from alcohol I dreamed of. At the same time, it suggested that a very high dose indeed, perhaps in excess of 400 milligrams a day, might be necessary, and this again raised a red flag in my mind about the safety of baclofen. Abstinence was not going to do me any good in the grave.

I took my new love to Parc de St.-Cloud for a stroll through the grounds. Once more I felt I was entering *la vie d'après*, "the life of afterward."

"You are like a little kid," she teased. "You think everything is marvelous. You tell me, 'Look at this flower, look at this tree . . . look how beautiful it is.' "

"But it is. It's gorgeous," I protested.

She laughed. "Okay, it's gorgeous, but why are you making such a fuss about it?"

In hindsight, I realize, on baclofen I was beginning to see beautiful days without the nostalgic melancholy that had shadowed me since childhood. I was beginning to live fully in the present.

I came upon a reference to a brand-new article in *The Lancet* by the University of Texas researcher B. A. Johnson et al. The article was entitled "Oral topiramate for treatment of alcohol: a randomised controlled trial," and the abstract described a twelve-week trial in which 150 alcohol-dependent people were given either placebo or increasing doses of topiramate, a drug thought to facilitate GABA activity in the brain. That caught my eye because baclofen affects GABA activity; perhaps topiramate did so more strongly. The abstract said that those receiving topiramate experienced "27.6% fewer heavy drinking days . . . , 26.2% more days abstinent . . . ," and similar reductions in craving for alcohol.[3]

The percentage differences were similar to those reported for naltrexone and acamprosate, which I had already taken with no effect. But I was impressed by the fact that the article was in *The Lancet*, one of the world's three most influential medical journals, along with *The New England Journal of Medicine* and *The Journal of the American Medical Association*. The other articles I had found were all in smaller, specialized journals. Moreover, the topiramate study was larger and longer than the baclofen studies in the other articles, and it was a randomized controlled trial, the gold standard of modern medicine. Last but not least, it was brand-new.

"This must be the cutting edge," I thought. It seemed like my best hope yet for achieving complete abstinence from alcohol. I went to the medical library at the Pompidou Centre to read the entire article and make a photocopy.

Over a ten-day period, I tapered my baclofen dose down to zero. I used my doctor's medical card to purchase topiramate, and then I followed the *Lancet* article's protocol, taking topiramate for a total of twelve weeks and escalating the dose from 25 to 300 milligrams a day.

During this twelve-week period, topiramate did not perceptibly reduce my craving for alcohol, and did not at all alleviate my anxiety and muscular tension, as baclofen did. Also unlike baclofen, topiramate had unpleasant side effects, including difficulty concentrating and impaired memory, that did not go away as I became used to taking it. In terms of both combating alcoholism and promoting a sense of well-being, baclofen proved far superior for me. I returned to wondering if a higher dose of baclofen than 180 milligrams a day could be safe.

It was time to let Philippe Coumel know what I had been exploring.

When I went to visit him in August, he was in the hospital and his appearance shocked me. He was clearly very ill, but his intelligent eyes and his smile were unchanged, and his mind remained razor sharp.

His wife was with him in the hospital room. It was the first time we had ever met. After a few moments, she excused herself to give Philippe and me some time alone.

I brought him up-to-date on my recent online investigations and my self-experiments with baclofen and topiramate. I described baclofen's very different effects on me compared to all the other medications I had taken for anxiety or alcoholism. And I outlined my reasons for surmising that my best future course of treatment was to increase my daily intake of baclofen until it produced complete abstinence or limiting side effects.

Just as he had when I was reporting my M.D. thesis findings, Philippe listened with penetrating attention, occasionally asking me to elaborate on changes in my anxiety and alcoholism symptoms in response to different medications. Forgetting his own concerns, my mentor, my friend, gave himself completely to helping me sharpen my self-diagnosis and my rationale for treating alcoholism with high-dose baclofen.

Philippe said, "Olivier, you have always been a splendid listener with your patients, and now you are giving yourself the same benefit: you are giving the most marvelous descriptions. Your supposition that muscular tension and addictive craving must be connected by an unknown mechanism makes perfect sense. Don't let yourself be crushed by disappointment if you are wrong. But your plan could work, and I believe it should work. I will look forward to hearing your results."

It had been four years since Philippe had spurred me on to save myself. He had so memorably written me, "I never let you down, and I will never drop you as a friend. More important, I cannot believe that a man of your intelligence cannot find the solution."

He had been true to his word. And I was doing everything I could to be true back to him.

7. Cutting Through Craving

A HISTORIC LATE-AUGUST HEAT WAVE struck Paris. Many elderly people died in this unusual heat.

My tragedy did not compare: I only lost my computer. It crashed totally, with no backup. All the key abstracts I had compiled to try to save my life were gone. A cold sweat broke out over my whole body, and I nearly fainted. I thought I might develop a heart attack. The calming effect of the 180 milligrams of baclofen a day I was taking evaporated in the face of this traumatic shock. I immediately took 80 more milligrams and lay down.

To my surprise and relief, within an hour I started to feel better. Without baclofen, I would have been in a hopeless state for days or weeks. Positive thoughts came to mind: "Look, you're alive. You can gather it all again as you did before." In fact, I had printed out the most important abstracts, and thanks to my good memory and a new set of online searches, I soon duplicated most of my research base. Regathering my confidence bit by bit, I reviewed all I had learned and inferred about alcoholism, addiction in general, and baclofen. And as I did I came to an important conclusion:

One characteristic that separates addiction from the vast majority of other diseases is that it is symptom-driven and symptom-dependent. In addiction, the symptoms *are* the disease.

In nearly all other diseases, symptoms do not drive the progression of the disease. When symptoms are discernible, they can often be suppressed, while the disease itself rages on in the body. Think of the fever of tuberculosis, the abdominal pain of pancreatic cancer, and the angina of severe coronary heart disease. Stopping the symptoms does nothing to stop the disease.

Many illnesses — say, forms of cancer and heart disease — are asymptomatic. Because patients experience no discernible symptoms, medicine speaks of these conditions as "silent killers," which are often detected too late to save the patient's life. But when it comes to addiction, it is impossible to separate it from its symptoms. Stopping the symptoms of addiction — the cravings, obsessive thoughts, and the motivation to consume an addictive substance or engage in an addictive behavior — would in fact stop the disease. The patient would go into complete remission.

Knocking out the symptoms of addiction would inactivate the disease by taking away all its weapons.

There is a similarly tight connection between illness and experiential symptoms in the preaddiction morbidities — such as anxiety and panic and depression — that I had heard so many addicts (myself among them) describe as the cause of their turn to addictive substances. Here, too, stopping the discernible symptoms stops the disease. If someone has pain from a cancerous tumor, it is necessary to both alleviate the pain and remove the tumor. If someone no longer feels anxious or depressed, there is nothing left to treat.

Craving for an addictive substance, or a compulsive behavior, is the primary symptom of addiction and compulsion in two senses. From the suffering patient's point of view, craving is the constant enemy that must be battled—even after years of abstinence. And, from the point of view of the disease process, craving is now recognized as the number-one cause of relapse.

Yet in other ways, craving remains a hotly contested subject in addiction research. Some researchers say that addictive craving is too elusive a concept to have practical value. To which I say: Like pain, it is only elusive if you don't have it.

The vast majority of researchers acknowledge the centrality of craving in addiction, and some seek to define distinctions between different categories of craving. In a 1999 paper in the journal *Alcohol and Alcoholism*, R. Verheul et al., of the Amsterdam Institute for Addiction Research at the University of Amsterdam, reviewed research on three types of craving, each thought to have its own distinctive pathway of neurotransmission in the brain: hedonistic "reward" craving; a desire for decreased tension dubbed "relief" craving; and "obsessive" craving, in which one is unable to stop thinking about the addictive substance or behavior. This paper and other studies have attempted to link the three types of craving to different manifestations of addiction, postulating for example that "reward" craving tends to define early-onset addiction and "relief" craving tends to define late-onset addiction.

As I considered the issue of craving in 2003, I thought that these distinctions might well prove important in medicine's ultimate understanding of addiction. Yet I also wondered how effectively they could be separated in terms of treatment. My alcoholism was very much a late-onset addiction, and most of my craving could best be described as craving for relief from extreme tension. But I also regularly experienced craving for reward—wanting to feel good for a change—and was frequently burdened by obsessive craving in which I could not stop thinking of alcohol.

I wondered just how different the different types of craving actually were. We like to think that it's the subtle differences that secretly, really count. But perhaps the common denominators in neurotransmission that have been observed in addicted people and animals count for far more than the subtle differences in neurotransmission do.

In this regard, it fascinated me that baclofen had suppressed laboratory animals' self-administration of alcohol, cocaine, heroin, methamphetamine, and nicotine. With enough baclofen, the animals lost their motivation to consume the addictive substance—whatever it was. The lab animals could not tell researchers whether reward, relief, or obsessive cravings were uppermost in their minds. It certainly made no sense to distinguish between early-onset and late-onset addiction in animals deliberately addicted to a substance as part of a scientific experiment. And they did not stop consuming addictive substances because they understood the behavior was detrimental to their health or had an awakening. But they stopped.

The more I learned, the more I came to believe that at a high enough dose of baclofen, I too could reach a point where I would lose the motivation to consume alcohol. But how high? Baclofen had suppressed laboratory animals' motivation to consume alcohol at 1 to 3 milligrams per kilogram of body weight; it had suppressed their motivation to consume a variety of other addictive substances at 1 to 5 milligrams per kilogram of body weight. The range of doses at which different individual laboratory animals stopped consuming the same addictive substance suggested that the severity of an individual's dependence might be a factor. My doctors told me that my alcoholism was extremely severe. So, again, how high a dose would I have to take?

And at what risk? It remained a distinct possibility that a high enough dose to suppress craving—my craving—could also kill me. Perhaps it would relax my muscles so much that I would stop breathing in my sleep. Although it seemed better to die with dignity in the search for a cure than to resign myself to the messy indignities of an alcohol-related demise, I had no death wish.

I struggled on. There were experiments with other treatments; other binges, other accidents. As the year waned, I mapped out a protocol for increasing my baclofen intake. Then, on January 8, 2004, I decided it was now or never. If I continued to follow my doctors' advice and the conventional treatments for alcoholism, I was going to keep lapsing into binges and eventually die from drinking. I had to take my treatment into my own hands.

To give my baclofen protocol a fresh start, I went down to a low dose of 30 milligrams and added 20 milligrams every third day, allowing an additional 20–40 milligrams a day to deal with heightened craving for alcohol or a spike in my stress level. Because my alcohol cravings were always worse in the afternoon and evening, I divided the baclofen into three unequal doses, taking less in the mornings and more later in the day. I planned to go as high as 300 milligrams a day, assuming there were no limiting side effects. That would be 4 milligrams of baclofen per kilogram of my body weight, above the dosage range, 1 to 3 milligrams per kilogram of body weight, shown to suppress motivation to consume alcohol in laboratory animals.

From the first day, my muscular tension and nervous anxiety began to subside and my sleep became more restful. If I took an extra 20–40 milligrams of baclofen when I experienced the first desire for alcohol, I only had to struggle with intense craving for about an hour before it subsided, without soon recurring strongly as it always had in the past.

The additional 20–40 milligrams of baclofen induced a state of deep relaxation followed by somnolence, which left me clearheaded. This was completely different from the mental fogginess induced by benzos like Valium. Even when I dropped off to sleep, I awoke feeling mentally sharp. (Based on my experience, cognitive enhancement is one of the characteristics of baclofen that deserves thorough study. Even when baclofen made me somnolent, I was struck by how clear my mind was. There were no interfering "parasite" thoughts, which usually invade and preoccupy the mind almost constantly in addiction.)

During the deep relaxation phase, I found that I could use the craving-coping skills taught in AA and CBT as I never could before. Baclofen enabled a thought process to intervene between craving and the compulsion to drink.

By Wednesday, February 11, I had reached 250 milligrams of baclofen a day. My friend Rebecca had convinced me to drive with her family to Megève, in the mountains, and we left early that afternoon. I loved her family, and was always happiest in the mountains; still, I was wary. A resort town would flood me with drinking stimuli, especially the sight of people relaxing with alcohol in the evenings. But I figured that if I avoided drinking places as much as possible, I would be fine.

At dinner on the first evening, Rebecca and her husband ordered wine for themselves and their daughters. No one drank more than a glass or two, I stuck to mineral water, and there was still a little wine in the bottle when we left the table.

Over the following days I took long hikes, sometimes alone and sometimes with others in the group. The mountain vistas and frequent fresh snow were exhilarating. I thought of skiing, but decided not to risk an injury that might interrupt my baclofen protocol.

On Saturday, February 14, thirty-seven days into the protocol, I reached a dose of 270 milligrams a day, nine times the amount that Giovanni Addolorato was using in his trials of baclofen to reduce alcoholics' craving. Rebecca wanted me to go with her that afternoon for tea at Le Lodge Park Hotel, the fanciest place in Megève. The hotel had a spacious bar and lounge area that was famous for people-watching as well as for the breathtaking views outside every window. I was apprehensive about seeing people drinking there, but I agreed to go.

We arrived around five o'clock, when there was still a little light to catch the splendid scenery. We found a table, and I picked up copies of *Le Monde* and the *International Herald Tribune*. I read the two newspapers religiously every day, but I also thought they would be a useful distraction from looking at people drinking.

We ordered tea, Rebecca settled into some people-watching, and I began reading. After five or ten minutes, I glanced up from the newspaper. I saw a man in an armchair to my right drinking a glass of something dark—whisky or cognac, I assumed—and felt neutral. I looked back down at the paper for another minute or two, before this neutral feeling registered consciously.

"That's interesting," I thought.

I looked up again at the man in the armchair. He had been

joined by a couple of friends and they were lifting glasses to each other in a toast. Again I felt neutral. In the years since the onset of my alcoholism, this had never happened. In five weeks, baclofen had made it happen.

Sweeping my eyes around the room, I dared to look at the bar with its gleaming bottles. They no longer called to me, as they had for so long. I saw people drinking various things: coffee and tea, soft drinks, beer, champagne, hard liquor. No alcohol thoughts came to mind; no craving for alcohol troubled me.

I thought, "I am in a fairy tale or a dream. In a moment the spell will break, and I will wake up to the horror of needing a drink."

I didn't.

Half an hour later, after Rebecca and I finished our tea, we went to meet her family for dinner. The spell didn't break; the dream didn't end. That evening, for the first time since my alcoholism began, I had no craving for alcohol.

We spent three more days in Megève. On the last afternoon, Rebecca and I rented skis and enjoyed a little time on the slopes. Her kids had been skiing every day, of course, and they teased us about waiting until the last minute. In the car going back to Paris in the evening, I wondered whether the craving for alcohol would return when I was home and in my usual routine.

It didn't.

I did not increase my baclofen dose at this point because 270 milligrams a day was producing intermittent somnolence that, unlike the somnolence at lower doses, did not go away. There was nothing uncomfortable about this. Quite the contrary, I had no anxiety whatsoever. But I sometimes felt too sleepy and on one occasion nodded off across the dinner table from a friend. For twelve days I remained at 270 milligrams with no return of craving for alcohol and no alcohol thoughts. I had not had a drunk dream since day fifteen of my protocol. Moreover I felt calmer and more physically relaxed than ever before in my life.

Then, over the following twelve days, I progressively reduced my baclofen dose to 120 milligrams. At this dosage I had no somnolence, yet craving for alcohol and alcohol thoughts did not return, and I also had no perceptible muscular tension or anxiety. Going up to 270 milligrams had apparently triggered a threshold response, which could now be maintained at the lower dosage.

Oddly enough, my calf muscles continued to twitch now and then. But the twitching never became the prelude to increasing muscular tension and rising anxiety, as it so frequently had in the past.

After day sixty-three of my baclofen protocol, March 11, I kept my daily dose at 120 milligrams, occasionally adding another 20–40 milligrams in stressful situations. I had emotional ups and downs, some of them very intense, as everyone does in life. But thanks to baclofen they no longer destabilized me to the extent that I experienced overwhelming anxiety or panic attacks.

The sense of being in a fairy tale or a dream stayed with me for quite a while. I was skeptical of what was happening, because I was living something that is supposed to be impossible for an alcoholic or addict: complete freedom from craving.

Over time I became used to a new reality in which I could live normally and function without alcohol and without any striving not to drink. It felt miraculous. As AA and CBT both advise, I at first avoided situations and places where alcohol might be present. But I realized before long that I did not have to be concerned about this. Even when socializing with friends who were drinking in a restaurant or at a party, I had no craving for alcohol.

The usual criterion for saying an alcoholic or addict is doing well is abstinence—success in resisting craving for alcohol or another addictive substance. I was not abstinent with regard to alcohol. I was completely and effortlessly *indifferent* to it.

Everyone noticed the change in me. In person they remarked on how clear-eyed and vital I looked. Even on the phone, they heard the difference in the tone of my voice. Friends and acquaintances said, "You are like a new man." They also praised me, very incorrectly in my view, by saying things such as "We admire you so much for not drinking." Maintaining abstinence despite powerful craving is meritorious and deserves praise. But as I tried to explain to everyone who complimented me on not drinking, I merited no praise because the change was entirely thanks to baclofen's suppressing my craving, calming my anxiety, and erasing my motivation to drink. It was difficult for my family and friends to grasp that my not drinking was effortless. I needed to talk to others in the medical community.

I was ready to share the good news with Philippe Coumel. Heartbreakingly, he had passed away earlier in the month.

At the end of June, I called my friend Boris Pasche and reached him at his lab in the hematology and oncology division of Northwestern University Medical School. No sooner had I said, "Hello, how are you," than Boris said, "Olivier, something wonderful has happened for you. I can hear it in your voice. You sound different than you ever have in the past."

"That is why I called you," I said, and went on to explain about my baclofen protocol. "It's as simple as one, two, three. One is that baclofen produces dose-dependent suppression of the motivation to consume addictive substances in laboratory rats. Two is that low-dose baclofen reduces addictive craving in human beings. And three is that high-dose baclofen, on the same ratio of 1 to 3 milligrams per kilogram of body weight as in the laboratory animals, has entirely suppressed my craving for alcohol and resolved my anxiety better than any other medicine I have tried. And as you know, I have tried them all. I want to share this with the medical community, but I am afraid I will not be credible as an alcoholic."

Boris said, "Ultimately, the facts will decide, and you have powerful facts to report. What you've done is fascinating. When are you sending me the paper?"

"What paper?"

"The paper you must write on your findings. I am a contributing editor at *JAMA* [*The Journal of the American Medical Association*] now, and I can pass it on to the right person."

Over the next weeks, I busied myself with drafting a self-case report on my alcoholism and the change brought about by high-dose baclofen in only five weeks. I was not sure at this point if I should try to publish the case report anonymously or with a pseudonym. I had outed myself as a physician with addiction in my own hospital seven years earlier. To do so in a published paper was an even more radical step, and there would be no going back. From then on, anyone who Googled my name would see that I was an alcoholic, or at the least an ex-alcoholic. Would I ever find a job if the case report included my name? I also worried about embarrassing my family, but fortunately Jean-Claude and Eva had no objection.

Weighing the personal risks against the potential public benefits, I recalled people I had met in detox and rehab. A number of them had died from alcoholism or other addictions. Others were still fighting for survival. Tentatively I decided that I would name myself in the case report in order to give it maximum impact. Revealing my identity would also make the point that those who suffer from addiction deserve to be treated with the same dignity and respect as sufferers from other diseases.

One thing missing from the baclofen-related research I had found so far was support for baclofen's safety at high doses. But then one day, searching for articles on "oral high-dose baclofen," I hit something promising. In 1991 C. R. Smith et al., of the Medical Rehabilitation Research and Training Center for Multiple Sclerosis at Albert Einstein College of Medicine, had published a paper in *Neurology* entitled "High-dose oral baclofen: experience in patients with multiple sclerosis." The abstract referred to MS patients taking more than 80 milligrams of baclofen a day and said that "taking a high dose was not associated with discontinuing treatment."[1]

I checked around Paris for the article, but could not find a library that carried *Neurology*. In August I learned that the library at the Necker Hospital had the journal. Students and most of the staff were away, and the library was nearly empty when I went there to read the article.

The article reported on MS patients taking up to 270 milligrams of oral baclofen, my own high point, for thirty-six months with no reported side effects. Equally important, the authors wrote, "Unfortunately, physicians tend to underutilize baclofen . . . Pinto et al. identified patients who had taken up to 225 mg daily for up to 30 months and emphasized that many patients need more than 100 mg daily and that side effects are only infrequently a persisting problem." Now I had ample proof that I was not an anomaly, and that oral baclofen was safe in doses much greater than the 30–60 milligrams addiction researchers were using in their human trials of the drug. But how much higher?

I searched for "baclofen overdose," and found the abstract of a 1986 article by R. Gerkin et al. in *Annals of Emergency Medicine*, which reported that a woman had been unsuccessful in committing suicide by taking "more than 2 g[rams] of baclofen . . . the largest ingestion of baclofen reported to date."[2] Not only had 2 grams of baclofen—almost seven and a half times the 270 milligrams that had suppressed my alcohol craving and more than sixteen and a half times my maintenance dose of 120 milligrams—proved nonlethal, but the woman had also made a complete recovery with no lingering side effects.

John Schaefer's Australian accent rang in my ears as I recalled his saying, "Olivier, it's a very safe drug." Given that the article on MS patients was published in *Neurology*, the leading journal in John's own field, I decided to call him and ask him about baclofen again.

Before I could tell him about the effect of baclofen on my alcoholism, John remarked on the healthy sound of my voice. He was delighted to hear about my recovery, and he laughed heartily when I said how afraid I had been to mention my drinking during our first conversation about baclofen.

I said, "Do you prescribe over 80 milligrams a day to your own patients, John?"

He said, "Sure."

"What's your limit? Do you go up to 100 milligrams?"

"Higher."

"200 milligrams?"

"Higher, depending on the individual case, of course."

"300 milligrams?"

"That's as far as I go."

"400 milligrams?"

"No, my boy, 300 milligrams a day is my limit. You can quote me on that in your paper."

John explained that 300 milligrams of oral baclofen a day was the conservative limit for neurologists of his generation, and that he had quite a few patients who took that much without any side effects. Younger neurologists tended to switch patients receiving over 120 milligrams a day to a spinal pump that had recently come on the market. But many neurologists saw no compelling reason to do this, given the common reports of infection and other complications from the spinal pump.

Hearing this, I regretted my inability to ask John about the dose earlier and save myself a year and a half of agonizing over how much I could safely take. But truly, the knowledge was better late than never.

In light of the successful experiments with high-dose baclofen in addicted laboratory animals and the routine prescribing of high-dose baclofen for comfort care of human patients in neurology, it perplexed me why addiction researchers used such small doses in their experiments with human beings. Could those in addiction medicine and research really be unaware of how neurologists had been using baclofen for decades? As I was to find out, the answer was yes, they were—an unfortunate result of the increasing specialization of medicine.

While I was drafting my case report, I went through intense emotional swings. In some moments I dared to hope that my paper could help bring relief to other alcoholics and addicts. In others I was sure that an alcoholic physician, even an ex-alcoholic physician, would never be taken seriously.

It seemed to me that as the only one who knew the secret code about baclofen, as it were, I must finish the article as soon as possible. I repeatedly told the woman typing the article for me, "If something happens to me before the article is finished, e-mail everything to Boris Pasche." She patiently kept telling me that she would.

Writing the paper was a considerable challenge, because I was describing something new in the annals of human addiction: not craving reduction but craving suppression; not abstinence or an aid to abstinence but complete, effortless indifference to alcohol, with simultaneous alleviation of comorbid anxiety.

"You made exist what did not exist before," said Jean-Claude, who offered me valuable feedback and suggestions after I had completed the draft. I was a little concerned that he might be biased in favor of the paper because he was my brother, but we had always been brutally honest with each other in intellectual matters, and his research achievements as an immunologist went far beyond mine as a cardiologist. Jean-Claude introduced the concept of apoptosis, programmed cell death, for the understanding of AIDS and other diseases in pioneering, sole-authored articles, and he has written many other important papers in collaboration with his research colleagues. He would never mince words with regard to medical and scientific questions.

One of the vital points I wanted to make in the case report was that alcoholics and other addicts tend to have a preexisting, lifelong dysphoria associated with disorders such as anxiety and depression. However, I feared that a journal editor or peer reviewers would argue that this was only an anecdotal claim based on my personal observation, and insist on cutting it. To my great relief, however, a major article substantiating my observation appeared at just this time. Writing in the August 2004 issue of *Archives of General Psychiatry*, Bridget F. Grant et al. reported on the U.S. National Institutes of Health's National Epidemiological Survey on Alcohol and Related Conditions (NESARC). NESARC's primary finding, which I cited in chapter 2, was that "associations between most substance use disorders and independent mood and anxiety disorders were overwhelmingly positive and significant."[3]

How I wished this article had been published years earlier! Nevertheless, I was grateful to have it now, and to be able to quote from it in the case report.

I e-mailed the draft to Boris Pasche, who gave it to the deputy editor of *JAMA*, Dr. Richard Glass, a psychiatrist and an expert in addiction medicine. Dr. Glass quickly e-mailed me to say that while he thought the paper was fascinating, *JAMA* never published case reports. He recommended that I send it to the journal *Alcohol and Alcoholism*, which is published by Oxford University Press for the British Medical Council on Alcohol.

Looking up the journal online, I saw that there were two coeditors-in-chief, one based in Edinburgh and the other in Belgium. The British Isles have a tradition of welcoming original ideas and being more open to innovation than is sometimes true on the European continent, and I hoped my paper would appeal to the Scottish editor, Dr. Jonathan Chick.

Jonathan Chick later told me that he had been so moved by reading my self-case report that he wondered if his emotional reaction might be biasing his editorial judgment. Following the normal editorial procedures, he sent the paper to two leading addiction researchers to review and comment on it, and their anonymous comments were passed along to me in due course. Both reviewers enthusiastically recommended publication, and one said the paper was "a precious cameo that deserves to be disseminated in the scientific community." The reviewers both said the paper would be more effective if it were shorter, and they offered a number of smaller suggestions for improving it.

After I completed revisions and resubmitted the article, Jonathan Chick very appropriately asked for one more thing: corroboration by one of my physicians. I phoned Jean-Paul Descombey, who gave me an appointment the next day, and who then wrote Chick:

> *I, the undersigned, Doctor Jean-Paul Descombey, former chief of psychiatry at Hôpital Ste.-Anne and member of the administrative council of the French Society of Alcohology, am in a position to offer the following testimony on Doctor Olivier Ameisen.*
>
> *1. Doctor Ameisen has been my patient since shortly after his return to France from the USA . . . He was suffering from alcohol addiction along with a strong neurotic component with symptoms of anxiety that were visible when not drowned by massive ingestion of alcohol (whisky).*
>
> *Despite many hospitalizations in various specialized settings, assiduous attendance at Alcoholics Anonymous meetings, and a positive relationship with me during sessions that were weekly as often as his state permitted it, Mr. Ameisen was never able to achieve sobriety for more than a few days during the years 2000–2002.*

The course of his disease was marked by numerous accidents, namely physical traumas related to his massive alcoholization. His somatic state deteriorated, worsened by the negligence of both his body and his living quarters. Apart from a few colleagues and friends, people close to him backed away, with the notable exception of a few AA friends, often themselves overwhelmed by the state and the behavior of Mr. Ameisen. Nevertheless, his biological parameters remained normal except for the [liver enzymes] GGTP [gamma-glutamyl transpeptidase] and the transaminases.

His state had reached the point that even a continuous psychiatric professional relationship became impossible or would risk turning into a simulated form of therapy devoid of honesty.

I did not see Mr. Ameisen again for over one year, although he occasionally phoned me to give his news.

2. Mr. Ameisen contacted me recently by telephone, giving me his (good) news in a clear and self-assured voice, very different from the voice I had experienced in all previous phone conversations.

He explained to me that he was self-treating himself with baclofen and writing a paper about this experience for publication in a specialized journal.

We decided to meet on 3 November 2004.

Mr. Ameisen's appearance and behavior at this meeting were spectacularly changed on every level: self-assured body language reflecting a sense of ease within himself, open face, clear skin, with no signs of chronic alcohol use, easy contact, neither self-conscious nor obsequious, clear speaking, sober, impeccable articulation, suitably attired without being overdressed.

In short, none of the signs of alcohol use which Mr. Ameisen had accustomed me to expect with him.

. . . One easily sees in him the person that could only be guessed at

during his period of "full alcoholization." He displays none of the con-
formist dulling behavior that one sometimes encounters in alcoholics
who are only "repentant." Also, no triumphalism whatsoever, since
Mr. Ameisen states that he would risk falling back into psychological
dependence toward alcohol if he were to discontinue baclofen.

It is not for me to infer what in this change is due to baclofen or
to any other associated factor . . . . But it is the facts—the change, the
rehabilitation—that strike me clearly; I am happy to furnish to Mr.
Ameisen testimony as a clinician and a therapist, or at the very least,
as a practitioner who had made all efforts to fulfil this goal.

Doctor Jean-Paul Descombey
Paris, 4 November 2004

In less than six weeks, short order for a scientific paper, my self-
case report was reviewed, revised, and accepted for publication.
It was slated to appear first in electronic form on December 13,
2004, and subsequently in the normal print edition of *Alcohol
and Alcoholism* (see the appendix for the full text of the article).

I briefly had second thoughts about becoming the first physician to admit to an addiction in a published paper. That no
physician had apparently done so before, even under a pseudonym, much less his or her real name, indicated how much there
was to lose. It was an agonizing decision. But I remembered
Philippe Coumel's words to me when I returned to Paris from
New York: "As a physician, how can you be embarrassed about
having a disease?" It was long since time for addiction to be seen
in proper moral terms as a disease like any other, and I could only
hope that publishing the paper under my real name would contribute to that understanding. Breaking this taboo was worth it
if it advanced the treatment of alcoholism.

8. The End of Addiction?

ON DECEMBER 12, 2004, the day before my self-case report's electronic publication by *Alcohol and Alcoholism*, I realized that I had not yet told my own alcoholism specialist, Dr. S., about my recovery or the case report. Over the previous year I had seen her infrequently, because I had not been making any progress with conventional alcoholism therapy. But she had always treated me with great kindness, and she deserved to hear about my experiences directly from me. I accordingly e-mailed her a copy of the self-case report with a brief cover note, and we arranged to meet in late January.

A week later, I heard from Giovanni Addolorato, whose articles on the effect of low-dose baclofen helped embolden me to try higher doses on myself. He wrote requesting a reprint of my report, which I immediately sent. Ten days after that, I saw online an abstract of a new paper by Addolorato on the use of baclofen in preventing alcohol withdrawal syndrome. He sent me a reprint at my request and wrote:

Many compliments for your paper published in Alcohol and Alcoholism; *a query: do you still continue the baclofen therapy (if yes, at the dose of)? Are you still abstinent?*

> *My best wishes*
> *Giovanni*

From this point on, Giovanni and I were on a first-name basis, as I soon was with his colleagues Giancarlo Colombo, Roberta Agabio, and Fabio Caputo. Giovanni and Giancarlo said that when I came to Italy they would hold a seminar on my self-case report and treatment model.

I was glowing with hope these days. Here I was, the author of the first peer-reviewed report of complete suppression of alcoholism symptoms—a report published in one of the world's leading medical journals on alcoholism. Concerned that I was going to be flooded with mail from interested physicians and researchers, I had rented a post office box and given that as my contact address in the self-case report, along with my e-mail address and telephone number. "It's only a matter of time," I thought, "before full-scale randomized trials of baclofen's effectiveness will be launched."

I felt as if I'd scaled Mount Everest. I'd barely made it to the base camp.

Late January came, and I arrived for my appointment with Dr. S. In the month or so since I'd sent her my article, she had not yet had an opportunity to read it, she told me, but she was delighted by the change in my condition, and she said that my self-case report would be the topic of the hospital alcohology department's staff meeting the following day.

I suggested that the next step was a study of baclofen's dose-dependent effectiveness for other alcoholics. She responded that I shouldn't worry about other alcoholics, but should concentrate on my own life now that my ordeal with alcoholism was over. She expressed skepticism that other alcoholics would even want to try baclofen, and warned me that agitating for baclofen studies would only alienate people in addiction medicine.

Her response was baffling, to say the least. In retrospect, I think it may have stemmed from her concern for me as her patient. She knew better than I how entrenched certain views were in the field and how difficult it would be to introduce a new perspective. And perhaps she did not quite trust in the fact of my recovery.

Before I left, she wanted to make an appointment to see me again in a month. Given that I had been completely disease-free for one year, I could not see the point of that.

Dr. S. then rewrote my standing prescription for baclofen. She reduced it from 180 milligrams a day to a maximum of 75 milligrams, because the higher dose I was taking was normally prescribed only for muscular issues—and she was not comfortable prescribing it for addiction, she said.

The complete remission of my alcoholism could not be maintained at that dosage. In addition to which, a daily dose of 120 milligrams of baclofen was indeed calming my chronic anxiety. In medicine there is something called off-label use, or off-label prescribing. It is common. Once a medication has been approved for a specific application, it is perfectly acceptable for physicians to prescribe it for other conditions. Over 23 percent of all prescriptions, and over 60 percent in cancer care, are off-label. The American Medical Association says that the deciding factor in off-label prescribing is "the best interest of the patient."[1]

The standard maximum dose for baclofen in France, as in the United States, is 80 milligrams. But as I had learned from John Schaefer, as well as from the Smith et al. paper on patients taking up to 270 milligrams a day, neurologists had been prescribing more than that off-label for a few decades without their patients experiencing any lasting side effects.

I decided not to press the point with Dr. S.

The meeting rattled me, but I regrouped, and on returning home e-mailed the head of Dr. S.'s department to say that I had heard about the plan to discuss my self-case report at the next day's staff meeting. Would he like me to attend to elaborate on my experiences or answer questions? He quickly e-mailed back, saying no thanks. He also sent his "Bravo to Jonathan Chick," the coeditor-in-chief of *Alcohol and Alcoholism*, for publishing my self-case report. Noting that the paper failed to specify the kind of anxiety I suffered, he suggested, "Perhaps [Dr.] Descombey could give the precise diagnosis." And finally: "Dr. S. will stay in touch with you for follow-up on your case."

It escaped me why the specific kind of anxiety I had should matter. That had not concerned Jonathan Chick or the two addiction research experts who had so strongly recommended the publication of my self-case report. The e-mail at least demonstrated that the head of Dr. S.'s department had read my paper. But it was disappointing, and rather odd in terms of usual practice, that a group of physicians preferred to discuss a paper in a medical journal without taking advantage of the opportunity to engage the author in question-and-answer, especially when the physician author was also the patient and had successfully experimented on himself with a treatment protocol of his own design. My eye was drawn to the statement "Dr. S. will stay in touch . . .

for follow-up on your case." That suggested pretty strongly that the department head did not take my paper seriously, but saw me only as a perhaps temporarily abstinent alcoholic.

A deafening silence ensued. Except for Giovanni Addolorato and a few of his colleagues in Italy, no one inside or outside the field of addiction research and treatment seemed to have any interest in the first peer-reviewed report of complete suppression of the deadly disease of alcoholism with alleviation of comorbid anxiety. I began to worry that my self-case report was largely going to be ignored, and that perhaps it deserved to be ignored because it was not really worthwhile.

In February my friend Georges Moroz, a psychiatrist and psychopharmacologist who does research on medications for anxiety, visited Paris from his home in New Jersey. Normally a reserved person, he told me, "Your paper is explosive!"

I said, "For an explosion, it's pretty silent."

"The fuse is lit. You've just got to get it in front of the right people. Baclofen affects GABA, so you should send it to George Koob. He's Mr. GABA. I bet he'll be fascinated."

A behavioral physiologist, George Koob chairs the Committee on the Neurobiology of Addictive Disorders at the Scripps Research Institute in La Jolla, California. Koob and his colleague Michel Le Moal are among the world's leading experts on the brain's reward mechanisms, which are crucial in addiction. Finding an e-mail address for Koob on one of his papers, I sent him a copy of my self-case report and asked for any feedback he might be able to give me. Time passed and I heard nothing from him.

The printed issue of *Alcohol and Alcoholism* containing my self-case report appeared in March. Professor Colin Martin, a clinical psychologist at the Chinese University of Hong Kong, wrote me an appreciative e-mail, congratulating me on the importance of my findings and my courage in revealing my identity. Apart from Giovanni Addolorato, he was the only person in the medical and research community to initiate contact with me on baclofen for nearly a year after the paper was published (and he remains one of only a handful of physicians and researchers to do so to date). I was puzzled that the first report in the medical literature of complete suppression of alcoholism, a deadly disease defined by the medical establishment as chronic and irreversible, had generated so little interest.

A bolt from the blue surprised me when the April 11, 2005, issue of *Business Week* ran an article, "Can Alcoholism Be Treated?" The article featured my self-experiment. Although the reporter, Catherine Arnst, had interviewed a number of addiction experts, she had never contacted me and instead had simply drawn information and quotations from my self-case report. That said, aside from a few minor errors (which she corrected in the online edition) she presented the main facts of the matter accurately and dramatically.

I briefly hoped that the *Business Week* article would lead to more contacts from the medical and research community or more media attention for baclofen. That hope soon faded.

Georges Moroz, Colin Martin, and Catherine Arnst—and before them, Boris Pasche and my brother, Jean-Claude—all coming from different backgrounds and none of them an expert in addiction, had immediately grasped that my treatment approach had nothing to do with conventional addiction therapies. That led me to wonder if people in addiction medicine and research might not be able to see beyond the dogma of their field— something that is common in every medical specialty, not to mention being a familiar fact of human nature—or if the experts like Dr. S. and her department chief saw gaping holes in my argument. But Richard Glass, the *JAMA* editor who had recommended that I submit the self-case report to *Alcohol and Alcoholism*, Jonathan Chick, and the report's two peer reviewers were experts on addiction, and they hadn't noticed any such holes.

Desperate for feedback that would give me a surer sense of my paper's value, I sent it to Jean Dausset, one of France's few living Nobel laureates in medicine. Although I knew he would want to look favorably on the paper because of our friendship, I also felt that he was too rigorous a scientist to let that bias his judgment. He would tell me plainly if he thought my experience with baclofen was a lucky anomaly. A few days later, his wife, Rosita, called. "Jean wants to see you," she said. I visited their lovely apartment in Saint-Germain for the first time in many months. They both greeted me warmly and said that it was wonderful to see me looking so well.

Jean gave me a hug. "You have discovered the treatment for addiction," he said.

"Well, perhaps only for my own alcoholism," I said.

"For addiction!" he declared.

We then discussed the report's implications. "Medical dogma can be slow to change," Jean warned.

Encouraged nonetheless by Jean's estimate of the self-case report's medical and scientific value, I decided to seize the initiative and send it to a number of researchers, asking for their feedback.

PubMed was a source not only of abstracts, but also of researchers' e-mail addresses, although not necessarily the most up-to-date ones. In May, as I was contemplating what to write to David Roberts, the physiologist whose studies of cocaine-addicted rats laid the foundation for all subsequent addiction research with baclofen, I got an e-mail from George Koob.

Apologizing for his slow reply, Professor Koob said that I'd written to an old e-mail address and told me, just as Georges Moroz had predicted, "I found your case history fascinating." Noting that he had just concluded an experiment on baclofen's ability to suppress alcohol intake in alcohol-dependent laboratory rats, he added, "I personally hope that our animal data and your ideas will ultimately translate to some consideration of baclofen-like compounds in the treatment of alcoholism."

Spurred by this encouraging e-mail, I sent my self-case report to David Roberts, expressing my profound thanks for the hope his papers had given me when I was investigating baclofen between binges. He quickly replied, "Please be assured that your letter has helped me regain my enthusiasm for doing further work with baclofen and related drugs. I also believe that by publishing your experiences you have helped convince a very skeptical readership that baclofen deserves a thorough assessment." He forwarded the self-case report to Anna Rose Childress, who wrote me in similar terms.

Koob later put me in touch with another of the world's leading addiction researchers, Charles O'Brien, Kenneth E. Appel Professor of Psychiatry at the University of Pennsylvania, whose medical center includes the Charles O'Brien Center for Addiction Treatment, and a senior colleague of Anna Rose Childress's.

Professor O'Brien wrote me, "Your paper has already influenced me and others. I believe that Anna Rose Childress has told you about our research with baclofen. The question, of course, is whether our dose is too low."

There was one physician-scientist in New York whose opinion I was especially eager to get: Jerome B. Posner, world-renowned as the founder of neuro-oncology. In addition to being a professor of neurology and neuroscience at Weill Cornell Medical College, Dr. Posner is Evelyn Frew American Cancer Society Clinical Research Professor and George C. Cotzias Chair of Neuro-oncology at Memorial Sloan-Kettering Cancer Center. Although we had been neighbors in the same apartment building and had said brief hellos to each other in the elevator and lobby, I didn't really know him and thought he might not remember me at all. But I so admired him. I sent him the self-case report with trepidation, because he had what my colleagues at New York Hospital had told me was a well-deserved reputation for demolishing faulty arguments with a few blunt words. He responded the very same day:

Dear Olivier,

Many thanks for the note and reprint. First, let me congratulate you on the successful treatment of your illness, of which I was unaware. Your treatment is reminiscent of the way in which George Cotzias was able to prove that L-dopa could successfully treat parkinsonism. Others had tried the drug with little success because they were unwilling to push the drug to full tolerance.

Sincerely,
Jerry

Coming from the Cotzias Chair of Neuro-oncology at Memorial Sloan-Kettering, there could be no greater words of encouragement.

The *Business Week* article had not triggered any contacts from researchers or the media. However, what it did trigger was, in a sense, more heartening—and heartbreaking. I began to hear from addicts and their families. I spent countless hours via e-mail and telephone answering questions about baclofen and advising people on how to speak to their physicians about it. In almost all cases, sadly, they could not convince their doctors to prescribe an unfamiliar medication off-label. I told the patients I would be glad to talk to their physicians about how to manage high-dose baclofen therapy. None contacted me.

One of the patients who tracked me down was Mr. A., a senior business executive in the Midwest. Mr. A. was dependent on alcohol, and he feared that if he kept drinking excessively he risked losing his career as well as his marriage. He also told me that he was seeing both a psychiatrist and a psychologist for treatment of anxiety and depression that preceded his drinking. But total abstinence was not Mr. A.'s aim. His job often required socializing with clients and staff, and his goal was to be able to drink alcohol normally, without losing control and endangering his professional and personal life.

AA and physicians say that moderate, safe, nondependent drinking is impossible for alcoholics. "Once a pickle, never a cucumber again," the saying goes. But it is the dream of many problem drinkers. "I wish I could enjoy a few drinks like a normal person," I often heard others (and myself) say in AA meetings and rehab.

After baclofen suppressed my alcoholism in February 2004, I had no interest in drinking. But eventually the question of how vulnerable I was to relapse began to prey on my mind. Would one drink plunge me back into the hell of alcoholism? Was I still in the disease, or thanks to baclofen was I now out of it?

In May 2005, sixteen months after my last drink, I put my recovery to the acid test by subjecting it to three successive challenges.

The first: while continuing to take my maintenance baclofen dose of 120 milligrams a day, I had three standard drinks (gin and tonics) over a few hours at a social gathering. Right away I observed that I had no urge to guzzle the first drink quickly, as I always did when I was dependent on alcohol. Instead I was content to sip it slowly over some forty minutes. The second gin and tonic, which I also drank slowly, produced a mild euphoria. I began a third gin and tonic, but was unable to finish it, an impossibility during my untreated alcohol dependence. The next morning I woke up feeling completely normal, without any of the remorse, fear, and guilt that accompanied my drinking in the past. Moreover, I had no craving whatsoever for alcohol, and in the following weeks, no alcohol thoughts or drunk dreams.

For the second challenge, I continued to take my maintenance baclofen dose of 120 milligrams a day, but this time I upped the alcohol. I had five standard drinks, also in a social gathering, this time vodka and tonics, consumed over a six-hour span. Again I had no urge to drink rapidly and experienced only a mild euphoria. But the following afternoon, I had a bout of alcohol craving.

An additional 40 milligrams of baclofen suppressed the craving within one hour.

Several hours later, craving for alcohol returned, suggesting that the greater volume of alcohol in the second challenge had reactivated my old craving cycle. Increasing my daily baclofen dose to a total of 180 milligrams completely suppressed the cravings. Over the next six days, I tapered my baclofen dose back down to 120 milligrams a day with no recurrence of craving. This was another indication, following the animal trials and my previous self-experimentation, that baclofen's symptom-suppression effects are dose-dependent; that higher doses may be necessary in times of stress; and that an effective maintenance dose is lower than the required symptom-suppressing dose.

Accordingly, the third and final challenge was to see if a higher-than-normal dose of baclofen would prevent cravings from occurring, even if I consumed a massive amount of alcohol, such as is ingested during heavy drinking or active relapse. The day of the challenge, I took a total of 140 milligrams of baclofen: 30 milligrams in the morning, 30 milligrams eight hours later, and 80 milligrams in the evening at the same time as beginning to drink a 750-milliliter bottle of Scotch. Over the rest of the evening, I drank four-fifths of the bottle, about 600 milliliters.

Despite a mild hangover the next day, I experienced no craving and no desire to continue drinking. That morning I took 140 milligrams of baclofen, and that evening I took 80 milligrams. For the following six days, I took three 60-milligram doses of baclofen, one each in the morning, afternoon, and evening, for a total of 180 milligrams a day, and then returned to my usual maintenance dose of 120 milligrams a day with no craving.

It was good to discover that with baclofen I could drink in a nondependent way. On rare occasions since then, I have had a glass or two of champagne, or a vodka tonic or gin and tonic, at gatherings with friends. But given all the alcohol I inflicted on my body during my illness, I prefer not to drink.

As far as Mr. A.'s alcohol dependence was concerned, his psychiatrist had tried him on oral naltrexone. A dose of 100 milligrams a day temporarily reduced his craving, but then had no benefit. Studies of oral naltrexone show that its effects commonly last for about three months and then fade. Increasing the naltrexone dose to 150 milligrams—an unusually high dose and thus off-label; 50 milligrams is standard—did nothing, but the psychiatrist was unwilling to prescribe baclofen off-label.

Mr. A. continued to see his psychiatrist and psychologist for anxiety and depression, and I advised him on finding another psychiatrist who was open to prescribing baclofen for his alcohol dependence. In the summer, after being turned down by a couple of doctors, he found William Bucknam, an addiction psychiatrist in Ann Arbor, who agreed to work with him and discuss the case with me.

Dr. Bucknam appropriately first wanted to see for himself how Mr. A. responded to conventional anticraving medications. He had Mr. A. keep taking 150 milligrams a day of oral naltrexone, and when that proved of no benefit combined it with 2 grams a day of acamprosate, which again had no positive effect on Mr. A.'s craving and drinking. Finally he tried him on topiramate, with even worse results. Not only did topiramate do nothing for his craving and drinking, it also impaired his word-recall memory. This was a disaster for Mr. A., because he often spoke before large audiences at business meetings and conventions. While taking these medications, Mr. A. continued to drink heavily, an average of twelve drinks at a time.

In September Mr. A. began taking baclofen, gradually increasing the dose over the course of a month to 100 milligrams a day. He contacted me daily by e-mail or phone, as Dr. Bucknam had urged him to do, so that I could coach him on what to expect from the medication and help him handle any problems that arose, and he was also reporting regularly to Dr. Bucknam and seeing him on a weekly basis.

Before the month was out, Mr. A. reported that he came home from his daily three-mile run one evening and, for the first time since his drinking became problematic, he reached into the refrigerator and took out a bottle of water instead of a beer. Ordinarily, he had three or four beers before dinner, with more alcohol while eating. This evening, he felt no desire to drink, although craving for alcohol returned later that evening, because he did not think of taking any more baclofen.

When Mr. A. reached 100 milligrams of baclofen, occasionally adding another 40 milligrams when he felt especially stressed, he said that heavy drinking became "an alien world" and called baclofen "my miracle drug." He never felt the urge to have more than three drinks at any one time. He could now drink moderately while socializing with clients and others, without the risk of losing control and drinking to excess. Moreover, he experienced no somnolence and no other side effects while increasing his baclofen dose to the 100–140 milligram range and maintaining it at that level.

Mr. A. continued to take an SSRI for his anxiety and depression. It seemed possible to me that he could dispense with the SSRI if he increased his baclofen dose. At doses above 140 milligrams of baclofen a day, however, Mr. A. experienced some somnolence. The evidence not only from my own case, but also from the safe long-term use of baclofen for comfort care in neurology patients, was that if he had taken a few days off work, the somnolence at the higher dose might well have passed. But he found the SSRI effective in managing his anxiety and depression and preferred to keep his baclofen dose at 100–140 milligrams.

Although I expected things to go well, I was enormously relieved. Meanwhile, as I learned around this time, another alcoholic in the United States had entirely ended his drinking thanks to high-dose baclofen.

On August 24, 2005, Dr. Jon Hallberg, a regular medical commentator on Minnesota Public Radio, reported on the air that a patient of his, "a hardcore alcoholic," had asked for baclofen after finding my self-case report online. "In my patient's case," Dr. Hallberg said, "[high-dose baclofen] has worked amazingly well. He was drinking a liter of hard liquor every day. And within a couple of days of taking this, he stopped."

So now we had three humans and a bunch of laboratory rats responding to baclofen. It remained to be seen if this therapeutic outcome would continue for Dr. Bucknam's and Dr. Hallberg's patients, as it had for me, but the early signs were good.

What I dreamed of were studies—randomized clinical trials to show either that others could achieve complete remission of addiction symptoms and consequences with baclofen, or that I was an anomaly. In a peer-reviewed letter to the editor of *The Journal of the American Medical Association*, I renewed the call I had made in my self-case report for randomized trials of high-dose baclofen. There was zero response.[2]

Here I was, not simply a documented alcoholic, but a doctor without a position at a university or a medical institute. On January 25, 2005, a little more than a month after my case report had been published, I was informed by the chairman of the department of medicine at Weill Cornell Medical College of his decision not to renew my appointment as clinical associate professor of medicine for 2004–2006, because of lack of participation in the department's teaching, clinical, administrative, or research efforts. I was very sad to see my association with this great institution end in this way after twenty-one years.

I had no means to mount a study of my own, and I didn't even have funds to travel to conferences to discuss baclofen's potential. Researchers interested in embarking on such a study admittedly faced many constraints. In the era of institutional medical science, securing grant money and other funding, clearing research protocols with ethics committees, running a laboratory, and seeing to the needs of staff and graduate and postdoctoral students all consume a great deal of time. The research projects that are in progress and others in the pipeline must be carried through and written up methodically. Microspecialization prevents many researchers in even closely related fields from cooperating with and learning from one another. In short, the business of modern medical science imposes its own agenda, and researchers are not free to drop what they are doing and shift scarce resources to investigate a new idea.

Last but by no means least, there was this obstacle: baclofen has been out of patent and available as a generic since the 1980s. That means no pharmaceutical company—and pharmaceutical companies pay most of the bill for the expensive human trials of addiction medicines—has a financial incentive to underwrite the large study needed to prove or refute baclofen's effectiveness.

I wondered if somehow I could get a study going in France. In June, it was suggested to me that I contact the psychiatrist and neurobiologist Renaud de Beaurepaire, the chief of psychiatry in one of Paris's health care sectors and director of the psychopharmacology laboratory at Hôpital Paul Guiraud. Looking up his publications, I saw that he did impressive research on addiction to nicotine and other drugs, as well as on personality disorders and neurotransmission. Dr. de Beaurepaire agreed to meet me, and I found him to be a tall, jovial man with a ready wit. We had a wide-ranging talk, in the course of which he said that the best person to get a human trial of high-dose baclofen going in France was a man I'll call Professor X. Others had advised me to contact Professor X. as well. I got in touch with him right away. He said he would be glad to talk to me. But he was very busy; it proved difficult to find a time when he could do so.

The frustration and anxiety I felt over not being able to generate action on baclofen and make it available to others suffering from addiction would probably have gotten the better of me and driven me back to drink, if I were not able to take the medication myself. Finally, five months later, on November 22, I met Professor X., who took Renaud de Beaurepaire and me to lunch. After a thorough discussion, Professor X. said, "Write a rationale for the study, and I will see what can be done."

The day before this lunch I had received an effusive letter from Professor Y., an internist at a Paris hospital, expressing interest in talking to me about my self-case report. I told Professor X. of Professor Y.'s letter, and before long it was agreed that both of them would participate if the study went forward.

I worked on the study on a pro bono basis full time through the end of 2005 and the beginning of 2006. I began by drafting a detailed rationale for what was planned to be a multicenter randomized trial comparing baclofen versus naltrexone for alcohol dependence. The maximum dose of the baclofen group would be 120 milligrams a day (although I argued for going higher), and the dose for the naltrexone group would be 50 milligrams a day. This, in spite of the fact that the Smith et al. study of high-dose oral baclofen in multiple sclerosis patients found that the greatest benefits were likely to occur above 100 milligrams, with no limiting side effects, and in spite of the evidence from animal trials and my own case.

Be that as it may, 120 milligrams was a major step in the right direction, and I hoped that the study would be the first in which patients achieved suppression of addiction. Dr. Bucknam's patient Mr. A. had experienced that result with less baclofen than I had needed, and the animal trials of baclofen for alcohol, cocaine, heroin, methamphetamine, and nicotine addiction all showed that the medication had beneficial effects over a range of doses.

I also drafted documents needed to submit the study proposal to France's Programme Hospitalier de Recherche Clinique (PHRC), the Hospital Program for Clinical Research. Among the most important of these was a section on the safety record of high-dose baclofen, which furnished the basis for the informed consent form that alcohol-dependent patients would sign to participate in the trial. The statisticians on the preliminary team assembled by Professors X. and Y. said that we needed at least 250 patients, 125 in each group, to achieve statistically significant results.

A couple of months later, Giancarlo Colombo wrote to suggest that we meet when he came to Paris in April for a two-day conference of the European Society for Biomedical Research on Alcoholism (ESBRA).

When I wrote Giancarlo that I looked forward to meeting him, but that I was not a member of ESBRA and did not know about the conference, he immediately offered to sponsor me as a new member of the society. Giancarlo wrote one of the two required letters of recommendation, and his wife and colleague, Roberta Agabio, wrote the other.

In the meantime I had sent my self-case report to Dr. Eliot L. Gardner, an expert on brain reward mechanisms in addiction, the director of the Laboratory of Behavioral Neuropharmacology at Albert Einstein College of Medicine of Yeshiva University in New York, and chief of the neuropsychopharmacology section of the Intramural Research Program of the National Institute on Drug Abuse (NIDA) of the U.S. National Institutes of Health. In early March Dr. Gardner e-mailed me:

> . . . *I applaud your work and wish you much success with your large multicenter trial of high-dose baclofen . . .*
>
> *And also let me say that I completely agree with you on the topic of craving suppression . . . You are on the right track. Please do not let small-witted people derail you.*
>
> *And I also completely share your skepticism about naltrexone,*

acamprosate, topiramate, low-dose baclofen, and rimonabant [as anti-craving agents] . . .

This was a great vote of confidence for the prospective PHRC study, and I happily shared it with Professors X. and Y. I then flew to New York City for the first time since I left in June 1999, my life and career as a cardiologist ruined by alcoholism. I was there to attend the seventy-fourth birthday party of my dear friend Arif Mardin, who was then seriously ill and who sadly died that summer, on the same day as my birthday. Walking the streets of Manhattan for the first time in seven years, I was flooded with bittersweet memories of past friends and experiences. It was emotionally wrenching to confront all that I had lost, but thanks to baclofen I was able to appreciate what I had gained as a person in my struggle against alcoholism and in my recovery.

It was exhilarating to be back in a city I loved so much. It felt like home. At the same time there was a different quality from the emotional excitement I was prone to before baclofen. Instead of the sense that I was in danger of being carried away by my emotions, I felt grounded and calm. After a few days, I returned to Paris, troubled by the state of Arif's health, but glad to have seen him and eager to bring the high-dose baclofen study to fruition.

The final study proposal had to be submitted to PHRC very soon.

The day before the deadline, Professors X. and Y. informed me that they had just decided to cancel the study as planned, and that their decision was final. They were no longer going to test high-dose baclofen, but instead a combination of high-dose baclofen and naltrexone versus naltrexone alone.

I was floored. This would not enable the study to say anything definitive about the value of high-dose baclofen. Another problem was that "baclotrexone," as I dubbed it, would in effect constitute a new medication with no known safety profile.

Overnight, the only randomized trial of high-dose baclofen to be planned and organized was dismantled before it started. Despite all my work on the study proposal, I now hoped that PHRC would reject it so that it did not spoil the chance for any future trials of high-dose baclofen.

Giancarlo Colombo had invited me to have dinner with him on April 12, the day before the start of the ESBRA conference. When I e-mailed to ask how I would recognize him, he told me he was two meters tall, or about six-foot-seven. I was still expecting an operatic, round, pasta-bellied fellow, but he turned out to be a slim, quiet, congenial man with whom I had a real meeting of the minds. In any case, I needn't have worried about missing him.

Over coffee on the terrace of La Rotonde and then at my suggestion over dinner at La Closerie des Lilas, Giancarlo asked all about my struggle with alcoholism and my history with baclofen, while I probed him about his research. At one point, I took out my doctor's identification card, without which I could never have taken baclofen, and said, "This has been my passport to life."

In return it was fascinating to hear Giancarlo describe the experiments in his lab that showed, following David Roberts's demonstration of baclofen's dose-dependent effects on rats addicted to cocaine, that enough baclofen made rats addicted to alcohol stop pressing the lever to receive it and spontaneously turn to drinking water instead. With expressive hand gestures,

Giancarlo mimed how the rats first eagerly pressed the lever for alcohol and then completely stopped doing so. The rats' leg strength remained normal, but they had lost their motivation to consume alcohol.

He also told me that my self-case report was now required reading for every new graduate and postdoctoral student joining his laboratory. He had grown exasperated with their saying of his baclofen experiments, "That's just for rats. We're interested in something that works in people." My paper was Giancarlo's preemptive response to such comments. That was gratifying to hear, and I described how stunned I'd been to have my paper not only enthusiastically recommended for publication in *Alcohol and Alcoholism* by both expert reviewers, but to see it described by one of the reviewers as a "precious cameo that deserved to be disseminated in the scientific community."

Giancarlo smiled. "I was that reviewer," he said.

The ESBRA conference was a wonderful opportunity to discuss both addiction in general and baclofen in particular with some of the world's leading researchers in the field. Giancarlo generously introduced me to a number of people, including George Koob, with whom I'd been in e-mail contact, but had not yet met. Over a private lunch at his invitation, Professor Koob remarked that my conceptual approach—postulating craving suppression rather than craving reduction—was a good fit with the experiments he and his colleagues were doing. "With our experiments and your ideas," he said jovially, "we may make some real progress."

The ESBRA conference also gave me the chance to meet, face to face, Jonathan Chick, the man responsible for publishing my self-case report. We had a warm talk. "In medicine," he said to me, "it can take up to a generation for a new approach to be accepted."

Emboldened by my conversations with Giancarlo Colombo and George Koob, I said, "I think things are already changing, and I'm determined to do everything I can to accelerate the process."

The first developments for baclofen therapy in addiction medicine after the conference were very positive. A few months earlier, in January, I had received an e-mail from Dr. Pascal Gache, head of the alcohology unit of the University Hospitals of Geneva in Switzerland. He had first learned about me when an alcoholic woman patient showed him an article about my experiences with baclofen that, thanks to a journalist friend of a friend, had recently run in a French magazine called *Top Santé* (Best Health). The magazine was not his usual reading matter, but he was intrigued by the mention of my self-case report in *Alcohol and Alcoholism*, and after reading it, he invited me to give a talk in Geneva in June, for which Geneva University would pay my train and hotel costs. This was a very welcome turn of events, and I immediately wrote back to accept his invitation.

In subsequent conversations, Dr. Gache said that he had four patients who seemed good candidates for high-dose baclofen therapy. All had failed to respond to conventional alcoholism treatments, including inpatient detoxification, rehab, and medications. Dr. Gache and I had several conversations about how to manage high-dose baclofen therapy, and over the course of the winter and spring we were periodically in touch about his patients' reactions to the drug. After several months, he could report that one patient had not responded well: he constantly fell asleep on baclofen. (I was glad that I had warned Pascal that none of his patients should drive or do anything hazardous while they were getting used to baclofen.) But the other three patients, the woman who had first shown him the *Top Santé* article and two men, were doing wonderfully.

These three patients found that baclofen suppressed their alcohol cravings at very different dosage levels. The woman patient had experienced craving suppression at 75 milligrams of baclofen a day. The other two patients required higher doses, with one of them taking 300 milligrams a day.

Dr. Gache shared with me an e-mail message from the woman patient, who wrote, "I am amazed that I no longer think of alcohol, especially during critical situations . . . It's fantastic. So far no somnolence, but very slight vertigo. I am thrilled at the state I am in. Thank you for proposing this treatment." The vertigo soon passed.

The other two patients expressed similar feelings. They also experienced minor side effects, including somnolence, but like the vertigo, the side effects were temporary.

In June I went to Geneva to give the lecture on baclofen therapy that Pascal Gache had arranged. It was both gratifying and amusing to find that Pascal had entitled my lecture "Coup de pied dans la fourmilière de l'alcoologie: l'important c'est la dose" (A kick in the anthill of alcohology: what's important is the dose). The subtitle was a play on Gilbert Bécaud's hit song "L'important c'est la rose" (What's important is the rose). Quite a few people

in the audience had read my report, and there were many penetrating questions about baclofen and the probable mechanisms
by which it could suppress addictive symptoms in both laboratory animals and human subjects.

Before I left Geneva, Pascal told me that he had identified
several other patients who seemed good candidates for baclofen
therapy. Like the first four, these men and women had failed to
respond to conventional alcoholism treatment, including both
outpatient and inpatient therapy and medications. We agreed
that Pascal would consult me about his baclofen patients, and
that I would advise him on a pro bono basis.

The other positive news was that Dr. Bucknam's patient Mr.
A. continued to thrive on his baclofen therapy of 100 milligrams
a day, with up to 40 milligrams more in times of stress. After ten
months, Mr. A. still had no alcohol cravings, still found 100 to
140 milligrams of baclofen mildly relaxing with no somnolence
or grogginess to interfere with his hectic worklife, and still drank
alcohol moderately in a nondependent fashion. This was in stark
contrast to his experience on other anticraving medications such
as naltrexone.

When Mr. A. drank, he experienced only a mild euphoria and
never wanted more than three drinks at a time. This kept him
well below the five drinks at a time for a man that are the diagnostic standard for problem drinking and bingeing—and well
below his previous hazardous intake.

Mr. A. informed me directly of another element in his state of
well-being: the end of his alcohol dependence had dramatically
improved his relationship with his wife, and he no longer feared
for the future of his marriage.

With my encouragement and consultation, Dr. Bucknam

drafted a case report on Mr. A., which he submitted to Jonathan Chick at *Alcohol and Alcoholism*. After the usual peer review process and revisions, the case report was accepted and Jonathan Chick scheduled it for electronic publication on December 15, 2006, almost exactly two years to the day after my self-case report.

Around the same time, I learned that PHRC had rejected the proposed study of "baclotrexone" versus naltrexone. There were concerns about the safety of "baclotrexone," as well as hesitancy about the planned 120 milligram doses of baclofen.

In one sense I was relieved, because "baclotrexone" was an untested drug combination and its safety was unknown, and because its use in the trial would have made it impossible to discover anything about and would also have cast doubt on the value of high-dose baclofen alone. But of course I was frustrated that there was no chance to carry out the multicenter trial of high-dose baclofen, as originally contemplated.

I would continue to work within normal academic channels to stimulate a randomized trial of high-dose baclofen. But at this point it seemed to me that if baclofen was to get a fair hearing, I would also have to go outside those channels and present the evidence to the public at large, including scientists, physicians, and addiction patients. I began to write this book.

"IT IS SO GOOD to see you as you were before," my brother, Jean-Claude, said.

"Not at all," I said. "I never felt this way before in my life. I may have seemed okay, but in reality I was miserable." Freed by baclofen not only from the biological prison of addiction, but also from the crippling anxiety that preceded it, I was finally at ease with myself and others. I felt that I was finally the person I was always meant to be.

As we reach the end of the first decade of the twenty-first century, many aspects of the addiction process remain unknown. But medical science is fitting large pieces of the puzzle together, and a comprehensive understanding of this deadly disease is beginning to emerge. Amid fierce competition by pharmaceutical companies to discover and patent an effective treatment for addiction, the evidence points to high-dose baclofen as the best hope for a cure.

According to the fourth edition of the American Psychiatric Association's *Diagnostic and Statistical Manual of Mental Disorders* (*DSM-IV*), addiction, or substance dependence, can be diagnosed with the presence of three or more of the following criteria in the same twelve-month period:

1. Tolerance to a substance, so that the same amount no longer has the desired effect and increased amounts are required to produce that effect.
2. Withdrawal dysphoria.
3. Loss of control during substance use, so that use is longer or more extreme than intended.
4. Inability to limit further use of the substance.
5. Substance use, including procuring the substance and withdrawing from it, occupies large amounts of time.
6. Substance use affects normal life activities.
7. Substance use continues despite recognition of its serious adverse effects.[1]

The fact that these symptoms and consequences all manifest themselves in one way or another in the mind and awareness of the substance-dependent person naturally suggests the hope, or expectation, that addiction is subject to conscious influence or control. On the one hand, this leads to moral judgments about substance-dependent people, that they lack virtue or willpower or require spiritual enlightenment. On the other hand, it points the way to nonjudgmental twelve-step programs, psychotherapy, and rehab, which aim to enhance substance-dependent people's ability to recognize and modify their unhealthy behaviors.

Addiction treatment based on twelve-step programs, psychotherapy, and rehab has remained virtually unchanged since the founding of AA in 1935. There is scarcely another major illness whose treatment has been static over the last seventy or more years. While these forms of addiction treatment have enabled a minority of substance-dependent people to remain abstinent, they have not enabled the vast majority of substance-dependent people to do so.

The far less static field of neurobiology, however, has, over the last few decades, evolved and developed in a way that offers greater hope for new addiction treatments. With increasing precision, neurobiology has shown how the symptoms and consequences of addiction are mediated at the molecular level by neurotransmission in the brain, especially that involving the neurotransmitters dopamine, gamma-aminobutyric acid (GABA), and glutamate. For example, dopamine plays what seems to be the leading role in the experience and recall of pleasant experiences, and thus is clearly crucial to addiction. But one transmitter always acts in concert with or opposition to another, and every brain activity recruits multiple neurotransmitters, which may play somewhat different roles in different combinations.

The receptors for different neurotransmitters respond directly or indirectly to many different substances, which in turn excite or slow the release of the neurotransmitters. Threshold responses mean that the amount of a substance can be crucial to its having one effect on neurotransmission rather than another. For example, low doses of alcohol activate mainly $GABA_A$ receptors, stimulating areas of the brain devoted to thinking, pleasure seeking, and relaxing the body. High doses also activate receptors for glutamate, disturbing learning and memory, as occurs in blackouts.

Taken together, the functions and characteristics of neurotransmitters and receptors determine how we respond physically, emotionally, and mentally to different substances and behaviors. Our responses — sensations, moods, images, and thoughts — become part of the process and contribute to their own propagation through self-organizing and self-reinforcing feedback loops. Thus an imbalance that generates overly anxious or depressed feelings may be imbalanced further by the strength of that feeling, helping anxiety or depression to recur with greater strength and frequency.

At the same time, this imbalanced neurotransmission is no more subject to conscious influence or control than any other organic disease process. Research has shown that closely similar patterns of neurotransmission apply not only to all drug addictions, but also to so-called nondrug addictions such as binge eating, compulsive gambling, compulsive shopping, and sex addiction. There is also a very close overlap with the neurotransmission seen in anxiety, depression, and impulse disorders.[2]

The identification of characteristic patterns of neurotransmission associated with both addiction and underlying dysphoria suggests that addicted patients can be helped with medication that affects brain activity. The first medication for alcoholism, disulfiram (Antabuse), might be said to do so indirectly. The primary effect of disulfiram is to prevent the body from metabolizing alcohol. This leads to the buildup of formaldehyde in the body, which makes people physically sick if they drink alcohol, the hope being that this will in turn create a mental aversion to drinking.

Beginning in 1984, with the FDA's approval of naltrexone for use in treating heroin addiction, a new class of addiction medications appeared that directly affect neurotransmission. Naltrexone (brand names Revia and Depade), which the FDA specifically approved for treating alcoholism in 1994, inhibits the release of dopamine by acting on the brain's opioid receptors. It was followed by medications such as acamprosate (brand name Campral), which reduces glutamate by acting on the NMDA receptors in the brain; topiramate (brand name Topamax), an anti epileptic drug that activates $GABA_A$ receptors and reduces glutamate; and ondansetron (brand name Zofran), which increases serotonin. These medications are known as anticraving agents, and they are used to reduce craving as an adjunct to twelve-step programs, psychotherapy, and rehab.

The craving-reduction approach was an important development in addiction medicine. It responded to the centrality of craving as the primary debilitating symptom of addiction and the primary predictor and cause of relapse, even after lengthy abstinence. Yet even the most enthusiastic proponents of the craving-reduction approach admit that it at best achieves only modest results.

Although European studies have shown somewhat greater effects in reduced craving, American studies have found acamprosate to be no better than placebo. All studies agree that acamprosate has no serious limiting side effects.

Besides acamprosate, the anticraving agents most commonly used in alcoholism treatment, naltrexone and topiramate, have been found in randomized trials to reduce craving, producing a modest decrease in the number of heavy drinking days and a modest increase in the period before the first heavy drinking day. The modest effects of oral naltrexone tend to fade after about three months; with injectable naltrexone (brand name Vivitrol), these effects have been shown to continue over a six month follow-up, but craving persisted throughout the trial and there was no progressive decrease in heavy drinking days.[3] In addition, naltrexone and topiramate have potential side effects that limit their use.

Naltrexone can damage the liver, which rules it out for patients with liver cirrhosis.

Topiramate, developed as an antiseizure drug and marketed under the brand name Topamax, commonly affects memory, thinking, speech, and movement. Some disgruntled patients have dubbed it "Dopamax." Topiramate can also produce kidney stones, and it carries a small but significant risk of triggering glaucoma, leading two eye specialists to write in an article in *JAMA* that "blindness is no less of a problem than alcohol dependence." Early in 2008, the FDA warned that topiramate may double the risk of suicidal thoughts and behaviors.[4]

The bottom-line measure for any treatment approach for a serious illness is a decrease in mortality and morbidity—meaning that fewer people are both dying from and being afflicted by the disease. In contrast to medication-induced reduction of high blood pressure, which is strongly correlated with a decrease in the mortality and morbidity associated with hypertension, medication-induced craving reduction has not been shown to decrease in any way the mortality and morbidity associated with addiction since the approach was introduced nearly two decades ago.

A new anticraving medication on the horizon, vigabatrin, will likely not change the picture. Marketed under the brand name Sabril, vigabatrin was fast-tracked for phase three human addiction treatment trials by the FDA in 2008. Vigabatrin has been shown to reduce craving for cocaine and methamphetamine, and there are plans to test it on alcohol dependence. Studies of vigabatrin in the treatment of epilepsy have reported that it is associated with a high rate of ocular toxicity and that 30 to 60 percent of the patients treated with it develop visual field constriction that is irreversible.

Given the documented ocular toxicity risk of vigabatrin and its yet unproven benefits, I would never have taken it during my alcoholism, even if there were no alternative. As a physician, I would not want to expose a patient to such a danger when there is an effective alternative in baclofen that has been shown safe over forty years of use.

Recent history has shown that once a medication is introduced on the market, the first patients to use it sometimes run a serious risk. The case of the anti-inflammatory Vioxx illustrates this. The drug came on the market in 1999 and was widely prescribed. But an FDA study found that 27,785 deaths and cardiac problems could have been caused by Vioxx between 1999 and 2004, and it was subsequently withdrawn from the market.

Two recently introduced drugs for smoking cessation, rimonabant (marketed as Acomplia) and varenicline (Chantix) also were reported to have serious potential side effects after they were put on the market. Rimonabant has been reported to greatly increase depression, and early in 2008 the FDA warned that varenicline may double suicidality.

We need to reassess what constitutes remission in addiction. The *DSM-IV* defines full remission from addiction as more than twelve months of abstinence, regardless of the presence of addictive craving and obsessive thoughts about the addictive substance. In other words, the patient still has crippling primary symptoms, and in no other disease would this qualify as full remission. When the World Health Organization (WHO) announced the preamble to its constitution in 1948, it defined health as not only the absence of impairment or disability, but the presence of well-being.

Even in the best scenario, anticraving agents such as naltrexone, acamprosate, and topiramate leave patients in an active disease state, in which they still must struggle, sometimes hour after hour, against addictive craving and obsessive thoughts of the addictive substance or behavior, symptoms that carry the risk of relapse and death. Moreover, these medications do not relieve the underlying dysphoria, such as preexisting anxiety or depression, that makes so many people vulnerable to addiction. In terms of the WHO's definition of health, they reduce, but do not eliminate, the impairment and disability of addiction, and they do not promote well-being by relieving chronic dysphoria.

Among addiction medicines, baclofen is unique to date in showing the ability to suppress, as opposed to reduce, motivation to consume alcohol, cocaine, heroin, nicotine, and amphetamine in animal studies. It is also unique among addiction medicines in its beneficial effect on dysphoria in human patients.

As I have already described, I postulated in 2003 that baclofen's dose-dependent ability to suppress animals' motivation to consume addictive substances could be transposed to human beings, and that baclofen would additionally promote well-being because of its effect on my underlying anxiety. I tested the postulate by self-experimenting with high-dose baclofen. My self-case report, "Complete and prolonged suppression of symptoms and consequences of alcohol-dependence using high-dose baclofen: a self-case report of a physician," described the success of the experiment, called for randomized trials of high-dose baclofen, and proposed a new treatment model for addiction, "integrating cure and well-being": "suppression of substance-dependence symptoms with alleviation of comorbid anxiety," or in more general terms, "the blockade of the clinical expression of addiction symptoms with simultaneous relief of underlying dysphoria." (See the appendix for the complete report.)

Subsequently, I have proposed in articles published in peer-reviewed medical journals, and in personal communications with members of the addiction research and treatment community, that anticraving agents should be classified as either craving-reduction agents (CRAs) or craving-suppression agents (CSAs). CRAs, including low-dose baclofen, do not raise addicted patients to the threshold of true remission. They keep patients in the disease, so to speak, whereas high-dose baclofen took me out of the disease of alcoholism and freed me from all its symptoms and consequences.

So far, high-dose baclofen is the only known CSA, but more CSAs should be sought and studied. No medication works effectively for everyone, and baclofen is surely no exception.

In February 2008, I was excited to read the abstract of a paper in the journal *Science* by D. T. George et al. entitled "Neurokinin 1 receptor antagonism as a possible therapy for alcoholism." According to the abstract, "LY686017 [a drug developed by Eli Lilly] suppressed spontaneous alcohol cravings, improved overall well-being, [and] blunted cravings induced by a challenge procedure." In a comment on the paper, its senior author, Dr. Markus Heilig, the clinical director of the National Institute on Alcohol Abuse and Alcoholism, said that LY686017 represented "a fairly new approach to treating alcoholism," because it targets "the anxiety that leads many alcoholics to reach for the bottle in the first place."[5]

In contrast to the abstract, the paper itself plainly said that LY686017 only reduced cravings in the study, as opposed to suppressing them as high-dose baclofen does. At the end of the trial, patients in the study still had persistent craving, as measured on standard craving scales. The imprecision in describing LY686017's effect is unfortunate; *The American Heritage Dictionary* says that to "suppress" something means to put an end to it or to halt it completely, not decrease it, and other dictionaries give similar definitions. Nonetheless, the language of the abstract signals a growing recognition that addiction medicine needs craving-suppression agents that will also address underlying dysphoria.

I would be glad to see baclofen joined by other craving-suppression agents, once they are shown to be as safe in long-term use as baclofen. In the meantime, baclofen is the best hope for addiction treatment. All the available data indicate that it is as safe for long-term use as it is effective. Late in 2007, Giovanni Addolorato et al. published an article in *The Lancet* reporting that low-dose baclofen could safely be used by people whose severe alcohol dependence had brought about liver cirrhosis.[6]

I have already discussed the safe use of high-dose oral baclofen for comfort care in neurology since the mid-1960s at doses up to 300 milligrams a day, ten times the amount given in trials to date with alcohol-dependent patients. After I published my self-case report, I learned that high-dose oral baclofen has been safely used to provide comfort care to children and adolescents as well as adult patients. In a study with an eight-year follow-up conducted at Columbia University Medical Center, children and adolescents with problems such as gait control were started on doses of 40 milligrams a day and received as much as 180 milligrams a day without limiting side effects.[7]

Yet for the past twenty years, addiction researchers have not budged above 30 milligrams a day in studies of alcoholism and 60 milligrams a day in studies of cocaine addiction. These doses translate, respectively, to about .5 milligram and 1 milligram per kilogram of body weight for the average adult male, well below the 1 to 3 milligrams per kilogram of body weight at which baclofen suppresses self-administration of alcohol and the 1 to 5 milligrams per kilogram of body weight at which it suppresses self-administration of other addictive substances in animal studies. The rationale for a 30 milligram a day limit in alcoholism studies, Giovanni Addolorato et al. have written, is that this dose "represents the minimum therapeutic dosage recommended by the drug manufacturer in order to avoid side-effects."[8]

The two potentially limiting side effects of high-dose baclofen are somnolence and muscular weakness, but they usually last at most a day or two and are always completely reversible. I experienced inconvenient somnolence at 270 milligrams of baclofen a day, but only milder somnolence at lower doses. I have none at my maintenance dose of 120 to 160 milligrams a day. And I have never experienced muscular weakness on baclofen.

Although I am the first person documented to achieve complete suppression of addiction through dose-dependent baclofen, I am not the last. I have been joined by Dr. Bucknam's patient, Mr. A., and by the patient whom Dr. Hallberg discussed on Minnesota Public Radio. In the June 2007 issue of the *Journal of Clinical Psychopharmacology*, Roberta Agabio et al. described an alcohol-dependent patient whose craving for alcohol was suppressed at only 75 milligrams of baclofen a day. At Hôpital Paul Guiraud in Paris, my friend Dr. Renaud de Beaurepaire is successfully treating with high-dose baclofen two alcoholic patients whose cases failed to respond to all conventional therapies.

In Geneva, Pascal Gache has now tried seventeen alcoholic patients on high-dose oral baclofen. Twelve patients have had a one-year follow-up. Two of these patients dropped out of treatment with high-dose baclofen, apparently from lack of motivation to control their drinking. Ten patients gave baclofen therapy a full trial, and nine achieved suppression of craving and other symptoms of alcoholism with daily doses ranging from 75 to 300 milligrams a day, within the limits that neurologists have safely used since the 1960s.

It is remarkable that nine of ten found a craving-suppressing dose that does not give them persistent somnolence or other troubling side effects. Neither placebo nor any other medication has ever produced such results. And as in my own case, all these patients achieved a craving-suppressing dose in only a few weeks. High-dose baclofen has an apparently unique ability to produce rapid-onset, effortless abstinence.

In this regard, it is worth noting that patients frequently stop taking naltrexone, acamprosate, and topiramate because they experience so little benefit from them. The problem of noncompliance in taking oral naltrexone led to the development of an injectable form. In contrast, the benefits of baclofen begin to be felt almost immediately in increased muscular relaxation and sense of well-being, which should increase compliance in taking it.

One of Dr. Gache's patients, the woman alcoholic who showed him the *Top Santé* article, visited me in Paris. She said, "I can't believe what has happened to me," and asked, "Can I call you Sigmund?"

I said, "Why Sigmund?"

"For Sigmund Freud."

"Well, I am not a big fan of his, so I would rather you called me Olivier."

She said, "People came from all over the world to see Sigmund Freud in Vienna. I had to come to Paris to see you face-to-face. I went to rehab all the time. Everything was falling apart. I could no longer function as a mother. Now I have a normal life."

It moved me greatly to receive this visit and hear these words, as it also did when Mr. A. and his wife made a point of seeing me when they were in Paris on vacation in the summer of 2007. Given the availability of my self-case report on the Internet, there may well be a number of other patients who have found true and lasting relief from baclofen, as prescribed by their physicians, without coming forward to break their anonymity.

In February 2008, I received an e-mail with the subject heading "Alcoholism & Baclofen. Sober 21 Months[.] Thank you for Saving My Life!!!" It was from a woman in Montana who first e-mailed me in October 2006. At that time she wrote,

> *I am a 47 year old woman . . . who has suffered with alcoholism most of my adult life. I have been a member of AA, attended thousands of meetings, have been in a total of 9 in-patient and out-patient rehabs.*
>
> *I have been to numerous physicians, counselors, psychologists, all with the same outcome. Relapse again and again . . .*

Without going into all the years of shame, fear, self loathing and suicidal thoughts, I truly believed I was losing my mind—not to mention my family, friends, jobs, and any sense of self.

In my heart of hearts I knew there had to be more going on with my disease, but I didn't know where else to turn . . . Many times I would say to my sons, "This may not happen in my lifetime, but someday there will be evidence of something more than just a psycho-social disease."

I finally took it upon myself to make an appointment with a neurologist . . . The night before my appointment my husband was on the internet and came upon your case report.

To make a very long story short, and with the support of [my neurologist] . . . [I] slowly began the process of taking baclofen . . . I now take 60 mgs. 3x's a day . . . I am happy to say that I have remained sober for the past six months!! Only once has that occurred and that was when I was in a rehab for 6 mos., back in 1993.

I wrote the woman back with congratulations and with warm thanks for her willingness to tell me her story. I asked her to keep in touch, but because of some unknown glitch did not receive her next message, dated January 2007, in which she wrote that she continued to do well on 180 milligrams of baclofen a day. Then came her message of February 2008 with the subject heading I've quoted. What is very touching is that she was concerned that my not having replied to her second message might mean that I had relapsed because I had stopped taking baclofen. I quickly wrote back to reassure her that I continue to take baclofen and to be free of alcoholism.

Exactly how baclofen produces craving suppression and alleviates underlying dysphoria must still be explained by further research. But important parts of the answer have been established. Baclofen affects the neurotransmitters dopamine, GABA, and glutamate. It enhances GABA activity, reduces glutamate, and through these effects reduces dopamine.[9] In so doing it seems to play a role in balancing the brain's reward mechanisms.

Dopamine release is stimulated by several drugs of abuse. In a 2003 article in *Synapse*, a leading neurology journal, researchers reported that baclofen "dose-dependently reduced the nicotine-, morphine-, and cocaine-evoked [dopamine] release" in animal trials. The abstract concludes, "Taken together, our data are in line with previous reports demonstrating the ability of baclofen to modulate . . . [dopamine] transmission and indicate baclofen as a putative candidate in the pharmacotherapy of polydrug abuse."[10] (In the jargon of science, "putative" means "likely," rather than "supposed" or "alleged.")

In addition to the fact that baclofen has been shown to dose-dependently suppress motivation to consume alcohol, cocaine, heroin, nicotine, and amphetamine in animals, low-dose baclofen has been shown in randomized trials with dependent patients to reduce craving for cocaine and opiates as well as alcohol, and, in an open trial, craving for food in binge eating and bulimia. As I pointed out in my paper in *Alcohol and Alcoholism*, these results suggest that baclofen's craving-suppressing effects might be transposed to humans for addictions besides alcoholism. They indicate that high-dose baclofen should also be tested in randomized trials for nondrug addictions as well as a variety of drug addictions including smoking.

Many drugs with sedative-hypnotic effects act on GABA. What distinguishes baclofen from all but one of them, however, is that it acts on the $GABA_B$ receptor as opposed to the $GABA_A$ receptor. For example, alcohol, barbiturates, topiramate, vigabatrin, and benzos like Valium all affect the $GABA_A$ receptor. Besides baclofen, the only other substance known to act on the $GABA_B$ receptor is gamma-hydroxybutyrate (GHB).

GHB occurs naturally in small amounts in human beings and many other living organisms. Natural, or endogenous, GHB has many sites of action in the brain, including a recently discovered GHB receptor. Synthetic, or exogenous, GHB was a fairly common childbirth anesthetic and sleep medication for some years in Europe. Under the brand name Alcover, it is used in Italy to treat alcoholism. But its use is much more tightly controlled in most other countries because of its potential as a drug of abuse. It is highly addictive, and it has been used as a date-rape drug.

The small amounts of endogenous GHB must perform a necessary role in the body. The nature of the role of endogenous GHB in the body remains unknown, but it seems to me likely to depend on the sedative-hypnotic effects of GHB and thus to be involved in the body's ability to relax and to recover from stress. In a recent peer-reviewed article in *Alcohol and Alcoholism* (see the appendix), I postulated that a GHB deficiency may underlie substance dependence through a $GABA_B$-mediated dysphoric syndrome. A biological deficit of GHB would thus be experienced as a loss of sedative effect, leading to anxiety, muscular tension, insomnia, and/or depression. Alcohol and other drugs would serve to "correct" these uncomfortable states. The fact that the sedative-hypnotic effects of GHB are mediated by the $GABA_B$ receptor could explain why baclofen, the only other substance known to act on that receptor, can be so useful against addiction and its underlying dysphoria. After the article was published, Giancarlo Colombo, the GHB researcher Fabio Caputo, George Koob, Michel Le Moal, Jerry Posner, and Dave Roberts told me they were very interested in the idea and thought it worth investigating.

I also discussed the role that GHB deficiency may play in alcoholism in a peer-reviewed article in *The American Journal of Drug and Alcohol Abuse*, commenting on an article in the journal by Felice Nava et al. about GHB's use in alcoholism treatment. (See Appendix, p. 309.)

In a reply to my article, Dr. Nava, writing on behalf of himself and his coauthors, including Gian Luigi Gessa, who is world-renowned in addiction medicine as a major figure in research on GHB, baclofen, and related topics, called my comment "appealing." He wrote, "In light of the . . . evidence [of GHB and baclofen both acting on the $GABA_B$ receptor] and our recent work, Dr. Ameisen is correct in pointing out that alcoholism may be a disease characterized by a GHB-deficiency in the brain . . . Furthermore, since baclofen has been shown to suppress both in animals and humans the intake of several drugs including alcohol, we may suppose a key role of the endogenous GHB not only in alcoholism but in several other forms of drug dependence." Dr. Nava concluded, "If [Ameisen's] hypothesis will be demonstrated, the role of endogenous GHB will be elucidated," something that has eluded medical science since Henri Laborit began studying GHB in connection with GABA in the 1960s.[11]

As I've described, I was initially intrigued by baclofen because of my conviction that my lifelong muscular tension was an important symptom of the anxiety that motivated my alcoholism. Recent research has suggested why baclofen's $GABA_B$-mediated muscle-relaxant effects could have so much potential in addiction treatment.

Addiction-related brain research has concentrated on the amygdala—part of the brain's limbic system, which processes physical sensations, feelings, and emotions—as the site where the most relevant neurotransmission occurs. The amygdala has also been shown to be prominently involved in the experience of anxiety. The neuroscientist Antonio Damasio and his colleagues at the University of Iowa and the University of Southern California have cast light on the insula, a neighboring brain region that is also part of the limbic system. The insula plays a crucial role in integrating feelings and desires, including addictive cravings, and making us conscious of them. Early in 2007, four of Professor Damasio's colleagues, the neuroscientists Antoine Bechara, Hanna Damasio, Nasir Naqvi, and David Rudrauf, reported in the journal *Science* that injuries to the insula suffered during strokes eliminated craving for nicotine in people who were previously addicted to smoking tobacco.[12]

When *Science* announced the insula finding, I was in New York City for discussions connected with this book, and I learned that Antonio Damasio and I share the same literary agent. Professor Damasio was also passing through New York, and we had a lengthy talk. Having read my self-case report, Professor Damasio said with a smile, "Your method is better than ours. You suppress craving with medicine. A stroke is not exactly the treatment one would recommend to a patient."

He continued, "I have an idea why baclofen could work."

I said, "I think I do, too."

Professor Damasio said, "What is it?"

I said, "Baclofen is a muscle relaxant, and I'm sure that the muscles play a direct role in the clinical expression of addiction."

Professor Damasio said, "I think you're right. The neurons in the insula are predominantly motor neurons that control muscular activity."

The chain of events within the body that leads to the dysphoria of anxiety or depression and to addictive craving thus may run something like this: Dysregulated neurotransmission could have its first perceptible effects on the muscles, and subsequently disturb our emotional feelings and thoughts. To treat the underlying dysphoria and addiction alike, we must cut the chain at its first link.

Much remains to be learned about baclofen, as I have said, but the value of investigating it thoroughly, including testing its efficacy against addiction in randomized trials, is fully established by what is already known about it.

Early in 2008, Professor Thomas Papo, chairman of the department of medicine at Bichat Hospital, one of the University of Paris's teaching hospitals, contacted me and said that Dr. Catherine DeAngelis, the editor-in-chief of *JAMA*, in which I have published two peer-reviewed papers on addiction, had told him about my work. This led Professor Papo to invite me to give a lecture at Bichat, which he entitled "Alcoholism: the new deal."

Around the same time, Professor Antoine Hadengue, chief of gastroenterology and hepatology at the University Hospitals of Geneva, invited me to lecture on baclofen there later in the spring, and George Koob asked me to consult on prospective baclofen experiments with a colleague of his at the University of California at San Diego. I was honored by both requests, and delighted to accept them.

Dose-dependent baclofen is slowly gaining the attention it has deserved since Dave Roberts's groundbreaking 1997 paper showed that it suppresses cocaine self-administration in animal trials. Despite these developments, I fear that a randomized trial of high-dose baclofen in human patients remains far off. Jonathan Chick may have been right when he warned me that it could take up to a generation for medicine to adopt a new treatment approach.

Meanwhile human trials of naltrexone, acamprosate, and topiramate have been mounted or are going forward, although these studies consistently show very modest results. No matter what the dose, these medications reduce, but do not suppress, the symptoms and consequences of addiction. This is in accordance with animal studies, which show that no matter what the dose, these medications, and likewise vigabatrin, reduce, but do not suppress, self-administration of addictive substances. In this regard, the key difference between baclofen on the one hand and acamprosate, naltrexone, topiramate, and vigabatrin on the other hand is that the latter drugs are under patent (oral naltrexone is available as a generic, but injectable naltrexone is under patent). Pharmaceutical companies readily fund research on them, and their sales representatives regularly visit doctor's offices to discuss their use (topiramate was FDA-approved for epilepsy, and it is prescribed for alcoholism off-label).

Baclofen is the one and only medication shown to suppress motivation to consume addictive substances in animal studies; it is the one and only medication shown to suppress the disease of addiction in human beings. Taken together, the data on high-dose baclofen amply support randomized clinical trials of its effectiveness for dependence on alcohol and other substances. Nearly all addiction medication trials are funded by pharmaceutical companies, however, and the cost-benefit analysis they must perform in the interest of shareholders dictates that they cannot spend money on baclofen, which is out of patent.

The cost-benefit analysis for society looks very different. The sum needed to fund a statistically significant trial of high-dose baclofen for alcohol abuse would be around half a million dollars. This is a small fraction of the costs that governments and corporations incur to treat the mortality and morbidity associated with alcohol, the most popular drug of abuse. Every year more than a hundred thousand people die from alcohol-related causes in the United States alone, around 270 people a day. Worldwide, two million people die every year from alcohol-related causes. The financial cost of alcohol-dependence-related lost workdays, hospitalizations, rehab, and other treatment has been estimated to be almost $200 billion a year in the United States alone. Similar costs arise with other drugs of abuse.[13]

When I wrote about high-dose baclofen to a physician-scientist responsible for directing addiction research at one of the world's most important government health institutes, he replied, "The chances of commercial success hinge on the patent life of a molecule, and we have our hands full with stuff that has that sort of potential." In other words, it does not matter how good a generic medicine is, or how many people die while the search for a patentable, likely inferior substitute drags on.

At a conference on alcoholism in 2007, I spoke to a world-renowned researcher about the need for a randomized clinical trial of high-dose baclofen. He said that he might look at baclofen for alcoholism one day and had the funding to do so, but in the meantime he had "other fish to fry." And then he laughed and said, "After all, it's not cancer."

As he walked away, I wished this man had been with me in the detox ward of a hospital a few years earlier, when drinking ruled my life. At the end of her rope, a woman patient burst out, "Why didn't God give me breast cancer? At least then my children would visit me."

Directly or indirectly, addiction kills as many people every year as any single form of cancer (not to mention the fact that smoking is the largest single cause of cancer). According to Brandeis University's Schneider Institute for Health Care, one in four U.S. deaths is attributable to alcohol, tobacco, or illegal drugs. Addiction's impact on the lives of the people who suffer from it, and their families, is no less devastating than cancer. Often it is more devastating, because of the social stigma it carries.

Lingering moral judgments about addiction as a self-inflicted malady, not a proper disease, constitute an enormous obstacle to the compassionate treatment of those who are substance-dependent. Such judgments ignore the overwhelming evidence that vulnerability to addiction is no more under the individual's control than cancer is. And cancer was once viewed in equally disparaging moral terms, until science slowly built up a better understanding of it. Just as some people persist in wanting to see cancer, or the failure to survive it, as somehow connected to a lack of positive thinking, so do many people inside and outside the medical community resist the trend to defining and understanding addiction as a biological disease.

On March 28, 2007, Senator Joseph Biden introduced a bill, the Recognizing Addiction as a Disease Act of 2007, to change the name of the National Institute on Drug Abuse to the National Institute on Diseases of Addiction, preserving the NIDA acronym, and to change the name of the National Institute on Alcohol Abuse and Alcoholism to the National Institute on Alcohol Disorders and Health.

Many scientists and physicians welcomed the proposed changes, noting that 10 percent of the population is vulnerable to becoming dependent on alcohol, and significant percentages are vulnerable to developing dependence on other drugs (this does not count the larger number who engage in hazardous drinking or drug use but are not dependent). Others criticized them as coddling addicts and encouraging victimhood.

Understanding addiction as a biological illness does not mean the end of the need for personal responsibility, motivation, and willpower in recovery. As the two dropouts from Pascal Gache's baclofen patient group show, a person must still want to stop using a drug of abuse. I have spoken to several alcohol-dependent people who resist the idea of taking baclofen because they are not sufficiently motivated to stop drinking. Unless we are going to subject people to enforced treatment, they must still want to get and stay well by taking appropriate medication.

Likewise, treating addiction with baclofen, or any medication that is shown to suppress addictive craving and motivation, does not spell the end of rehab, twelve-step programs like AA and NA, and addiction-related cognitive behavioral therapy. To the contrary, it will give them all new life.

The sad fact is that relapse rates after rehab are extremely high, and have even been estimated to be up to 90 percent. Twelve-step programs also have a very high relapse rate. Precise numbers for failure to achieve or maintain abstinence despite faithful participation in AA, NA, and addiction-related CBT are hard to come by. To some extent, this is because of the anonymity practiced in AA and similar programs, which makes it difficult to obtain patient data.[14]

Only a small fraction of substance-dependent people join twelve-step groups or go to rehab or outpatient treatment programs, and only a small fraction of them become abstinent. The high cost of addiction treatment plays a significant role in this, but so do the poor results of all conventional addiction treatments.

A stay in rehab or participation in an outpatient program could provide the perfect setting to establish an individual's effective dose of baclofen or a newly developed craving-suppression agent under medical supervision. With this, success rates of these programs would improve, which would then encourage more people with addiction to try them.

Addiction is indeed a complex disease with biological and non-biological components. However, I could not utilize the life lessons of AA and CBT, many of which I was taught in rehab, until baclofen suppressed my craving and controlled my underlying anxiety. Desperately trying as hard as possible to stay with the program, only to relapse because of overwhelming craving, is the rule, not the exception, for people afflicted with the disease of addiction. It defies common sense, as well as the accumulating scientific evidence, to say that all these people are deficient in willpower, moral virtue, and/or spiritual faith.

Until a randomized clinical trial of dose-dependent baclofen is mounted, I ask all physicians who treat addiction to consider prescribing baclofen off-label for care of those patients who remain ill despite existing therapies and have no alternative treatment for a devastating and often deadly disease. For physicians and patients alike, the scientific papers reprinted in the appendix offer a starting point for discussing baclofen and deciding whether it is appropriate on a case by case basis. As Dr. Markus Heilig, clinical director of the National Institute on Alcohol Abuse and Alcoholism at the NIH wrote me, "There is certainly nothing wrong with physicians prescribing [baclofen] off-label."[15]

In the interest of public health and on behalf of all who suffer from addiction, I also call on government health agencies and officials, politicians, nongovernmental health organizations, and citizens to support full-scale randomized clinical trials of high-dose baclofen. There is a recent model for this activism in the development of the so-called AIDS cocktail of retroviral drugs, which dramatically reduced the mortality and morbidity associated with AIDS. With the same energy and commitment on the part of addiction patients, their families, and advocates for their care, it need not take a generation to mount the randomized trials required to establish definitively the safety and efficacy of baclofen and the value of craving suppression as a treatment model for both drug and nondrug addictions.

On a sunny day shortly before the manuscript of this book was due at the publisher, I went to visit my parents' graves in the Montparnasse Cemetery. I go there now and then. Following Jewish tradition, I place on their graves a few stones that I have picked up on a walk in the park or a visit to the seashore or the mountains. And I stay by the graves while I talk to my parents in my mind, letting them know that I am finally well and that alcohol is no longer a part of my life. I tell them, too, about others who have gotten well thanks to baclofen.

In these moments I mourn their passing and I miss them and I feel close to them, sensations that are not in conflict with one another but in harmony. For I have no regrets. I feel the loss of so much because of alcoholism: the heartbreaking damage to my family, especially to my mother's last years and my relationship with Jean-Claude and Eva, the extreme disruption of my personal life, the collapse of my career as a cardiologist. Yet no human life is without suffering, and we must all do our best to learn from it.

Instead of being regretful, I am grateful. I give thanks for my loving parents and their shining example; for all that I have learned about myself and others, including the extraordinary wisdom for living of AA; for all the ways I have been challenged to grow and change; for the friends who stood by me in my illness and helped rescue me from despair; for the joys of music and laughter, and the beauty and harmony of nature, which sustained me in dark hours; for baclofen; and for all the blessings of the end of my addiction, especially my reconciliation with Jean-Claude and Eva and the new stability in my personal life. Last but not least, I give thanks for the opportunity to become a physician, my parents' crowning gift to me. I hope this book honors that gift and helps others to end their addictions.

This appendix reprints abstracts and articles concerning baclofen's efficacy in addiction treatment. My self-case report describes the first case in the medical literature of the complete suppression of alcoholism, and two subsequent case reports also describe baclofen's dose-dependent suppression of alcoholism. The three case reports are followed by abstracts and articles on several related topics: low-dose baclofen's ability to reduce alcohol cravings and anxiety; baclofen's dose-dependent suppression of the motivation to consume cocaine, heroin, alcohol, nicotine, and amphetamine in animal studies; the long-term safety of high-dose baclofen in comfort care in neurology; the overwhelming prevalence in addicted patients of preexisting anxiety and mood disorders, which demonstrates the need for a medication, such as baclofen, that can also address underlying dysphoria in addiction; and the possibility that one of the reasons for baclofen's effectiveness as a medication for addiction is that it compensates for a deficiency of GHB, a naturally occurring substance that has many sites of action in the body.

BACLOFEN AND COMPLETE SUPPRESSION OF ALCOHOLISM

Case Report 1

Alcohol and Alcoholism vol. 40, no. 2, pp. 147–150, 2005

Complete and prolonged suppression of symptoms and consequences of alcohol-dependence using high-dose baclofen: a self-case report of a physician

Olivier Ameisen

ABSTRACT

Aims: To test whether the dose-dependent motivation-suppressing effect of baclofen in animals could be transposed to humans, and suppress craving and sustain abstinence. Methods: Neurologists safely use up to 300 mg/day (10 times the dosage currently used for alcohol dependence) of high-dose oral baclofen, to control spasticity, in order to avoid invasive therapy. I am a physician with alcohol dependence and comorbid anxiety. I self-prescribed high-dose baclofen, starting at 30 mg/day, with 20 mg increments every third day and an (optional) additional 20–40 mg/day for cravings. Results: Cravings became easier to combat. After reaching the craving-suppression dose of 270 mg/day (3.6 mg/kg) after 5 weeks, I became and have remained free of alcohol dependence symptoms effortlessly for the ninth consecutive month. Anxiety is well controlled. Somnolence disappeared with a dosage reduction to 120 mg/ day, now used for the ninth consecutive month. Conclusions: High-dose baclofen induced complete and prolonged suppression of symptoms and consequences of alcohol dependence, and relieved anxiety. This model, integrating cure and well-being, should be tested in randomized trials, under medical surveillance. It offers a new concept: medication-induced, dose-dependent, complete and prolonged suppression of substance-dependence symptoms with alleviation of comorbid anxiety.

INTRODUCTION

Alcohol dependence symptoms (craving, preoccupation) are defined as chronic (Morse and Flavin, 1992), and current therapeutic approaches are based on the idea that such symptoms can be attenuated but not suppressed. Therefore, medical trials set abstinence with lower-grade craving as the declared goal (Addolorato *et al.*, 2000, 2002a; Pelc *et al.*, 2002; Froehlich *et al.*, 2003; Johnson *et al.*, 2003, 2004).

I am a physician diagnosed with alcohol dependence and comorbid anxiety disorder according to the Diagnostic and Statistical Manual of Mental Disorders fourth edition (DSM-IV) (American Psychiatric Association, 1994). I had been hospitalized for acute withdrawal seizures. Anxiety disorder had long preceded addiction.

I had tried recommended dosages of medications proposed for promotion of abstinence and reduction of craving (see Patient and Methods). I had achieved prolonged abstinence with and without medications. But I had always experienced cravings and preoccupation with alcohol, and achieving abstinence in such conditions required daily planning as well as constant and full attention.

Baclofen is a potent gamma-aminobutyric acid (GABA$_B$) receptor agonist clinically used to control spasticity (Davidoff, 1985):

(i) In alcohol-dependent patients, low-dose baclofen at 30 mg/day (-0.5 mg/kg) was shown to be effective in promoting abstinence, reducing alcohol craving and consumption, with no limiting side-effects (Addolorato *et al.*, 2000, 2002a,b).

(ii) In rats, at doses up to 10 times higher (5 mg/kg), baclofen suppresses cocaine self-administration, motivation to consume alcohol and attenuates self-administration of cocaine, alcohol, heroin, nicotine and D-amphetamine (Roberts and Andrews, 1997; Shoaib *et al.*, 1998; Xi and Stein, 1999; Colombo *et al.*, 2000, 2003; Fattore *et al.*, 2002; Brebner *et al.*, 2004). Effects are dose-dependent for each substance. For alcohol, up to 3 mg/kg are required.

(iii) In multiple sclerosis, neurologists safely use long-term high-dose oral baclofen (270 mg/day), to control spasticity, in order to protect patients from risks of invasive intrathecal therapy (Smith *et al.*, 1991). Given the safety record of baclofen since 1967, neurologists with experience in spasticity do not hesitate to use up to 300 mg/day of baclofen, as long as somnolence and/or muscular weakness do not limit treatment (John Schaefer, Cornell University Medical College, personal communication). In the highest recorded baclofen overdose (acute ingestion of 2 g), the patient survived (Gerkin *et al.*, 1986).

I postulated the notion that dose-dependent suppressing effects could be transposed to humans and that by using baclofen in dose ranges used in animal studies, one might reach a critical dose at which craving and motivation to drink alcohol might be suppressed in alcoholics, thus substantially reducing relapse risk.

Baclofen has also been used successfully in anxiety disorders (Breslow *et al.*, 1989; Drake *et al.*, 2003), and was shown to be effective in ameliorating some affective disturbances in alcoholic patients, including anxiety and depression (Krupitsky *et al.*, 1993; Addolorato *et al.*, 2002a,b). Anxiety is an overwhelmingly prevalent comorbidity of alcoholism (Grant *et al.*, 2004), and efficacy on anxiety has not been shown for other agents used for alcohol dependence (disulfiram, naltrexone, acamprosate or topiramate). I had used baclofen for > 1 year (2002–2003) to reduce anxiety. I had progressively increased the dosage to 180 mg/day, which improved personal and general well-being considerably, but did not suppress cravings and alcohol relapses. Being unaware then that higher dosages were safe, I had not exceeded 180 mg/day.

By analysing the literature, I subsequently realized that baclofen was the only monotherapy that could, in theory, completely suppress cravings, while alleviating comorbid anxiety simultaneously. Although my doctors remained unconvinced, I decided to self-prescribe high-dose baclofen, choosing 300 mg/day (4 mg/kg) as the maximal daily dosage, as long as side-effects were not limiting.

PATIENT AND METHODS

On January 9, 2004, I was a 50-year-old white French-American male physician with alcohol dependence and comorbid pre-existing anxiety disorder. Since 1997, there had been numerous emergency hospitalizations, emergency room visits, detoxifications, years of inpatient and outpatient rehabilitation treatments. I bear no medical sequelae. On a typical drinking day, I consumed ~750 ml of Scotch. Treatment had included 500 mg/day of disulfiram (I did drink while taking it). Thereafter, I had consecutively and for each medication been on 12–18 months of naltrexone (50 mg/day), acamprosate (2 g/day) and baclofen (180 mg/

day). I have subsequently been on topiramate (300 mg/day) for 3 months. Naltrexone and acamprosate had been discontinued because there had been no perceptible effects on cravings or relapse reduction. During this time, I benefited from cognitive behavioural therapy (CBT) and Alcoholics Anonymous (AA) meetings. I attended around two AA meetings a day, making roughly 700 meetings a year, over a period of 7 years.

Anxiety was refractory to buspirone, specific serotonin re-uptake inhibitors, valproate and carbamazepine. In May 2003, hoping to achieve complete abstinence, I tapered baclofen and self-prescribed topiramate following an outlined schedule (Johnson *et al.*, 2003). I continued with 300 mg/day of topiramate for 3 months despite side-effects (memory, speech). Topiramate had no efficacy in reducing anxiety and I suffered a severe relapse.

On January 9, 2004, day 1 of post-relapse abstinence, I started oral baclofen monotherapy: 10 mg three times daily (30 mg/day), adding 20 mg/day every third day; optional 20–40 mg/day p.r.n. at a time was available for cravings or important inter-current stress or anxiety. Since cravings appeared during afternoons or evenings, dosages were divided unequally: lower in mornings, i.e. on day 31 (230 mg/day) I took 50 mg, then 90 mg, then 90 mg.

Primary outcome measures included, in addition to abstinence from alcohol, the personal assessment of indifference to alcohol (speech, sight, places or odour in restaurants) under any circumstances (stressful situations or anxiety), of cravings, preoccupation and alcohol dreams.

Other outcome measures included the personal assessment of anxiety, muscular tension, quality of sleep, general well-being and side-effects of baclofen. Blood tests assessing haematological parameters, biochemistry, including liver enzymes, were performed at the third and fifth months.

RESULTS

I have not had a drink since January 9, 2004. Detoxification was marked by less malaise than with benzodiazepines. From day 1, anxiety was substantially reduced, muscular tension had begun to subside and sleep had become restful. At the onset of cravings, I took an additional 20–40 mg of baclofen that induced a state of deep relaxation within the hour, followed by somnolence. During the deep relaxation phase it was much easier for me to use CBT and AA techniques to resist drinking. During cravings, the knowledge that I could reliably limit the struggle to 1 h with the additional baclofen dose was very useful. Since day 15 not one alcohol dream occurred (normally more than once a month). On day 37 (February 14, 2004), on 270 mg/day of baclofen (3.6 mg/kg), I experienced no craving or desire for alcohol for the first time in my alcoholic life. Even in a restaurant with friends, I was indifferent to people drinking. This had never occurred before. Somnolence prevented me from increasing the dosage of baclofen further, and there was no need for the extra 20–40 mg dose. For 12 days, at 270 mg/day, absence of craving persisted, and I remained indifferent to alcohol. In this condition, somnolence became an inconvenient side-effect, and I therefore progressively reduced the dosage to 120 mg/day (1.6 mg/kg) from days 49–63. Since day 63 I have stabilized the dosage around this value with occasional additions of 40 mg p.r.n. in stressful situations. I have not experienced somnolence again; muscular weakness never occurred and there were no other side-effects. Blood tests remained within normal limits.

At the end of my ninth month of complete liberation from symptoms of alcohol dependence, I remain indifferent to alcohol. Abstinence has become natural to me. I no longer plan my life around alcohol. Alcohol thoughts no longer occur. I undertook personal and professional projects, which I was unable to do before as I had to anticipate consequences of unpredictable drinking episodes (cancelling appointments when possible and blackouts). As taught in CBT, I avoided places, situations, social settings, and vacations where alcohol might have been present. I no longer notice liquor sections in supermarkets. Some of these changes have been pointed out to me by relatives and friends.

I no longer suffer anticipatory anxiety of relapse, of embarrassing or dangerous alcohol-related situations. I am no longer depressed about having an incurable stigmatizing disease.

Liberation from symptoms of alcohol dependence substantially improved my self-esteem.

DISCUSSION

I have never come across a report of complete medication-induced suppression of craving or other symptoms and consequences of alcohol dependence in AA, CBT, rehabilitation centres or in the medical literature.

Here, I describe how, using high-dose baclofen, I succeeded in completely suppressing all signs and consequences of alcohol dependence, while simultaneously and for the first time controlling comorbid refractory anxiety for the ninth consecutive month. However, I wish to underline the 'personal point of view' aspect of this report, since I did not use validated scales to evaluate cravings, anxiety and depression.

Notion of symptom-suppressing dose (SSD)

The baclofen dosage that suppressed my craving and other symptoms of alcohol dependence (SSD) was 270 mg/day (nine times the dosage used in clinical alcohol dependence studies). But the subsequent maintenance dose of ~120 mg/day (1.6 mg/kg) that controlled anxiety prevented craving from reoccurring altogether. This suggests that the maintenance dose is much lower than the SSD. I attained the SSD empirically. In clinical trials, I believe that the SSD (leading to complete indifference to repeated exposure to the strongest cues) should be determined clinically, based on the patient's feedback to the physician and the use of validated scales. I had no choice but to initiate and conduct dose escalation under my sole supervision. But escalation should be tested solely under properly designed studies and should be not replicated by any patient without a strict medical surveillance, which may require an inpatient condition, because of risks associated with somnolence, possible muscular weakness and other side-effects of baclofen.

Issue of well-being, comorbidity and compliance
My alcoholism did not appear in a vacuum: chronic anxiety had long preceded alcoholism. I used alcohol as a tranquilizer until it became an addiction. Associations between alcohol and most substance use disorders and independent mood and anxiety disorders are overwhelmingly positive and significant (Grant *et al.*, 2004). Alleviation of anxiety promotes well-being, which renders 'extra' relief from alcohol useless.

A recent trial established the superiority of topiramate over placebo in improving the quality of life of alcohol-dependent individuals (Johnson *et al.*, 2004). The authors point out that such effects (that were not assessed beyond the 12-week duration of the trial) may be obtained only with moderately dependent alcoholics. The severity of my dependence and anxiety might explain why I did not benefit from topiramate.

A recent multicentre trial showed the advantage of monthly intramuscular naltrexone depot over oral naltrexone in improving the total abstinence rate because of compliance issues with oral naltrexone (Kranzler *et al.*, 2004). Naltrexone—as disulfiram, acamprosate and topimarate—does not claim efficacy in reducing symptoms of anxiety. In contrast, baclofen, by its additional effect on anxiety, encourages compliance and represented an effective monotherapy for me.

Deep relaxation

During cravings, it had always been extremely difficult for me to apply CBT techniques because the efforts required induced anxiety in such a context. In contrast, in the first 37 days during which cravings were present (escalating baclofen doses), when deep relaxation occurred after an additional baclofen dose, it was much easier for me to use CBT and AA techniques to combat cravings and avoid drinking than before. Deep relaxation reliably occurred within the hour after an additional 20–40 mg of baclofen.

Tolerance

Tolerance, though uncommon, has been reported in spasticity after years of intrathecal baclofen therapy, requiring minor adjustments in dosage (Nielsen *et al.*, 2002). Should tolerance develop, there is ample room for me to safely increase the dosage until other medications demonstrate efficacy.

Possible mechanisms of action of baclofen

Medications that facilitate GABA neurotransmission (baclofen, topiramate) show promise in treatment of alcohol and cocaine dependence (Addolorato *et al.*, 2000, 2002a,b; Johnson *et al.*, 2003, 2004; Shoptaw *et al.*, 2003; Kampman *et al.*, 2004). GABA neurotransmission is an important common denominator in the pathophysiology of anxiety and mood disorders (Brambilla *et al.*, 2003; Nemeroff, 2003). GABA modulation is a highly probable mechanism by which the clinical expression of alcohol dependence is blocked by baclofen. However, at high doses, recruitment of additional mechanism(s) by baclofen cannot be excluded. Behaviours that resemble human diagnostic criteria for addiction have been recently described in rats (Deroche-Gamonet *et al.*, 2004). This new animal model should allow further research on the mechanisms by which baclofen reverses dependence.

Chronic treatment

Currently, I use baclofen primarily to control anxiety. It is impossible for me to know whether symptoms of dependence would reoccur, and at which lower dosage, since I have not contemplated weaning myself off baclofen. Would conscious cognition that I have remained indifferent to alcohol for several months modify my behavioural response if symptoms were to reoccur? I believe that the new situation created by baclofen-mediated suppression of symptoms of alcohol dependence offers a window of opportunity to explore the effects of other approaches, such as CBT, in helping reduce or suppress requirement for life-long baclofen treatment. Moreover, the necessity for life-long baclofen treatment could be studied in the newly described addiction model in rats (Deroche-Gamonet *et al.*, 2004).

The major limitation of this report is that it is a self-case report, not a study. But it suggests a new concept of treatment: the blockade of the expression of substance dependence symptoms with simultaneous intervention on anxiety. This case could result from a placebo effect, but I believe this to be unlikely since there has been no report of such complete and prolonged effects in clinical trials. The efficacy of high-dose baclofen should be tested for reproducibility in randomized trials under strict medical surveillance to confirm the validity of the concept of dose-dependent suppression of symptoms of alcohol dependence.

ACKNOWLEDGEMENTS

A physician's signed corroboration of the author's self-report has been provided by Dr Jean-Paul Descombey, former chief of psychiatry at Hôpital Sainte-Anne, Paris, and a member of the Administrative Council of the French Society of Alcohology. He has known the author for the last 5 years. The author states that he has no financial or other connections with any company marketing baclofen, or other conflict of interest.

REFERENCES

Addolorato, G., Caputo, F., Capristo, E. *et al.* (2000) Ability of baclofen in reducing alcohol craving and intake: II —preliminary clinical evidence. *Alcoholism: Clinical and Experimental Research* 24, 67–71.

Addolorato, G., Caputo, F., Capristo, E. *et al.* (2002a) Baclofen efficacy in reducing alcohol craving and intake: a preliminary double-blind randomized controlled study. *Alcohol and Alcoholism* 37, 504–508.

Addolorato, G., Caputo, F., Capristo, E. *et al.* (2002b) Rapid suppression of alcohol withdrawal syndrome by baclofen. *American Journal of Medicine* 112, 226–229.

American Psychiatric Association (1994) *Diagnostic and Statistical Manual of Mental Disorders.* APA, Washington, DC.

Brambilla, P., Perez, J., Barale, F. *et al.* (2003) GABAergic dysfunction in mood disorders. *Molecular Psychiatry* 8, 715, 721–737.

Brebner, K., Ahn, S. and Phillips, A. G. (2004) Attenuation of D-amphetamine self-administration by baclofen in the rat: behavioral and neurochemical correlates. *Psychopharmacology (Berlin)* Jul 22 [Epub ahead of print].

Breslow, M. F., Fankhauser, M. P., Potter, R. L. *et al.* (1989) Role of gamma-aminobutyric acid in antipanic drug efficacy. *American Journal of Psychiatry* 146, 353–356.

Colombo, G., Agabio, R., Carai, M. A. *et al.* (2000) Ability of baclofen in reducing alcohol intake and withdrawal severity: I. Preclinical evidence. *Alcoholism: Clinical and Experimental Research* 24, 58–66.

Colombo, G., Vacca, G., Serra, S. *et al.* (2003) Baclofen suppresses motivation to consume alcohol in rats. *Psychopharmacology (Berlin)* 167, 221–224 [Epub April 1, 2003].

Davidoff, R. A. (1985) Antispasticity drugs: mechanisms of action. *Annals of Neurology* 17, 107–116.

Deroche-Gamonet, V., Belin, D. and Piazza, P. V. (2004) Evidence for addiction-like behavior in the rat. *Science* **305**, 1014–1017.

Drake, R. G., Davis, L. L., Cates, M. E. *et al.* (2003) Baclofen treatment for chronic posttraumatic stress disorder. *The Annals of Pharmacotherapy* **37**, 1177–1181.

Fattore, L., Cossu, G., Martellotta, M. C. *et al.* (2002) Baclofen antagonizes intravenous self-administration of nicotine in mice and rats. *Alcohol and Alcoholism* **37**, 495–498.

Froehlich, J., O'Malley, S., Hyytia, P. *et al.* (2003) Preclinical and clinical studies on naltrexone: what have they taught each other? *Alcoholism: Clinical and Experimental Research* **27**, 533–539.

Gerkin, R., Curry, S. C., Vance, M. V. *et al.* (1986) First-order elimination kinetics following baclofen overdose. *Annals of Emergency Medicine* **15**, 843–846.

Grant, B. F., Stinson, F. S., Dawson, D. A. *et al.* (2004) Prevalence and co-occurrence of substance use disorders and independent mood and anxiety disorders: results from the National Epidemiologic Survey on Alcohol and Related Conditions. *Archives of General Psychiatry* **61**, 807–816.

Johnson, B. A., Ait-Daoud, N., Bowden, C. L. *et al.* (2003) Oral topiramate for treatment of alcohol dependence: a randomized controlled trial. *Lancet* **361**, 1677–1685.

Johnson, B. A., Ait-Daoud, N., Akhtar, F. Z. *et al.* (2004) Oral topiramate reduces the consequences of drinking and improves the quality of life of alcohol-dependent individuals: a randomized controlled trial. *Archives of General Psychiatry* **61**, 905–912.

Kampman, K. M., Pettinati, H., Lynch, K. G. *et al.* (2004) A pilot trial of topiramate for the treatment of cocaine dependence. *Drug and Alcohol Dependence* **75**, 233–240.

Kranzler, H. R., Wesson, D. R., Billot, L. *et al.* (2004) Naltrexone depot for treatment of alcohol dependence: a multicenter, randomized, placebo-controlled clinical trial. *Alcoholism: Clinical and Experimental Research* **28**, 1051–1059.

Krupitsky, E. M., Burakov, A. M., Ivanov, V. B. *et al.* (1993) Baclofen administration for the treatment of affective disorders in alcoholic patients. *Drug and Alcohol Dependence* **33**, 157–163.

Morse, R. M. and Flavin, D. K. (1992) The definition of alcoholism. The Joint Committee of the National Council on Alcoholism and Drug Dependence and the American Society of Addiction Medicine to Study the Definition and Criteria for the Diagnosis of Alcoholism. *The Journal of the American Medical Association* **268**, 1012–1014.

Nemeroff, C. B. (2003) The role of GABA in the pathophysiology and treatment of anxiety disorders. *Psychopharmacological Bulletin* **37**, 133–146.

Nielsen, J. F., Hansen, H. J., Sunde, N. *et al.* (2002) Evidence of tolerance to baclofen in treatment of severe spasticity with intrathecal baclofen. *Clinical Neurology and Neurosurgery* **104**, 142–145.

Pelc, I., Ansoms, C., Lehert, P. *et al.* (2002) The European NEAT program: an integrated approach using acamprosate and psychosocial support for the prevention of relapse in alcohol-dependent patients with a statistical modeling of therapy success prediction. *Alcoholism: Clinical and Experimental Research* **26**, 1529–1538.

Roberts, D. C. and Andrews, M. M. (1997) Baclofen suppression of cocaine self-administration: demonstration using a discrete trials procedure. *Psychopharmacology (Berlin)* **131**, 271–277.

Shoaib, M., Swanner, L. S., Beyer, C. E. *et al.* (1998) The GABA$_B$ agonist baclofen modifies cocaine self-administration in rats. *Behavioral Pharmacology* **9**, 195–206.

Shoptaw, S., Yang, X., Rotheram-Fuller, E. J. *et al.* (2003) Randomized placebo-controlled trial of baclofen for cocaine dependence: preliminary effects for individuals with chronic patterns of cocaine use. *The Journal of Clinical Psychiatry* **64**, 1440–1448.

Smith, C. R., LaRocca, N. G., Giesser, B. S. *et al.* (1991) High-dose oral baclofen: experience in patients with multiple sclerosis. *Neurology* **41**, 1829–1831.

Xi, Z. X. and Stein, E. A. (1999) Baclofen inhibits heroin self-administration behavior and mesolimbic dopamine release. *The Journal of Pharmacology and Experimental Therapeutics* **290**, 1369–1374.

Alcohol and Alcoholism vol. 42, no. 2, pp. 158–160, 2007

Suppression of symptoms of alcohol dependence and craving using high-dose baclofen

William Bucknam

ABSTRACT

Aims: To further test whether the baclofen-induced suppression of motivation to consume alcohol in animals could be transposed to humans. Methods: A patient who had neither tolerated nor benefited from other alcohol treatment modalities was put on trial with baclofen on a dosage up to 140 mg/day. Results: The patient reported dramatic reduction in cravings for and preoccupation with alcohol. Conclusions: High-dose baclofen therapy was associated with complete and prolonged suppression of symptoms and consequences of alcohol-dependence.

INTRODUCTION

In the past decade, scientists have made important progress toward understanding the neurobiology underlying drug and alcohol addiction. Consequent development of new pharmacotherapies has been shown to substantially improve the outcomes of patients treated with standard alcohol therapies (individual and/or group supportive psychotherapy, cognitive behavioral therapy; 12-step programs). FDA approval has been granted for three agents thus far. Listed in order of FDA approval dates, these are disulfiram, oral naltrexone, acamprosate, and recently an extended release (30 day) injectable suspension of naltrexone. The latter, having just been released, has not yet had widespread use in clinical settings. Although Garbutt *et al.* (2005) did associate injectable naltrexone with a lower number of heavy drinking days per month in alcohol-dependent individuals, the number did not continue to diminish over the long duration of the trial. This may be because naltrexone has never been shown to completely eliminate craving for alcohol. Craving has been shown in some studies to predict drinking behavior (Bottlender and Soyka, 2004). Craving remains, nonetheless, an ill-defined concept. Clinical assessment of craving remains of unclear value. Reduction of heavy drinking days has been previously established in randomized trials with the oral naltrexone (Balldin *et al.*, 2003), topiramate (Johnson *et al.*, 2003), baclofen dosed 10 mg t.i.d. (Addolorato *et al.*, 2002), and in an open-label trial of acamprosate (Soyka and Chick, 2003).

In validated animal models for craving for alcohol (Koob, 2000), one of these agents, baclofen, which is a $GABA_B$ receptor agonist, has been shown in high dose to completely suppress motivation to consume alcohol. The suppressing effect is dose-dependent (Colombo *et al.*, 2003). Acamprosate has also been shown to reduce self-administration of alcohol in alcohol-preferring rats (Cowen *et al.*, 2005). Naltrexone reduced but did not eliminate self-administration of alcohol. Animal data are not available for topiramate (Ameisen, 2005a).

Anxiety disorders (Breslow *et al.*, 1989; Drake *et al.*, 2003) and anxiety associated with affective disorders (Addolorato *et al.*, 2002a,b, 2006) have been shown to be ameliorated by baclofen. Clinically significant anxiety is commonly comorbid with alcohol dependence (Grant *et al.*, 2004). Efficacy on anxiety has not been shown for other agents used for alcohol dependence (Ameisen, 2005b). Thus it appears, upon review of the literature, that baclofen is the only agent capable of completely suppressing cravings, while alleviating comorbid anxiety.

The data presented thus far was previously reported in a letter to the editor of *Journal of the American Medical Association* (Ameisen, 2005a) and in a case study authored by Olivier Ameisen, MD, who used himself as the subject of study (Ameisen, 2005b). Dr. Ameisen had previously tried recommended dosages of disulfiram, oral naltrexone, acamprosate, and topiramate and had had extended periods of abstinence utilizing CBT and extensive involvement in alcoholics anonymous (AA). He nevertheless persisted to have alcohol cravings and anxiety symptoms, which had predated his alcohol dependence, despite trials of buspirone, selective serotonin reuptake inhibitors, valproate and carbamazepine. Hypothesizing that the dose-dependent suppression of alcohol consumption (3 mg/kg body wt) in animals could be transposed in humans, he subjected himself to a trial. He self-prescribed baclofen up to 270 mg/day (3.6 mg/kg body wt) during the first 37 days and experienced, for the first time in his alcoholic life, the absence of craving for alcohol. Indeed, he reported a state of complete and persistent indifference to alcohol, along with substantial reduction of anxiety, for a duration of 9 months at the time of his report. For reasons of somnolence, he subsequently reduced his dosage to 120 mg/day and used extra 40 mg p.r.n. stressful situations. The somnolence abated and he never experienced muscle weakness or other side effects. Blood tests remained within normal limits.

PATIENT AND METHODS

Mr. A is a 59-year-old married successful businessman who frequently presides over national conventions and speaks before hundreds of people. He enjoys a stable home life, does not smoke, has no other chronic medical illnesses, and exercises regularly. He sought my services as an addiction psychiatrist in May 2005 despite having a beneficial ongoing relationship with both a psychologist and a psychiatrist for the management of depression and anxiety. He had been given a diagnosis of major depressive disorder. His symptoms had responded to paroxetine over the previous 2–3 years. Prior to taking paroxetine he had had trials of fluoxetine, citalopram, and sertraline which he considered to have been tainted by his heavier alcohol consumption at the time. He spontaneously identified himself as an alcoholic and presented a strong family history of the same. He presented with a strong distaste for AA meetings, which he had tried, and refused to consider returning. He was not interested in a recommendation for outpatient chemical dependency programming. In counseling sessions he was advised to pursue abstinence from alcohol.

His ardent desire, however, was to be able to control his drinking so as to not have it continue, in its unpredictable fashion, to embarrass and/or episodically incapacitate him in his professional endeavors. Toward that end, he had already completed the Drinkwise program offered through the University of Michigan. This program utilizes CBT techniques to assist those with an alcohol abuse diagnosis to be able to drink in a controlled fashion, if they so choose. It did not work for him, which appropriately led him to his own conclusion that he had alcohol dependence rather than alcohol abuse.

Through his other psychiatrist he had already taken oral naltrexone. A dosage of 100 mg/day had initially been necessary before he noticed any attenuation of his alcohol cravings. This was short-lived, however, and by the time he presented to me he was taking 150 mg/day with no apparent benefit. He was still consuming an average of 35 drinks distributed over a week and up to 12 drinks per occasion. He remained concerned about the potential damage such drinking might do to his

health, professional and home life. I recommended he continue naltrexone at 150 mg/day and added acamprosate 2 g/day. After 1 month,
that did not reduce his craving or drinking so I offered a trial of topiramate in its place. Topiramate, similarly, offered no benefit and was associated with word-finding difficulties, a side-effect he could not abide.

At this juncture, September 2005, a trial of baclofen was agreed
upon. Scales to evaluate craving and laboratory parameters were not
used. Over the first month he gradually increased his dosage to 100 mg/
day, taken on a t.i.d. schedule, and reported a completely satisfactory
response. He felt that drinking was now "an alien world" to him. On occasion, when stressed, he increased his dosage to 140 mg/day. He experienced only mild relaxation, not sedation, as a side-effect. This benefit
did not abate, as had been his experience with naltrexone, and he continued to report baclofen as "my miracle drug." If he chose to drink his
consumption was never more than 12 per week, or 3 per occasion, and
his sense of euphoria from that was dulled. With the guidance of his
other psychiatrist he discontinued the paroxetine, experienced return
of depression and anxiety, had a brief unsuccessful trial on Effexor XR
75 mg, and returned to paroxetine.

DISCUSSION

Having worked with chemically dependent individuals struggling for
recovery for over 20 years, I am a supporter of AA and Narcotics Anonymous (NA) and believe connection with those organizations to be the
most likely route toward quality recovery. With or without such a connection, however, I have repeatedly been faced with the patient who,
despite his or her apparent best efforts, has not been successful at resisting the impulse to relapse, even when I believe I have successfully
treated psychiatric comorbidity. I have experienced such patients ben-

efiting from either oral naltrexone, acamprosate, or the combination of both. I make disulfiram available to patients whom I believe it will help, but do not rely upon it to reduce the phenomenon of craving. I have yet to treat anyone with injectable naltrexone.

Mr. A is an individual whom I believe represents a very large number of patients who do not experience a satisfactory anti-craving response to either the current FDA-approved medications for alcohol dependence or to topiramate. My report is that he has experienced a satisfactory response to high-dose baclofen that has been sustained over ten months without significant side-effect. Tolerance has not developed, whereas it had with oral naltrexone. Tolerance to baclofen has uncommonly been reported only after years of intrathecal use for severe spasticity (Nielsen *et al.*, 2002). In contrast with Dr. Ameisen's experience, use of a selective serotonin reuptake inhibitor (SSRI; paroxetine) did appear to be necessary as baclofen by itself did not satisfactorily reduce Mr. A's anxiety or depression.

Being a case study, this report is obviously limited. Placebo response is a possibility. If that is the case, however, there is no apparent explanation for why it did not appear in trials of either naltrexone or acamprosate, alone or in combination, or with topiramate. Given the nearly four decades of use of high-dose baclofen for the long-term comfort care of patients with muscular spasticity from various neurological conditions (spinal injuries, multiple sclerosis), and the absence of report of serious or irreversible adverse effect, baclofen may be a safe, effective and well-tolerated adjunct to our treatment efforts with this population. Hypotension, changes in glucose control in diabetics, sedation and changes in seizure control are potential side-effects. Randomized trials of high-dose baclofen should be conducted to test elimination of alcohol craving and its potential consequences.

ACKNOWLEDGEMENT

I am grateful to Dr. Ameisen for his support and the sharing of his experience.

REFERENCES

Addolorato, G., Caputo, F., Capristo, E. *et al.* (2002a) Baclofen efficacy in reducing alcohol craving and intake: a preliminary double-blind randomized controlled study. *Alcohol and Alcoholism* 37, 504–508.

Addolorato, G., Caputo, F., Capristo, E. *et al.* (2002b) Rapid suppression of alcohol withdrawal syndrome by baclofen. *American Journal of Medicine* 112, 226–229.

Addolorato, G., Leggio, L., Abenavoli, L. *et al.* (2006) Baclofen in the treatment of alcohol withdrawal syndrome: a comparative study vs diazepam. *American Journal of Medicine* 119, 276.e13–276.e18.

Ameisen, O. (2005a) Naltrexone treatment for alcohol dependency. *Journal of the American Medical Association* 294, 899–900; author reply 900.

Ameisen, O. (2005b) Complete and prolonged suppression of symptoms and consequences of alcohol-dependence using high-dose baclofen: a self-case report of a physician. *Alcohol and Alcoholism* 40, 147–150.

Balldin, J., Berglund, M., Borg, S. *et al.* (2003) A 6-month controlled naltrexone study: combined effect with cognitive behavioral therapy in outpatient treatment of alcohol dependence. *Alcohol and Clinical Experimental Research* 27, 1142–1149.

Bottlender, M. and Soyka, M. (2004) Impact of craving on alcohol relapse during, and 12 months following, outpatient treatment. *Alcohol and Alcoholism* 39, 357–361.

Breslow, M. F., Fankhauser, M. P., Potter, R. L. *et al.* (1989) Role of gamma-aminobutyric acid in antipanic drug efficacy. *American Journal of Psychiatry* 146, 353–356.

Colombo, G., Vacca, G., Serra, S. *et al.* (2003) Baclofen suppresses motivation to consume alcohol in rats. *Psychopharmacology (Berlin)* 167, 221–224.

Cowen, M. S., Adams, C., Kraehenbuehl, T. *et al.* (2005) The acute anti-craving effect of acamprosate in alcohol-preferring rats is associated with modulation of the mesolimbic dopamine system. *Addiction Biology* 10, 233–242.

Drake, R. G., Davis, L. L., Cates, M. E. *et al.* (2003) Baclofen treatment for chronic posttraumatic stress disorder. *The Annals of Pharmacotherapy* 37, 1177–1181.

Garbutt, J. C., Kranzler, H. R., O'Malley, S. S. *et al.* (2005) Vivitrex Study Group. Efficacy and tolerability of long-acting injectable naltrexone for alcohol dependence: a randomized controlled trial. *Journal of the American Medical Association* 293, 1617–1625.

Grant, B. F., Stinson, F. S., Dawson, D. A. *et al.* (2004) Prevalence and co-occurrence of substance use disorders and independent mood and anxiety disorders: results from the National Epidemiologic Survey on Alcohol and Related Disorders. *Archives of General Psychiatry* 61, 807–816.

Johnson, B. A., Ait-Daoud, N., Bowden, C. L. *et al.* (2003) Oral topiramate for treatment of alcohol dependence: a randomized controlled trial. *Lancet* 361, 1677–1685.

Koob, G. F. (2000) Animal models of craving for ethanol. *Addiction* 95(Suppl 2), 573–581.

Nielsen, J. F., Hansen, H. J., Sunde, N. *et al.* (2002) Evidence of tolerance to baclofen in treatment of severe spasticity with intrathecal baclofen. *Clinical Neurology and Neurosurgery* 104, 142–145.

Soyka, M. and Chick, J. (2003) Use of acamprosate and opioid antagonists in the treatment of alcohol dependence: a European perspective. *American Journal of Addiction* 12(Suppl 1), 569–580.

Case Report 3

Journal of Clinical Psychopharmacology vol. 27, no. 3, pp. 319–320, 2007

Baclofen suppresses alcohol intake and craving for alcohol in a schizophrenic alcohol-dependent patient: a case report

To the Editors:

Alcohol use disorders (AUDs) are common in patients with schizophrenia. The Epidemiologic Catchment Area Study[1] indicated that approximately one third of patients with schizophrenia have a lifetime diagnosis of AUDs. An excessive alcohol intake produces negative consequences on schizophrenic patients, such as increased relapses, more hospitalizations, and increased violence and suicide attempts.[2] Therefore, decreasing alcohol consumption in patients with schizophrenia should be considered a major goal in their treatment programs. It has recently been demonstrated that the prototypic agonist of the γ-aminobutyric acid ($GABA_B$) receptor, baclofen, widely used to control spasticity,[3] reduced alcohol consumption and obsessive thinking of alcohol,[4,5] as well as symptoms of alcohol withdrawal syndrome[6] in human alcoholics. A recent paper also reported that higher doses of baclofen completely suppressed alcohol consumption and craving for alcohol.[7] These studies also reported that use of baclofen in alcohol-dependent patients appeared to be safe and manageable. Baclofen was tested in schizophrenic patients to evaluate its effect on tardive dyskinesia, an adverse effect of neuroleptic drugs, or schizophrenic symptoms.[8–10] The results of these studies suggested that baclofen was similar to placebo in both effects. However, baclofen administration—up to 90 mg daily—did not result in any worsening of schizophrenic symptoms.[8,9,11–13] Moreover, a recent case report described the efficacy and safety of baclofen in decreasing craving for cocaine in a patient with cocaine dependence and schizoaffective disorder.[14] Considering the efficacy of baclofen in reducing alcohol intake in alcoholics and in view of the fact that it did not worsen schizophrenic symptoms, baclofen administration to the patient described here was aimed at evaluating the effectiveness and safety profile of baclofen in an alcohol-dependent schizophrenic patient.

CASE REPORT

In 1999, a 49-year-old male outpatient was admitted to the Division of Psychiatry, University of Cagliari, Italy, having persecutory and referential delusions, visual hallucinations, affective flattening, and avolition. Details provided by his relatives revealed an early onset of heavy alcohol drinking and schizophrenic symptoms at approximately the age of 28 years.

Daily alcohol intake, as reported by both the patient himself and his relatives, averaged approximately 2 L of wine (approximately 16 drinks per day). After frequent episodes of alcohol intoxication and/or exacerbation of schizophrenic symptoms, he had been admitted several times to medical and psychiatric hospitals with a diagnosis of alcohol dependence and paranoid schizophrenia (in accordance with *Diagnostic and Statistical Manual of Mental Disorders, Fourth Edition* criteria) and treated with haloperidol and benzodiazepines. He had also been treated with disulfiram and had attended Alcoholics Anonymous meetings, without any apparent beneficial effect in terms of reduction of alcohol intake. From 1999 to 2005, he was admitted to the hospital approximately once a year because of severe episodes of acute alcohol intoxication. In July 2005, we proposed to the patient and his family a new pharmacological treatment to decrease his alcohol consumption. Specifically, the possibility of using baclofen was discussed. Written informed consent was obtained. Before the first baclofen administration, a blood sample was collected for evaluation of the following indicators of heavy alcohol drinking: mean corpuscular volume of red blood cells, aspartate aminotransferase, alanine aminotransferase, and g-glutamyl transpeptidase. A schedule was drawn up providing for patient examination once a day for the first 3 days, once a week for the first 4 weeks, and subsequently once every 2 weeks. A breathalyzer test, using the Alco-Sensor IV breathalyzer apparatus (Syen Elettronica, Gardigiano di Scorzè, Venezia, Italy), was administered at each visit to evaluate the patient's breath alcohol concentration. At each visit, the following rating scales were administered to the patient: Zung Self-rating Depression Scale, Spielberger State Anxiety Inventory, Brief Psychiatric Rating Scale (BPRS), Clinical Global Impression (CGI)–Improvement and –Severity Scales, a visual analog scale (VAS) of craving severity and Obsessive Compulsive Drinking Scale (OCDS15) in its validated form in Italian.[16] Alcohol intake was self-reported by the patient and confirmed by a family member. Possible side effects related to baclofen therapy were also recorded. Treatment with baclofen started with the dose of 5 mg, per os, 3 times a day for 3 days; starting from day 4, the dose was increased to 10 mg, 3 times a day. The patient attended all scheduled visits and regularly took the baclofen pills as indicated by counting the returned tablets. He did not report any side effect, with the sole exception of a mild degree of sedation at the very beginning of the treatment. He stopped drinking from the first week of treatment; breath alcohol concentrations were negative throughout the treatment. OCDS and VAS scores were virtually suppressed from the first 4 weeks of treatment (Table 1). Indexes of severity of schizophrenic symptoms tended to decrease during treatment (Table 1). Conversely, anxiety and depression severity scores were not modified by baclofen administration.

In line with the reduction in alcohol intake, value of mean corpuscular volume decreased from 101 to 94 fL over treatment with baclofen. The patient reported the consumption of 1 drink in week 18. Subsequently, taking into account the recently reported beneficial effects induced by relatively high doses of baclofen (up to 270 mg/d) on alcohol consumption and craving for alcohol,[7] the dose of baclofen was increased to 25 mg, 3 times a day. After 1 year of treatment, the latter remains the only episode of alcohol drinking, as the patient demonstrated near-complete suppression of alcohol drinking and craving for a 48-week period.

TABLE 1. Scores of Different Rating Scales for Psychiatric Disorders and Alcohol Craving in an Alcohol-Dependent Schizophrenic Patient Treated with Baclofen

Rating Scales	Week									
	0	1	2	3	4	8	12	16	20	24
BPRS	36	33	33	30	29	25	33	29	33	26
CGI-S	6	6	6	6	5	5	4	4	4	4
CGI-I	7	3	3	3	3	3	2	2	2	1
OCDS	34	7	15	6	0	5	3	6	4	9
VAS	25	30	23	23	13	6	1	0	0	0
ZUNG	41	41	40	42	38	44	40	42	40	40
STAI	42	38	47	38	41	42	32	35	42	42

Values in week 0 are baseline values (before the start of treatment with baclofen). Weeks 1 to 24 are time elapsed from the start of the treatment with baclofen.

BPRS indicates Brief Psychiatric Rating Scale, CGI-S, CGI-Severity; CGI-I, CGI-Improvement; OCDS, Obsessive Compulsive Drinking Scale; VAS, visual analog scale; ZUNG, Zung Self-rating Depression Scale; STAI, Spielberger State Anxiety Inventory.

DISCUSSION

Suppression, or at least reduction, of alcohol drinking is 1 of the major goals in the treatment of patients affected by schizophrenia and alcohol dependence.[2] However, research to evaluate effective pharmacotherapies for patients diagnosed with AUDs and psychiatric comorbidity is still in its infancy. To our knowledge, this is the first case of a schizophrenic alcohol-dependent patient treated with baclofen in an attempt to decrease his alcohol consumption. Consistent with previous reports,[11-13] treatment with baclofen did not worsen schizophrenic symptoms in our patient, as indicated by the scores of BPRS and CGI. Vice versa, treatment with baclofen resulted in a virtually complete suppression of alcohol drinking, without occurrence of any relevant side effects. This observation is in agreement with the results of 2 recent studies which demonstrated that treatment with baclofen induced a significant reduction in alcohol intake and craving for alcohol.[4,5] Of interest, another GABAergic medication has recently been suggested to be effective in alcohol-dependent schizophrenic patients. A recent case report indeed described how the GABAergic antiepileptic drug, topiramate, suppressed alcohol intake in a patient affected by alcohol dependence and schizophrenia.[17] In conclusion, the present observation suggests that baclofen may be evaluated in future, properly designed studies as a novel pharmacotherapy for patients affected by alcohol dependence and schizophrenia.

Roberta Agabio, MD*†
Priamo Marras, MD†
Giovanni Addolorato, MD‡
Bernardo Carpiniello, MD†
Gian Luigi Gessa, MD*
*Bernard B. Brodie Department of Neuroscience
and †Division of Psychiatry

Department of Public Health

University of Cagliari

Cagliari, Italy

‡Institute of Internal Medicine

Catholic University

Rome, Italy

agabio@unica.it

REFERENCES

1. Regier DA, Farmer ME, Rae DS, et al. Comorbidity of mental disorders with alcohol and other drug abuse. Results from the Epidemiologic Catchment Area (ECA) Study. *J Am Med Assoc.* 1990;**264**:2511–2518.

2. Le Fauve CE, Litten RZ, Randall CL, et al. Pharmacological treatment of alcohol abuse/dependence with psychiatric comorbidity. *Alcohol Clin Exp Res.* 2004;**28**:302–312.

3. Davidoff RA. Antispasticity drugs: mechanisms of action. *Ann Neurol.* 1985; **17**:107–116.

4. Addolorato G, Caputo F, Capristo E, et al. Baclofen efficacy in reducing alcohol craving and intake—a preliminary double blind randomised controlled study. *Alcohol Alcohol.* 2002; **37**:504–508.

5. Flannery BA, Garbutt JC, Cody MW, et al. Baclofen for alcohol dependence: a preliminary open-label study. *Alcohol Clin Exp Res.* 2004;**28**:1517–1523.

6. Addolorato G, Leggio L, Abenavoli L, et al. Baclofen in the treatment of alcohol withdrawal syndrome: a comparative study vs diazepam. *Am J Med.* 2006;**119**:e13–e18.

7. Ameisen O. Complete and prolonged suppression of symptoms and consequences of alcohol-dependence using high-dose baclofen: a self-case report of a physician. *Alcohol Alcohol.* 2005;**40**:147–150.

8. Gulmann NC, Bahr B, Andersen B, et al. A double-blind trial of baclofen against placebo in the treatment of schizophrenia. *Acta Psychiatr Scand.* 1976; **54**:287–293.

9. Bigelow LB, Nasrallah H, Carman J, et al. Baclofen treatment in chronic schizophrenia: a clinical trial. *Am J Psychiatry*. 1977;**134**:318–320.

10. Soares KV, McGrath JJ. The treatment of tardive dyskinesia—a systematic review and meta-analysis. *Schizophr Res*. 1999;**39**:1–16.

11. Glazer WM, Moore DC, Bowers MB. The treatment of tardive dyskinesia with baclofen. *Psychopharmacology (Berlin)*. 1985;**87**:480–483.

12. Itil TM, Herkert E, Schneider SJ, et al. Baclofen in the treatment of tardive dyskinesia: open label study. *Acta Ther*. 1980;**6**:315–323.

13. Nair NP, Yassa R, Ruiz-Navarro J, et al. Baclofen in the treatment of tardive dyskinesia. *Am J Psychiatry*. 1978;**135**:1562–1563.

14. Kaplan GB, McRoberts RL 3rd, Smokler HJ. Baclofen as adjunctive treatment for a patient with cocaine dependence and schizoaffective disorder. *J Clin Psychopharmacol*. 2004;**24**:574–575.

15. Anton RF, Moak DH, Latham PK. The obsessive compulsive drinking scale: a new method of assessing outcome in alcoholism treatment studies. *Arch Gen Psychiatry*. 1996;**53**:225–231.

16. Janiri L, Calvosa F, Dario T, et al. The Italian version of the obsessive-compulsive drinking scale: validation, comparison with the other versions and difference between type 1– and type 2–like alcoholics. *Drug Alcohol Depend*. 2004;**74**:187–195.

17. Huguelet P, Morand-Collomb S. Effect of topiramate augmentation on two patients suffering from schizophrenia or bipolar disorder with comorbid alcohol abuse. *Pharmacol Res*. 2005;**52**:392–394.

Full Article

Alcohol and Alcoholism vol. 37, no. 5, pp. 504–508, 2002

Baclofen efficacy in reducing alcohol craving and intake: a preliminary double-blind randomized controlled study

Giovanni Addolorato, Fabio Caputo, Esmeralda Capristo, Marco Domenicali, Mauro Bernardi, Luigi Janiri, Roberta Agabio, Giancarlo Colombo, Gian Luigi Gessa, and Giovanni Gasbarrini

Institute of Internal Medicine and Institute of Psychiatry, Catholic University of Rome, Rome, 'G. Fontana' Centre for the Study and Treatment of the Alcohol Addiction, University of Bologna, Bologna, 'Bernard B. Brodie' Department of Neuroscience, University of Cagliari, C.N.R. Institute of Neurogenetics and Neuropharmacology, Cagliari and Neuroscienze S.c.a r.l., Cagliari, Italy

ABSTRACT

Aims: The γ-aminobutyric acid ($GABA_B$) receptor agonist, baclofen, has recently been shown to reduce alcohol intake in alcohol-preferring rats and alcohol consumption and craving for alcohol in an open study in humans. The present study was aimed at providing a first evaluation of the efficacy of baclofen in inducing and maintaining abstinence and reducing craving for alcohol in alcohol-dependent patients in a double-blind placebo-controlled design. Methods: A total of 39 alcohol-dependent patients were consecutively enrolled in the study. After 12–24 h of abstinence from alcohol, patients were randomly divided into two groups. Twenty patients were treated with baclofen and 19 with placebo. Drug and placebo were orally administered for 30 consecutive days. Baclofen was administered at the dose of 15 mg/day for the first 3 days and 30 mg/day for the subsequent 27 days, divided into three daily doses. Patients were monitored as out-patients on a weekly basis. At each visit alcohol intake, abstinence from alcohol, alcohol craving and changes in affective disorders were evaluated. Results: A higher percentage of subjects totally abstinent from alcohol and a higher number of cumulative abstinence days throughout the study period were found in the baclofen, compared to the placebo, group. A decrease in the obsessive and compulsive components of craving was found in the baclofen compared to the placebo group; likewise, alcohol intake was reduced in the baclofen group. A decrease in state anxiety was found in the baclofen compared to the placebo group. No significant difference was found between the two groups in terms of current depressive symptoms. Baclofen proved to be easily manageable and no patient discontinued treatment due to the presence of side-effects. No patient was affected by craving for the drug and/or drug abuse. Conclusions: Baclofen proved to be effective in inducing abstinence from alcohol and reducing alcohol craving and consumption in alcoholics. With the limits posed by the small number of subjects involved, the results of this preliminary double-blind study suggest that baclofen may represent a potentially useful drug in the treatment of alcohol-dependent patients and thus merits further investigations.

INTRODUCTION

In recent years, the use of pharmacotherapy together with psychosocial interventions (including Alcoholics Anonymous and various counselling approaches) has enhanced the percentage of success in maintaining alcoholic patients in remission and assisting the development of a life-style compatible with long-term alcohol abstinence. However, to date, drugs with proven efficacy are very few (see Garbutt *et al.*, 1999; Swift, 1999; Kranzler, 2000) and the discovery of new medications capable of positively affecting the components of alcohol dependence syndrome, such as craving and loss of control on drinking or protracted abstinence symptoms, would represent an important step forward in the treatment of patients with alcohol problems (see Garbutt *et al.*, 1999).

Baclofen is a potent and stereoselective γ-aminobutyric acid ($GABA_B$) receptor agonist used clinically to control spasticity (Davidoff, 1985). Recent preclinical experiments have demonstrated the efficacy of baclofen in suppressing both alcohol withdrawal signs in rats made physically dependent on alcohol and voluntary alcohol intake in alcohol-preferring rats (Colombo *et al.*, 2000, 2002). Moreover, preliminary clinical open studies have confirmed the ability of baclofen to reduce alcohol craving and intake (Addolorato *et al.*, 2000*b*) and alcohol with-drawal symptoms (Addolorato *et al.*, 2002) in alcohol-dependent patients.

The present double-blind randomized placebo-controlled study was performed in order to determine the efficacy of short-term baclofen administration on craving for alcohol, alcohol intake and abstinence from alcohol in patients affected by alcoholism.

PATIENTS AND METHODS

A total of 39 alcohol-dependent patients (mean age ± SD: 47.3 ± 10.5 years; mean daily drinks: 14.2 ± 7.9; mean years of addiction: 11.8 ± 4.2) were consecutively admitted to the study. Inclusion criteria were: (1) age ranging from 18 to 70 years; (2) diagnosis of current alcohol dependence according to DSM-IV criteria (American Psychiatric Association, 1994); (3) last alcohol intake reported to have taken place in the 24 h preceding observation; (4) presence of a referred family member. Exclusion criteria were the presence of: (1) severe liver, kidney, heart or lung diseases; (2) psychopathological illness undergoing treatment with psychoactive drugs, epilepsy or epileptiform convulsion; (3) addiction to drugs other than nicotine. Each patient was required to provide his/her informed consent after having received information on the characteristics, dosing rate and possible side-effects of the drug, as well as on the possibility of dropping out of the study at any time. The study protocol fully complied with the guidelines of the Ethics Committees of the Università Cattolica in Rome and of the University of Bologna, where the study was performed.

Patients were randomized in two groups; 20 patients were treated with baclofen (mean age: 45.8 ± 10.6 years; mean daily drinks: 17.6 ± 7.5; mean years of addiction: 12.6 ± 4.8) and 19 patients with placebo (mean age: 48.8 ± 10.4 years; mean daily drinks: 10.7 ± 6.7; mean years of addiction: 11.0 ± 3.4). Patients were recruited among those contacting our Alcohol Treatment Units. Randomization was performed as follows: the 39 consecutive patients received either baclofen or placebo in a double-blind fashion. Baclofen and placebo were entrusted to a referred family member. Placebo tablets were identical in size, colour, shape and taste to baclofen tablets. Baclofen or placebo was orally administered for 4 consecutive weeks. For the first 3 days, baclofen was administered at a dose of 15 mg/day refracted in three times/day; subsequently, the daily dose of baclofen was increased to 30 mg/day refracted in three times/day. The dose prescribed was chosen on the basis of the results obtained in a previous open clinical study (Addolorato *et al.*, 2000*b*), and represents the minimum therapeutic dosage recommended by the drug manufacturer in order to avoid side-effects.

In cases where symptoms of alcohol withdrawal could not have been controlled effectively by baclofen or placebo, a 'rescue' protocol would have been adopted, based on administration of diazepam (0.5–0.75 mg/kg body weight). However, no patients required this treatment intervention.

All patients were strongly advised against the use of drugs capable of potentially affecting craving for alcohol. Specifically, the use of benzodiazepines, antidepressants, metadoxine, naltrexone, acamprosate, γ-hydroxybutyric acid (GHB), as well as alcohol-sensitizing drugs (e.g. disulfiram) was not allowed during the study period and subsequent follow-up.

Each subject was checked as an out-patient every week for the duration of the study; at each visit, routine psychological support counselling as previously described (Addolorato *et al.*, 1993) was provided by the same professional staff. Craving level was evaluated by administration of the Obsessive Compulsive Drinking Scale (OCDS) at the start of the study (To) and at each weekly out-patient visit (T1–T4). The OCDS is a validated scale consisting of two subscales which evaluate the obsessive and compulsive components of craving (Anton *et al.*, 1995). Abstinence from alcohol was evaluated, at each out-patient visit, on the basis of: (1) patient's self-evaluation [reporting alcohol intake as the mean number of standard drinks consumed per day (one standard drink equal to 12 g of absolute alcohol) (Secretary of Health and Human Services, 1997)]; (2) family member interview; (3) determination of alcohol concentration in blood and saliva by QED (Enzymatics Inc., Horsham, UK). Cumulative abstinent duration (CAD), defined as the total number of days of abstinence, was also calculated in both the baclofen and placebo groups. Further, main biological markers of alcohol abuse [aspartate aminotransferase (AST), alanine aminotransferase (ALT), γ-glutamyl-transpeptidase (GGT) and mean cell volume (MCV)] were determined at the start (To) and at the end (T4) of the study. Finally, possible changes in state anxiety and current depression were assessed by means of the State and Trait Inventory test, Y1 axes (Spielberg *et al.*, 1983), and Zung Self-rating Depression Scale (Zung *et al.*, 1965), respectively.

At drug discontinuation, the presence of possible side-effects due to drug suspension was recorded on a weekly basis for the first 4 weeks.

Statistical evaluation of patients' age, years of addiction and CAD in the baclofen and placebo groups was performed by the Mann–Whitney test. The number of drop-outs and of patients maintaining abstinence in the two groups were compared using the Fisher exact test for a 2×2 table [treatment (baclofen; placebo) × drop-out (presence; absence) or treatment (baclofen; placebo) × abstinence (presence; absence)]. The numbers of patients maintaining abstinence and CAD were analysed with the intention-to-treat principles (see Lehert, 1993), i.e. entering into the analysis any randomized patient, including drop-outs. In this analysis, it was assumed that all patients who terminated treatment before the end of the study were abstinence failures and CAD was calculated on the data available at the time of the last weekly visit. Analysis of the effect of baclofen on daily drinks, OCDS scales, scales of state anxiety and depression, and main biological markers of alcohol misuse was performed by the two-way (treatment × time) analysis of covariance (ANCOVA) with repeated measures on the time factor, and baseline data as covariance.

RESULTS

No statistically significant difference in mean age and mean years of addiction was found between the two groups ($P > 0.05$, Mann–Whitney test).

A schematic diagram on recruitment, group allocation, treatment retention and success in achieving and maintaining complete abstinence is presented in Figure 1. Although statistical significance was not reached ($P = 0.06$, Fisher's exact test), the number of drop-outs was lower in the baclofen than in the placebo group; indeed, three subjects in the baclofen group (corresponding to 15.0%) and eight subjects in the placebo group (42.1%) dropped out and were excluded from further statistical analyses.

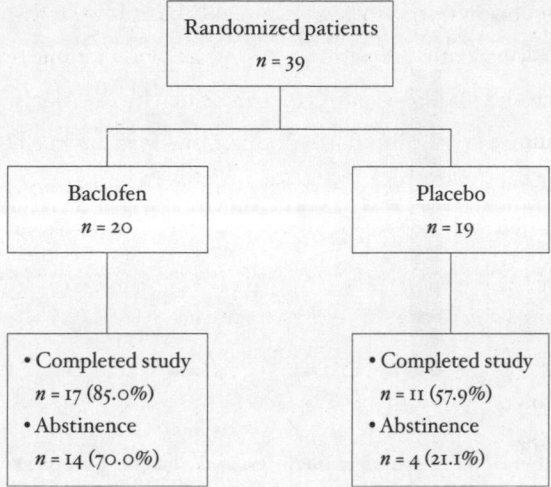

Fig. 1. Diagram on recruitment, group allocation, treatment retention and success in achieving and maintaining complete abstinence.

A significantly higher number of patients who achieved and maintained abstinence throughout the experimental period was found in the group of patients treated with baclofen (14 out of 20, corresponding to 70.0%) compared to subjects treated with placebo (four out of 19, or 21.1%) ($P < 0.005$; Fisher's exact test). CAD was ~3-fold higher in baclofen- than placebo-treated patients [19.6 ± 2.6 and 6.3 ± 2.4 (mean ± SEM), respectively; $P < 0.005$, Mann–Whitney test].

Figure 2 shows daily alcohol intake in the two groups of patients at the different observation times of the study. ANCOVA revealed a significant effect of treatment on alcohol intake [$F_{treatment}(1,78) = 10.71$, $P < 0.005$; $F_{time}(3,78) = 1.38$, $P > 0.05$]. In the baclofen group, the mean number of daily drinks was virtually completely suppressed within the first week of the treatment, being reduced from ~18 (value at To) to

< 0.5 (values at T1–T4); in the placebo group, the daily drinks were reduced from approximately a mean number of 10 (T0) to 3.5–4.5 (T1–T4).

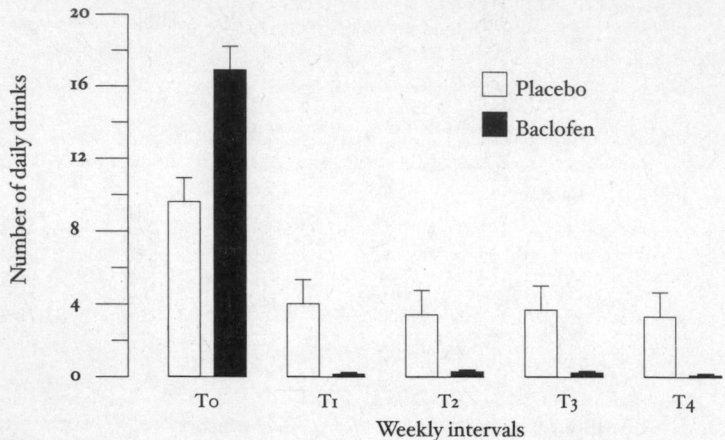

Fig. 2. Number of daily drinks in baclofen and placebo groups at T0 (baseline) and over the four weekly visits (T1–T4). Each value is the mean ± SEM of 17 patients in the baclofen group and 11 in the placebo group.

Figure 3 (top panel) shows the craving score in the two groups of patients at the different observation times. ANCOVA showed a significant effect of both treatment and time on total OCDS score [$F_{treatment}$ (1,78) = 5.65, $P < 0.05$; F_{time}(3,78) = 10.30, $P < 0.00005$]. From T1 to T4, the score in the baclofen group was constantly lower than that moni-

Fig. 3. Obsessive Compulsive Drinking Scale (OCDS) total (top panel), OCDS Compulsive Drinking subscale (centre panel) and OCDS Obsessive Drinking subscale (bottom panel) scores in baclofen and placebo groups at T0 (baseline) and over the four weekly visits (T1–T4). Each value is the mean ± SEM of 17 patients in the baclofen group and 11 in the placebo group.

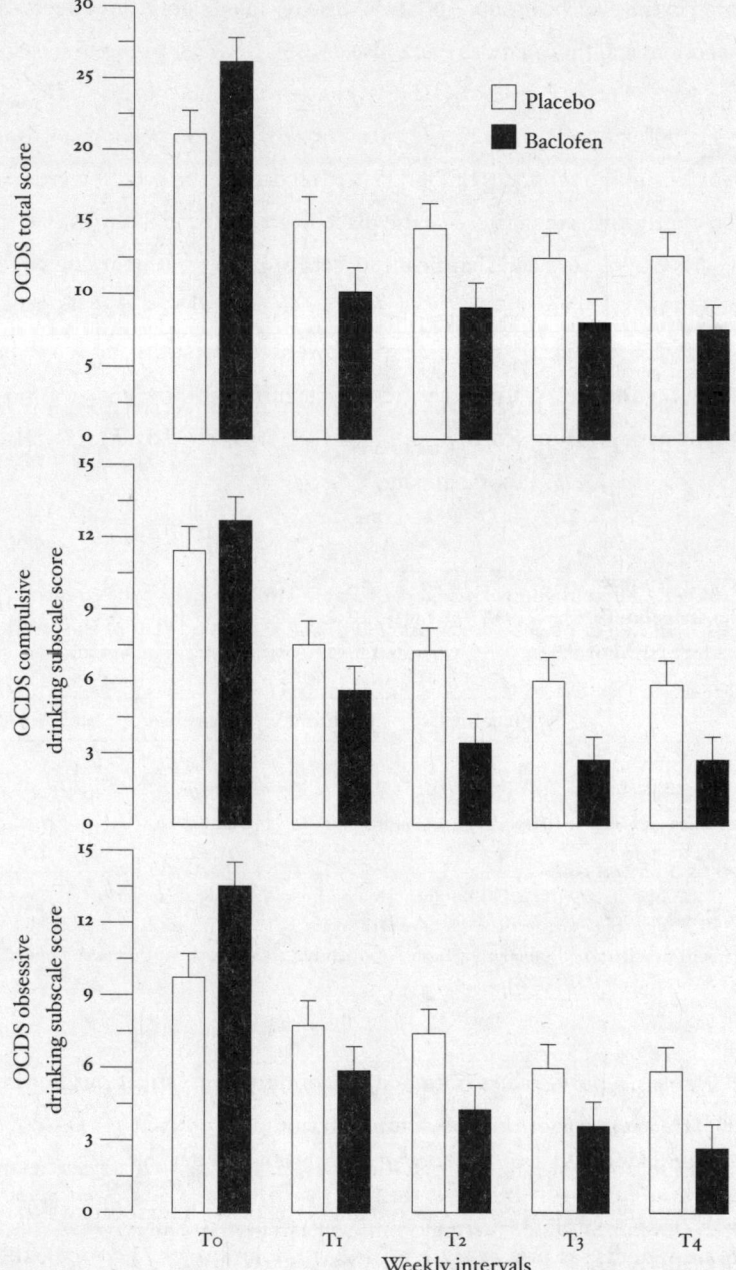

tored in the placebo group. ANCOVA also revealed significant effects of treatment and time on both compulsive [$F_{treatment}(1,78) = 4.60, P < 0.05; F_{time}(3,78) = 6.40, P < 0.0005$] (Fig. 3, centre panel) and obsessive [$F_{treatment}(1,78) = 5.06, P < 0.05; F_{time}(3,78) = 11.53, P < 0.00005$] (Fig. 3, bottom panel) drinking subscales of OCDS, with scores in the baclofen groups constantly lower than those of the placebo group throughout T1–T4.

ANCOVA revealed significant effects of both treatment and time factors on state anxiety [$F_{treatment}(1,78) = 4.62, P < 0.05; F_{time}(3,78) = 3.05, P < 0.05$] (Fig. 4, top panel), with lower scores in the baclofen than placebo group at T1–T4. In contrast, no significant difference was observed in depression score [$F_{treatment}(1,78) = 0.70, P > 0.05; F_{time}(3,78) = 2.28, P > 0.05$] (Fig. 4, bottom panel).

TABLE 1. **Main biological markers of alcohol misuse in patients treated with baclofen or placebo at the start (To) and at the end (T4) of the study**

	To		T4	
	Placebo	Baclofen	Placebo	Baclofen
MCV (μm²)	95.3 ± 2.8	95.7 ± 2.1	95.0 ± 2.7	93.7 ± 1.9
GGT (81–99 U/l)	103.6 ± 24.8	150.9 ± 41.8	50.5 ± 11.2	56.9 ± 16.7
AST (7–45 U/l)	45.6 ± 9.0	56.9± 13.3	26.9 ± 5.7	31.2 ± 7.4
ALT (7–45 U/l)	46.4 ± 8.6	62.7± 13.1	25.7 ± 3.9	32.1 ± 4.8

MCV, mean cell volume; GGT, γ-glutamyltranspeptidase; AST, aspartate aminotransferase; ALT, alanine aminotransferase. Each value is the mean ± SEM of 17 patients in the baclofen group (with the exception of the GGT data for 16 patients) and 11 patients in the placebo group.

Table 1 reports values obtained in laboratory investigations before and after baclofen or placebo administration.

No serious systemic or single-organ event leading to drug cessation was reported and no patient discontinued the drug. Tolerability was fair in all patients; as previously reported (Addolorato *et al.*, 2000*b*), the

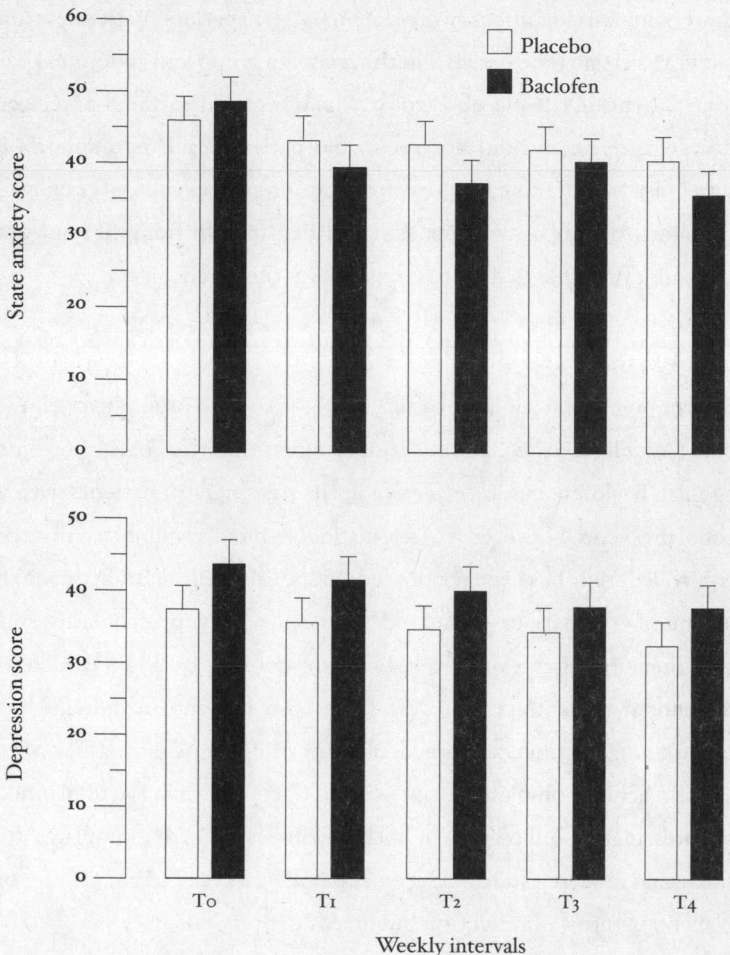

Fig. 4. State anxiety score, evaluated by the State Anxiety Inventory Test (STAI-Y1), and current depression score, evaluated by the Zung Self-rating Depression Scale, in baclofen and placebo groups at T0 (baseline) and over the four weekly visits (T1–T4). Each value is the mean ± SEM of 17 patients in the baclofen group and 11 in the placebo group.

most common side-effects were sleepiness (two patients), tiredness (one patient), vertigo (one patient) in the baclofen group and abdominal pain (one patient) in the placebo group, which resolved within 1–2 weeks of drug treatment and did not recur. No patient reported euphoria or other pleasant effects caused by the drug. No subject showed craving for baclofen. At drug discontinuation, neither drug withdrawal syndrome nor side-effect due to drug suspension was observed.

DISCUSSION

Recent preclinical (Colombo *et al.*, 2000, 2002) and preliminary clinical data (Addolorato *et al.*, 2000*b*, 2002) suggest that the $GABA_B$ receptor agonist, baclofen, may be effective in the treatment of patients with alcohol problems. However, to date, no double-blind, randomized placebo-controlled study has been conducted. In spite of the limitation due to the low number of patients evaluated, the results of the present study indicate that administration of relatively low doses of baclofen to alcohol-dependent patients is more effective than placebo in inducing and maintaining abstinence from alcohol (both in terms of number of patients reaching complete abstinence and CAD), reducing alcohol intake, suppressing alcohol craving in both its 'obsessive' and 'compulsive' features, and reducing state anxiety. Baclofen, however, did not differ from placebo in terms of reduction of current depression.

In agreement with our previous observation (Addolorato *et al.*, 2000*b*), abstinence from alcohol or reduction in alcohol intake was achieved within the first week of baclofen treatment and was maintained throughout the treatment period. The increased efficacy of baclofen over placebo may be related to its suppressant effect on craving; indeed, the drug produced a rapid decrease in the 'compulsive' and 'obsessive' components of craving, as indicated by the immediate reduction in mean score of both OCDS subscales. It is noteworthy that an anti-craving effect of baclofen has already been observed with other substances of abuse, particularly cocaine in cocaine users (Ling *et al.*, 1998). The anti-craving effect of baclofen may depend on its ability to interfere with the neuronal substrates mediating the reinforcing properties of ethanol. $GABA_B$ receptors located in the ventral tegmental area (VTA) have been reported to control the activity of mesolimbic dopamine neurons, a major neural pathway in the regulation of the reinforcing properties of addictive drugs, including alcohol (see Di Chiara, 1995; Koob *et al.*, 1998; Spanagel and Weiss, 1999). Accordingly, pharmacological stimulation of VTA $GABA_B$ receptors has been found to inhibit the firing activity of these neurons (Kalivas, 1993) as well as basal (Yoshida *et al.*, 1994) and alcohol-stimulated (Carta *et al.*, 2001) dopamine release from their terminals in the nucleus accumbens.

Moreover, it is conceivable that the suppressing effect of baclofen on alcohol withdrawal symptomatology (Addolorato *et al.*, 2002) may have helped the patients to achieve and maintain alcohol abstinence.

In contrast to the observation by Krupitsky *et al.* (1993) that baclofen ameliorates affective disorders in alcoholics, in the present study baclofen was found to be effective in reducing state anxiety, but not current depression. It may be hypothesized that the decrease in state anxiety found in the present study and the decrease in depression observed by Krupitsky *et al.* (1993) in alcoholics after a 3-week treatment with baclofen were secondary to the ability of baclofen to achieve both a rapid detoxification (Addolorato *et al.*, 2002) and a decrease in craving, resulting in a rapid reduction of physical and psychological symptoms. Finally, it should be emphasized that the absence of a significant decrease in Zung depression scale score in the present study could be influenced by the relatively low score recorded in some patients at the start of the study.

In agreement with both previous observations (Krupitsky *et al.*, 1993; Ling *et al.*, 1998; Addolorato *et al.*, 2000*a*), baclofen proved to be devoid of serious side-effects in alcoholics. Moreover, side-effects were present only during the first week of the treatment.

Preclinical data suggest that baclofen might be liable to misuse since the drug shares several pharmacological effects with the alcohol-mimicking agent, γ-hydroxybutyrate (GHB), and craving for and abuse of GHB have been observed in different alcoholic patients (see Addolorato *et al.*, 2000*a*). However, baclofen failed to show euphorigenic effects and no patient consumed the drug above the prescribed dose. The lack of misuse liability of baclofen is an important factor in pharmacological treatments of alcohol and other substance addictions.

In conclusion, with the limits of the low number of patients recruited and the short time of observation, the results of the present preliminary double-blind study confirm that baclofen, because of its anti-craving and anti-reward action on the one hand, and safety on the other, may have an important role in the treatment of patients with alcohol problems. Future studies with larger patient samples and longer periods of observation are surely warranted to confirm the results of the present study.

ACKNOWLEDGEMENTS

This study was supported by grants from Associazione Ricerca in Medicina, Bologna-Rome, Italy. The authors are grateful to C. Ancona, MD and R. Mascianà, MD (Università Cattolica, Rome, Italy), F. Lorenzini MD (University of Bologna, Bologna, Italy), S. Serra and G. Vacca (Neuroscienze S.c.a.r.l., Cagliari, Italy) for technical support, and to A. Farmer for language editing of the manuscript.

REFERENCES

Addolorato, G., Viaggi, M., Gentilini, L., Castelli, E., Nicastro, P., Stefanini, G. F. and Gasbarrini, G. (1993) Alcohol addiction: evaluation of the therapeutic effectiveness of self-managed self-help group in the maintenance of abstinence from alcohol. *Alcologia, European Journal of Alcohol Studies* 5, 261–263.

Addolorato, G., Caputo, F., Capristo, E., Stefanini, G. F. and Gasbarrini, G. (2000*a*) Gamma-hydroxybutyric acid: efficacy, potential abuse and dependence in the treatment of alcohol addiction. *Alcohol* 20, 217–222.

Addolorato, G., Caputo, F., Capristo, E., Colombo, G., Gessa, G. L. and Gasbarrini, G. (2000*b*) Ability of baclofen in reducing alcohol craving and intake: II—preliminary clinical evidence. *Alcoholism: Clinical and Experimental Research* 24, 67–71.

Addolorato, G., Caputo, F., Capristo, E., Janiri, L., Bernardi, M., Agabio, R., Colombo, G., Gessa, G. L. and Gasbarrini, G. (2002) Rapid suppression of alcohol withdrawal syndrome by baclofen. *American Journal of Medicine* 112, 226–229.

American Psychiatric Association (1994) *Diagnostic and Statistical Manual of Mental Disorders*, 4th edn. American Psychiatric Association, Washington, DC.

Anton, R. F., Moak, D. H. and Latham, P. (1995) The Obsessive Compulsive Drinking Scale: a self-rated instrument for the quantification of thoughts about alcohol and drinking behavior. *Alcoholism: Clinical and Experimental Research* 19, 92–99.

Carta, G., Satta, R., Pani, L., Colombo, G., Gessa, G. L. and Nava, F. (2001) Baclofen suppression of alcohol-induced dopamine release in the nucleus accumbens. *Pharmacological Research* 43 (Suppl. A), 35.

Colombo, G., Agabio, R., Carai, M. A. M., Lobina, C., Pani, M., Reali, R., Addolorato, G. and Gessa, G. L. (2000) Baclofen ability in reducing alcohol intake and withdrawal severity: I—preclinical evidence. *Alcoholism: Clinical and Experimental Research* 24, 58–66.

Colombo, G., Serra, S., Brunetti, G., Atzori, G., Pani, M., Vacca, G., Addolorato, G., Froestl, W., Carai M. A. M. and Gessa, G. L. (2002) The GABA$_B$ receptor agonists baclofen and CGP 44532 prevent acquisition of alcohol drinking behavior in alcohol-preferring rats. *Alcohol and Alcoholism* 37, 499–503.

Davidoff, R. A. (1985) Antispasticity drugs: mechanisms of action. *Annals of Neurology* 17, 107–116.

Di Chiara, G. (1995) The role of dopamine in drug abuse viewed from the perspective of its role in motivation. *Drug and Alcohol Dependence* 38, 95–137.

Garbutt, J. C., West, S. L., Carey, T. S., Lohr, K. N. and Crews, F. T. (1999) Pharmacological treatment of alcohol dependence: a review of the evidence. *Journal of the American Medical Association* 281, 1318–1325.

Kalivas, P. W. (1993) Neurotransmitter regulation of dopamine neurons in the ventral tegmental area. *Brain Research Reviews* 18, 75–113.

Koob, G. F., Sanna, P. P. and Bloom, F. E. (1998) Neuroscience of addiction. *Neuron* 21, 467–476.

Kranzler, H. R. (2000) Pharmacotherapy of alcoholism: gaps in knowledge and opportunities for research. *Alcohol and Alcoholism* 35, 537–547.

Krupitsky, E. M., Burakov, A. M., Ivanov, V. B., Krandashova, G. F., Lapin, I. P., Grienko, A. J. and Borodkin, Y. S. (1993) Baclofen administration for the treatment of affective disorders in alcoholic patients. *Drug and Alcohol Dependence* 33, 157–163.

Lehert, P. (1993) Review and discussion of statistical analysis of controlled clinical trials in alcoholism. *Alcohol and Alcoholism* 28 (Suppl. 2), 157–163.

Ling, W., Shoptaw, S. and Majewska, D. (1998) Baclofen as a cocaine anti-craving medication: a preliminary clinical study. *Neuropsychopharmacology* 18, 403–404.

Secretary of Health and Human Services (1997) *Ninth Special Report to the U.S. Congress on Alcohol and Health*, NIH publication no. 97-4017. Government Printing Office, Washington, DC.

Spanagel, R. and Weiss, F. (1999) The dopamine hypothesis of reward: past and current status. *Trends in Neurosciences* 22, 521–527.

Spielberg, C. D., Gorsuch, R. L. and Lushene, R. E. (1983) *Manual for the State and Trait Anxiety Inventory*. Consulting Psychologist Press, Palo Alto, CA.

Swift, R. M. (1999) Drug therapy for alcohol dependence. *New England Journal of Medicine* 340, 1482–1490.

Yoshida, M., Yokoo, H., Tanaka, T., Emoto, H. and Tanaka, M. (1994) Opposite changes in the mesolimbic metabolism in the nerve terminal and cell body sites induced by locally infused baclofen in the rat. *Brain Research* 636, 111–114.

Zung, W. W., Richards, C. B. and Short, M. J. (1965) Self-rating depression scale in an outpatient clinic. Further validation of the SDS. *Archives of General Psychiatry* 13, 508–515.

Abstract

Addolorato G., Leggio L., Ferrulli A., et al. (2007) Effectiveness and safety of baclofen for maintenance of alcohol abstinence in alcohol-dependent patients with liver cirrhosis: randomised, double-blind controlled study. *Lancet*, 370(9603) (8 December 2007–14 December 2007), 1915–1922.

SUMMARY

Background

Intervention to achieve alcohol abstinence represents the most effective treatment for alcohol-dependent patients with liver cirrhosis; however, anticraving drugs might worsen liver disease. We aimed to investigate the effectiveness and safety of baclofen in achieving and maintaining alcohol abstinence in patients with liver cirrhosis.

Methods

Between October, 2003, and November, 2006, 148 alcohol-dependent patients with liver cirrhosis were referred to the Institute of Internal Medicine, Rome, Italy. 84 were randomly allocated either oral baclofen or placebo for 12 weeks. Primary outcome was proportion of patients achieving and maintaining alcohol abstinence. Measures of this outcome were total alcohol abstinence and cumulative abstinence duration, which were assessed at outpatient visits. Relapse was defined as alcohol intake of more than four drinks per day or overall consumption of 14 or more drinks per week over a period of at least 4 weeks. Analysis was by intention to treat. This study is registered with ClinicalTrials.gov, number NCT00525252.

Findings

Of 42 patients allocated baclofen, 30 (71%) achieved and maintained abstinence compared with 12 (29%) of 42 assigned placebo (odds ratio 6·3 [95% CI 2·4–16·1]; p = 0·0001). The number of dropouts (termination of treatment) did not differ between the baclofen (6/42 [14%]) and placebo (13/42 [31%]) groups (p = 0·12). Cumulative abstinence duration was about twofold higher in patients allocated baclofen than in those assigned placebo (mean 62·8 [SE 5·4] *vs* 30·8 [5·5] days; p = 0·001). No hepatic side-effects were recorded.

Interpretation

Baclofen is effective at promoting alcohol abstinence in alcohol-dependent patients with liver cirrhosis. The drug is well tolerated and could have an important role in treatment of these individuals.

BACLOFEN AND ANXIETY

Abstract 1

Breslow, M. F., Fankhauser, M. P., Potter, R. L., et al. (1989) Role of gamma-aminobutyric acid in antipanic drug efficacy. *American Journal of Psychiatry* 146, 353–356.

All effective pharmacologic agents used to treat panic disorder augment gamma-aminobutyric acid (GABA) transmission. Anxiolytics and antidepressants that lack GABA activity are not effective in panic disorder. To test the hypothesis that GABA activity is a component of antipanic drug efficacy, the authors treated nine medication-free panic disorder subjects with oral baclofen (30 mg/day for 4 weeks) in a double-blind, placebo-controlled crossover trial. Baclofen, a selective GABA agonist, was significantly more effective than placebo in reducing the number of panic attacks and scores on the Hamilton anxiety scale, Zung scale, and Katz-R nervousness subscale. The authors discuss possible mechanisms of antipanic drug efficacy.

Krupitsky, E. M., Burakov, A. M., Ivanov, V. B., et al. (1993)
Baclofen administration for the treatment of affective disorders
in alcoholic patients. *Drug and Alcohol Dependence* 33, 157–163.

Ninety alcoholic patients with the secondary affective disorders (anxiety, depression) were divided into four groups. Patients in the first group received $GABA_B$ receptor ligands (baclofen), those in the second group, diazepam, those in the third group, amitriptyline and those in the fourth group, placebo. The results of clinical, psychological (tests of Spielberger, Zung and MMPI), and electrophysiological (superslow omega-potential) investigations showed that baclofen is an effective drug for affective disturbances in alcoholic patients, with efficacy superior to placebo and equal to diazepam and amitriptyline. At the same time baclofen does not have the side-effects and complications of the latter. Significant changes in platelet MAO_B activity and the dopamine, serotonin and GABA concentrations in blood after treatment were not found in the four patient groups. The peripheral metabolism of GABA and monoamines do not seem to be related to the development of secondary affective disorders in alcoholic patients. This investigation encourages the search for drugs acting on the affective psychopathology of $GABA_B$ receptor ligands.

Drake, R. G., Davis, L. L., Cates, M. E. et al. (2003) Baclofen treatment for chronic posttraumatic stress disorder. *The Annals of Pharmacotherapy* 37, 1177–1181.

OBJECTIVE

Previous studies have shown the efficacy of gamma-aminobutyric acid B ($GABA_B$) receptor agonists in treating anxiety in patients with panic disorder and in treating depression and anxiety in alcoholic patients. We hypothesized that baclofen, a $GABA_B$ agonist, would be an effective treatment in the symptomatic management of veterans with chronic posttraumatic stress disorder (PTSD).

METHODS

Fourteen male veterans with chronic, combat-related PTSD were enrolled in an open-label, 8-week, monotherapy trial of baclofen titrated to a maximum of 80 mg/d in 3 divided doses. The primary outcome measure was the Clinician-Administered PTSD Scale (CAPS), and secondary outcome measures included the Hamilton Rating Scale for Anxiety, the Hamilton Rating Scale for Depression, the Global Assessment of Functioning Scale, and the Clinical Global Impressions.

RESULTS

In the 11 patients who completed the 8-week trial, the mean total CAPS score decreased significantly from baseline (from 82.9 ± 16.1 to 63.5 ± 21.2). The avoidance and hyperarousal subscales showed significant decreases (from 36.2 ± 6.2 to 26.5 ± 9.6 and from 31.9 ± 6.5 to 22.1 ± 7.1, respectively), whereas the re-experiencing subscale remained unchanged. Significant improvements were also noted on all secondary outcome measures. Treatment response was noted within the first 4 weeks of treatment and was maintained throughout the trial. Baclofen therapy was well tolerated, as only 1 patient dropped out due to adverse effects.

CONCLUSIONS

Baclofen therapy was effective in treating both the PTSD symptoms and accompanying depression and anxiety in patients with chronic PTSD due to combat. Larger, double-blind, placebo-controlled studies are needed to confirm the efficacy of baclofen in the treatment of PTSD.

BACLOFEN IN ANIMAL STUDIES: DOSE-DEPENDENT EFFECTS

Abstract 1

Roberts, D. C., and Andrews, M. M. (1997) Baclofen suppression of cocaine self-administration: demonstration using a discrete trials procedure. *Psychopharmacology (Berlin)* 131, 271–277.

We have previously reported that rats display a circadian pattern of cocaine self-administration if access to drug is limited to 10-min discrete trials that are separated by at least 20 min. In the present study, the pattern of cocaine intake (1.5 mg/kg per injection) was studied in two large groups of animals that were maintained on different 12-h light/dark cycles (3 a.m. to 3 p.m. versus 10 a.m. to 10 p.m.). Regardless of the time of light onset, a circadian pattern of cocaine self-administration was observed. Maximum cocaine intake occurred during the final 6 h of the dark period and was followed by a relative abstinence period during the light phase. This highly predictable pattern of drug taking behavior provided an opportunity to explore the effect of baclofen, a $GABA_B$ agonist, on the initiation of self-administration behavior. In two separate studies, acute treatment with baclofen (1.25–5.0 mg/kg) was shown to suppress cocaine intake for at least 4 h. Baclofen had no significant effect on responding for food reinforcement. Previous results have indicated that baclofen appears to reduce specifically the motivation to respond for cocaine. Together, these data suggest that baclofen should be considered as a possible pharmacotherapeutic agent in cocaine addiction.

Xi, Z. X., and Stein, E. A. (1999) Baclofen inhibits
heroin self-administration behavior and mesolimbic
dopamine release.
The Journal of Pharmacology and Experimental Therapeutics 290, 1369–1374.

An emerging hypothesis to explain the mechanism of heroin-induced positive reinforcement states that opiates inhibit gamma-aminobutyric acid (GABA)-ergic interneurons within the mesocorticolimbic dopamine (DA) system to disinhibit DA neurons. In support of this hypothesis, we report that the development of heroin self-administration (SA) behavior in drug-naive rats and the maintenance of SA behavior in heroin-trained rats were both suppressed when the $GABA_B$ receptor agonist baclofen was coadministered with heroin. Microinjections of baclofen into the ventral tegmental area (VTA), but not the nucleus accumbens, decreased heroin reinforcement as indicated by a compensatory increase in SA behavior. Additionally, baclofen administered alone or along with heroin dose-dependently reduced heroin-induced DA release. This effect was blocked partially by intra-VTA infusion of the $GABA_B$ antagonist 2-hydroxysaclofen, suggesting an additional, perhaps $GABA_A$ receptor-mediated, disinhibitory effect. Taken together, these experiments, for the first time, demonstrate that heroin-reinforced SA behavior and nucleus accumbens DA release are mediated predominantly by $GABA_B$ receptors in the VTA and suggest that baclofen may be an effective agent in the treatment of opiate abuse.

Colombo, G., Vacca, G., Serra, S., et al. (2003) Baclofen suppresses motivation to consume alcohol in rats. *Psychopharmacology (Berlin)* 167, 221–224.

RATIONALE

Recent studies demonstrated that treatment with the gamma-aminobutyric acid ($GABA_B$) receptor agonist baclofen reduced alcohol intake in selectively bred Sardinian alcohol-preferring (sP) rats tested under the home-cage, two-bottle choice regimen.

OBJECTIVES

The present study investigated the effect of baclofen on the appetitive, rather than consummatory, aspects of alcohol ingestion in sP rats.

METHODS

Rats were trained to lever-press for oral alcohol (10%, v/v) or sucrose (3%, w/v) under a fixed-ratio schedule of 4. Once self-administration behavior was established, alcohol intake averaged approximately 0.7 g/kg over the 30-min session. Subsequently, the effect of the acute administration of baclofen (0, 1, 2 and 3 mg/kg, i.p.) on the extinction responding for alcohol and sucrose (defined as the maximal number of lever responses reached in the absence of reinforcement and used as index of motivation to consume alcohol and sucrose) was evaluated.

RESULTS

All doses of baclofen produced a marked suppression of extinction responding for alcohol. Conversely, only the 3-mg/kg baclofen dose significantly affected extinction responding for sucrose. A separate open-field test indicated that baclofen (0, 1, 2 and 3 mg/kg, i.p.) did not affect spontaneous motor activity in sP rats.

CONCLUSIONS

These results suggest that baclofen may specifically reduce the motivational properties of alcohol; further, these results are in agreement with the recently reported anti-craving potential of baclofen in alcoholics.

Fattore, L., Cossu, G., Martellotta, M. C. et al. (2002) Baclofen antagonizes intravenous self-administration of nicotine in mice and rats. *Alcohol and Alcoholism* 37, 495–498.

Aims: γ-Aminobutyric acid (GABA)-ergic transmission plays an important role in modulating reinforcing effects of different drugs of misuse. In particular, stimulation of $GABA_B$ receptors negatively influences self-administration of cocaine, heroin, nicotine, alcohol and γ-hydroxybutyric acid. The effect and specificity of the $GABA_B$ agonist baclofen on nicotine misuse were studied on two animal models of self-administration. Methods: The effects of RS baclofen and the two isomers R baclofen and S baclofen were studied on the acute nicotine self-administration in drug-naïve mice. The effect of RS baclofen was also studied in rats trained to chronically self-administer nicotine under a continuous reinforcement (FR1) schedule. Results: RS baclofen antagonizes nicotine intravenous self-administration at doses of 1.25–2.5 mg/kg intraperitoneally (i.p.). Furthermore, this effect is sterospecific. R baclofen completely prevented nicotine self-administration at the dose of 0.625 mg/kg i.p., whereas S baclofen was inactive up to the dose of 2.5 mg/kg i.p. In rats trained to self-administer nicotine, pretreatment with RS baclofen at the dose of 2.5 mg/kg i.p. significantly increased the rate of responding for nicotine. This effect was similar to the effect obtained when rats were pretreated with the nicotine central receptor antagonist mecamylamine (1 mg/kg i.p.). Conclusions: These data show that baclofen is able to antagonize nicotine-rewarding effects in mice and rats and suggest its potential clinical utility for the treatment of nicotine misuse.

Brebner, K., Ahn, S., and Phillips, A. G. (2005) Attenuation of d-amphetamine
self-administration by baclofen in the rat: behavioral and neurochemical
correlates. *Psychopharmacology (Berlin)* 177, 409–417.

RATIONALE

Recent reports have demonstrated that gamma-aminobutyric acid
(GABA)-ergic compounds attenuate the reinforcing effects of cocaine
in rats. Baclofen, a $GABA_B$ receptor agonist, appears to be particularly
effective in this respect, suggesting that $GABA_B$ receptor activation is
critically involved in mediating anti-cocaine effects. Amphetamine, like
cocaine, is a psychomotor stimulant with high abuse potential in humans.

OBJECTIVES

The purpose of the present investigation was to determine whether
baclofen may attenuate the reinforcing effects of d-amphetamine
(dAMPH) in rats. Dose-response curves were generated to examine the
effect of three doses of baclofen (1.8, 3.2 or 5.6 mg/kg, IP) on dAMPH
intravenous self-administration (IVSA). Separate groups were trained
to self-administer two doses of dAMPH (0.1 mg/kg or 0.2 mg/kg per injection) under either a fixed-ratio (FR) or progressive ratio (PR) schedule of reinforcement. Microdialysis was performed in an additional

group of rats to examine the effect of baclofen on dAMPH-induced increases in dopamine (DA) efflux in the nucleus accumbens (NAc).

RESULTS

Pretreatment with baclofen produced dose-dependent reductions in responding for dAMPH under both the FR and PR schedules, and attenuated dAMPH-induced increases in DA levels in the NAc.

CONCLUSION

These results add to previous findings showing that baclofen attenuates the reinforcing effects of psychostimulant drugs, and suggest that further investigation into the effects of GABA$_B$ receptor agonists on drug self-administration is warranted.

Full Article

Neurology 41 (1991), 1829–1831

High-dose oral baclofen: experience in patients with multiple sclerosis

Charles R. Smith, MD; Nicholas G. LaRocca, PhD; Barbara S. Giesser, MD; and Labe C. Scheinberg, MD.

ABSTRACT

We reviewed a 10% random sample of charts from an outpatient clinic for multiple sclerosis to determine the frequency with which baclofen was prescribed for spasticity in high doses (> 80 mg/d). About 20% of patients had taken high-dose baclofen, and 15% were still receiving a high dose. Taking a high dose was not associated with discontinuing treatment.

Spasticity, a frequent problem in multiple sclerosis (MS), can limit daytime function and interfere with sleep. Severe spasticity can result in fibrous contractures predisposing to pressure sores.[1] Baclofen is the treatment of choice for spasticity of spinal origin,[2] but not all patients respond to baclofen in the manufacturer's recommended dosage range of 40 to 80 mg/d. Some patients experience adverse effects while others derive insufficient benefit. Some clinicians will prescribe beyond the recommended maximum when a satisfactory effect does not occur within the usual dosage range.[1] However, there are no published data on how frequently high doses of baclofen are given, what the range of dosage is, or whether patients on high doses are more likely to discontinue treatment because of adverse effects.

To gather some data concerning baclofen use in the management of spasticity in MS, we completed a chart review for a 10% random sample of all patients actively followed at a large MS outpatient center. Our purpose was to generate estimates of the frequency of baclofen usage at various dosage levels. Of particular interest were those patients at or above the recommended maximum dosage of 80 mg/d. Since it was a simple chart review, we did not design this study to address directly safety and efficacy issues.

METHODS

A chart review was completed for a 10% random sample of all patients with MS (n = 1,120) actively followed at the Medical Rehabilitation Research and Training Center for MS of the Albert Einstein College of Medicine. Demographics and history of baclofen use, if any, were recorded. Specifically, the highest dose, current dose, duration of therapy (both overall and at the highest dose), and the reason for stepdown or discontinuation were recorded.

RESULTS

Demographics. A total of 112 charts were analyzed. The mean age was 45.2 years (SD, 13.5; range, 18 to 75). The mean duration of MS was 12.9 years (SD, 9.6; range, 5 months to 50.5 years). Women comprised 66% of the sample. As a predominately female, middle-aged sample with a several-year history of MS, this sample closely parallels the patient population at the Center.

Analysis of baclofen use. The average duration of therapy with any dose of baclofen was 43.7 months (SD, 37.6 months; range, 1 to 132 months). The average duration at the highest recorded dose was 15.8 months (SD, 16.4 months; range, 1 to 63 months).

Table 1 presents data on baclofen prescription in terms of the history of baclofen use. While 59% (n = 66/112) were currently taking baclofen, 66% (n = 74/112) had taken it at some time while a patient at the Center. Thus, the majority of patients treated at this Center receive baclofen on an ongoing basis. Of those still taking baclofen, the majority (n = 45/66 or 68%) were receiving baclofen at the highest dose they had ever gotten.

TABLE 1. History of baclofen use

	No.	%
Baclofen ever used	74/112	66
Baclofen still being used	66/112	59
Baclofen dose ever > 80 mg	15/74	20
Baclofen dose still > 80 mg	10/66	15
Baclofen discontinued	8/74	11
Baclofen dose ever reduced	24/74	32

As expected, use of high-dose baclofen was frequent, with 15% of patients currently on baclofen receiving more than 80 mg ($\leq$180 mg, 85%; >80 mg, 15%; mean, 59.7 mg; SD, 44.5 mg; range, 5 to 270 mg). When the maximum dosage recorded was considered and patients who had discontinued were included, the percentage of patients who had received more than 80 mg rose to 20% ($\leq$180 mg, 80%; >80 mg, 20%; mean, 65.6 mg; SD, 49.2 mg; range, 15 to 280 mg). For those patients currently receiving >80 mg (n = 10), the mean dose of baclofen was 141 mg (SD, 50.7), and for those who had ever taken >80 mg (n = 15), the mean dose was 137 mg (SD, 60.2). Table 2 gives the distribution of baclofen dosage for the entire sample.

TABLE 2. Distribution of baclofen dosage

Dose range	Highest dose (N = 74)		Current dose (N = 66)	
	No.	%	No.	%
<20	12	16	11	16
21–40	17	24	22	33
41–60	15	20	10	15
61–80	15	20	13	20
81–100	6	8	3	5
101–120	4	5	2	3
>120	5	7	5	8

Of the eight patients who had discontinued baclofen, none were taking more than 60 mg (<80 mg, 100%; mean, 27.5 mg; SD, 18.3 mg; range, 5 to 60 mg). The most common reasons for stopping baclofen (table 3) were lack of benefit as observed by the patient or physician (n = 4) and weakness (n = 3). One patient discontinued treatment because of urinary incontinence and one because of nausea. No reason was recorded for another patient. Two patients had two reasons for discontinuing baclofen. Only two patients sought advice from their physician before stopping the drug.

Of the 24 patients who had ever reduced their dosage from their maximum recorded levels (table 3), the most common reason was weakness (n = 15). For eight of these, dosage reduction was suggested by their physician. Two additional patients reduced the dose because of drowsiness, one each because of nausea, urinary incontinence, and lack of additional benefit, and three for unstated reasons. In one patient, the dose was reduced by the physician because of an episode of possible confusion reported by the family.

TABLE 3. Reasons for discontinuing or ever reducing baclofen dose

	Discontinued*	Reduced
Lack of benefit	4	1
Weakness	3	15
Nausea	1	1
Urinary incontinence	1	1
Drowsiness	0	2
Confusion	0	1
Not stated	1	3
Total	10*	24

*Two of eight patients had two reasons for discontinuing baclofen.

Relationships between baclofen use and patient characteristics were examined. Compared with women, there was a nonsignificant trend for men to be more likely to have received baclofen (men = 78.9%; women = 59.5%; p = 0.064). Otherwise, there were no sex differences. Patients who had received baclofen were significantly older (48.5 years versus 38.7 years; $p >$ 0.001) and had MS longer (14.9 years versus 9.2 years; $p >$ 0.01) than those who had never taken baclofen, probably because spasticity is more likely to appear or to get worse as the disease progresses. However, there was no relationship between age or duration of illness and either the highest dose recorded or the current dose.

DISCUSSION

Baclofen is an effective drug for the treatment of spasticity of spinal origin.[3] Adverse effects are generally mild and transient.[4] Unfortunately, physicians tend to underutilize baclofen because the recommended maximum is 80 mg/d.[5,6] As patients may suffer serious complications because of inadequate spasticity relief,[1] it is important to alleviate at least some of the more serious manifestations of severe spasticity, such as lower limb flexor spasms. Although high-dose baclofen has never been studied prospectively, our experience suggests that MS patients can readily tolerate relatively large doses.

There are several references to long-term, high-dose baclofen treatment for spasticity. Jones and Lance[7] summarized their experience with 113 patients with spasticity treated with baclofen for up to 6 years. Baclofen dosage ranged from 30 to 200 mg daily with the mean varying from 60 to 110 mg depending on the cause of spasticity. Treatment was abandoned in only four patients because of intolerable side effects, and another 20% required a reduction in dosage. Pedersen et al.[8] treated patients with up to 100 mg of baclofen daily for more than 3 years. Adverse effects were transient but more frequent at higher doses. Pinto et al.[9] identified patients who had taken up to 225 mg daily for up to 30 months and emphasized that many patients need more than 100 mg daily and that side effects are only infrequently a persisting problem.

The present study did not attempt to collect objective evidence indicating that doses of baclofen in excess of 80 mg/d are safe or result in increased benefit. However, the results of this retrospective study do suggest that doses in excess of 80 mg/d are used rather frequently in clinical practice and should be considered when more aggressive management of spasticity is indicated. Our study also suggests that adverse effects may only rarely be important as obstacles in determining the best dose.

Recently, considerable interest has been generated by reports of the efficacy of intrathecal baclofen.[10] While a welcome addition to the management of refractory spasticity, this treatment is expensive, invasive, and prone to complications. We hope that patients being considered for intrathecal baclofen will first be given an adequate trial with oral baclofen or other oral antispastic medications such as diazepam and dantrolene sodium.

This brief chart review confirmed that use of high-dose baclofen is fairly frequent in a large MS center. The results also suggested that high dosages are not associated with discontinuation of the medication, although there is a reduction of dose from highest recorded levels for a significant proportion of patients using >80 mg (n = 5/15). On the basis of these data, no conclusions can be drawn concerning the safety or efficacy of high doses of baclofen. However, given that high dosing is frequent enough in MS, the results do strongly suggest that patient needs and response to therapy, and not some arbitrary maximum, should determine the optimal dose.

REFERENCES

1. Smith CR, Aisen ML, Scheinberg L. Symptomatic management of multiple sclerosis. In: McDonald WI, Silberberg DH, eds. *Multiple sclerosis*. London: Butterworths, 1986: 166–183.

2. Katz RT. Management of spasticity. *Am J Phys Med Rehabil* 1988;**67**:108–116.

3. Feldman RG, Kelly-Hayes M, Conomy JP, Foley JM. Baclofen for spasticity in multiple sclerosis. *Neurology* 1978; **28**:1094–1098.

4. Young RR. Treatment of spastic paraparesis. *N Engl J Med* 1989;**320**: 1553–1555.

5. Delwaide P. Oral treatment of spasticity with current muscle relaxants. In: Marsden D, ed. *Treating spasticity: pharmacological advances*. Bern: Hans Huber, 1989:31–37.

6. Whyte J, Robinson KM. Pharmacologic management. In: Glenn MB, Whyte J, eds. *The practical management of spasticity in children and adults*. Philadelphia: Lea & Febiger, 1990:10.1–10.26.

7. Jones RF, Lance JW. Baclofen (Lioresal®) in the long term management of spasticity. *Med J Aust* 1976;**1**:654–657.

8. Pedersen E, Arlien-Soborg P, Grynderup V, Henriksen O. GABA derivative in spasticity. *Acta Neurol Scand* 1970;46:257–266.

9. Pinto O de S, Polikar M, Debono G. Results of international clinical trials with Lioresal®. *Postgrad Med J* 1972;48(suppl):18–23.

10. Penn RD, Savoy SM, Corcos D, et al. Intrathecal baclofen for severe spinal spasticity. *N Engl J Med* 1989;320:1517–1521.

ADDICTION AND PREEXISTING ANXIETY AND MOOD DISORDERS

Abstract

Grant, B. F., Stinson, F. S., Dawson, D. A., et al. (2004) Prevalence and co-occurrence of substance use disorders and independent mood and anxiety disorders: results from the National Epidemiologic Survey on Alcohol and Related Conditions. *Archives of General Psychiatry* 61, 807–816.

Background: Uncertainties exist about the prevalence and comorbidity of substance use disorders and independent mood and anxiety disorders. Objective: To present nationally representative data on the prevalence and comorbidity of DSM-IV alcohol and drug use disorders and independent mood and anxiety disorders (including only those that are not substance induced and that are not due to a general medical condition). Design: Face-to-face survey. Setting: The United States. Participants: Household and group quarters' residents. Main Outcome Measures: Prevalence and associations of substance use disorders and independent mood and anxiety disorders. Results: The prevalences of 12-month DSM-IV independent mood and anxiety disorders in the US population were 9.21% (95% confidence interval [CI], 8.78%–9.64%) and 11.08%

(95% CI, 10.43%–11.73%), respectively. The rate of substance use disorders was 9.35% (95% CI, 8.86%–9.84%). Only a few individuals with mood or anxiety disorders were classified as having only substance-induced disorders. Associations between most substance use disorders and independent mood and anxiety disorders were positive and significant (P<.05). Conclusions: Substance use disorders and mood and anxiety disorders that develop independently of intoxication and withdrawal are among the most prevalent psychiatric disorders in the United States. Associations between most substance use disorders and independent mood and anxiety disorders were overwhelmingly positive and significant, suggesting that treatment for a comorbid mood or anxiety disorder should not be withheld from individuals with substance use disorders.

Hypothesis

Ameisen, O. (2007) Gamma-hydroxybutyrate (GHB)-deficiency in alcohol-dependence? *Alcohol and Alcoholism* 42, 506.

I wish to propose a hypothesis that could help explain some of the effects of baclofen in alcohol dependence that are described in Dr. Bucknam's case study (Bucknam, 2007) and in my self-case report (Ameisen, 2005). At a behavioural level, alcohol, baclofen and GHB all share sedative/hypnotic effects in humans. Clinical trials have shown baclofen to reduce anxiety in alcoholic (Krupitsky *et al.*, 1993; Addolorato *et al.*, 2002) and non-alcoholic (Breslow *et al.*, 1989; Drake *et al.*, 2003) patients alike. And somnolence is an overwhelmingly prevalent side effect of baclofen. Yet unlike other sedative/hypnotics (benzodiazepines, meprobamate, barbiturates), baclofen and GHB have been specifically shown to reduce craving in alcoholic patients (Addolorato *et al.*, 2002; Caputo *et al.*, 2003; Nava *et al.*, 2006). In animals, effects of baclofen on anxiety are more heterogeneous. While some studies demonstrate that baclofen has sedative activity (Carai *et al.*, 2004), lack of anxiolytic activity (Dalvi and Rodgers, 1996) and even anxiogenic actions (Car and Wisniewska, 2006) have also been reported. Also, while there are reports showing baclofen to increase severity of alcohol withdrawal in animals (Humeniuk *et al*., 1994), the efficacy of baclofen in the treatment of acute withdrawal syndrome has been shown to be comparable to that of diazepam in clinical trials (Addolorato *et al*., 2006). In mice, Carai *et al.* established that the sedative/hypnotic effect of GHB is, like that of baclofen, mediated by the stimulation of $GABA_B$ receptors (Carai *et al*., 2001) which adds support to the hypothesis that the $GABA_B$ receptor constitutes a central site of action of GHB. Functionally, both baclofen and GHB increase a potassium current and decrease the H-current in hippocampal neurons via $GABA_B$ receptor (Schweitzer *et al*., 2004). Of alcohol, GHB and baclofen, only one is a naturally occurring molecule: GHB. This leads me to raise the hypothesis that a primary dysfunction in GHB, such as a quantitative or functional deficit, could be partly responsible for the dysphoric syndrome (anxiety, insomnia, muscular tension . . .) that precedes and later coexists with alcohol dependence. And that baclofen effect could compensate for some of the deficit of $GABA_B$-mediated effect of GHB, and suppress dysphoria and dependence. Most sedative/hypnotics can cause dependence. In clinical practice, of these two agents that stimulate $GABA_B$ receptors, GHB causes dependence, while dependence has not been reported with baclofen. This could be related to GHB's many sites of action aside from $GABA_B$. Animal studies should be performed to test this hypothesis. Of interest, a GHB receptor has recently [been] characterized in the human brain.

REFERENCES

Addolorato, G., Caputo, F., Capristo, E. *et al*. (2002) Baclofen efficacy in reducing alcohol craving and intake: a preliminary double-blind randomized controlled study. *Alcohol and Alcoholism* **37**, 504–508.

Addolorato, G., Leggio, L., Abenavoli, L. *et al*. (2006) Baclofen in the treatment of alcohol withdrawal syndrome: a comparative study vs diazepam. *American Journal of Medicine* **119**, 276.e13–8.

Ameisen, O. (2005) Complete and prolonged suppression of symptoms and consequences of alcohol-dependence using high-dose baclofen: a self-case report of a physician. *Alcohol and Alcoholism* 40, 147–150.

Andriamampandry, C., Taleb, O., Kemmel, V. *et al.* (2007) Cloning and functional characterization of a gamma-hydroxybutyrate receptor identified in the human brain. *FASEB J.* 3, 885–895.

Breslow, M. F., Fankhauser, M. P., Potter, R. L. *et al.* (1989) Role of gamma-aminobutyric acid in antipanic drug efficacy. *American Journal of Psychiatry* 146, 353–356.

Bucknam, W. (2007) Suppression of symptoms of alcohol dependence and craving using high-dose baclofen. *Alcohol and Alcoholism* 42, 158–160.

Caputo, F., Addolorato, G. and Lorenzini, F. (2003) Gamma-hydroxybutyric acid versus naltrexone in maintaining alcohol abstinence: an open randomized comparative study. *Drug and Alcohol Dependence* 70, 85–91.

Car, H. and Wisniewska, R. J. (2006) Effects of baclofen and L-AP4 in passive avoidance test in rats after hypoxia-induced amnesia. *Pharmacological Reports* 58, 91–100.

Carai, M. A., Colombo, G., Brunetti, G. *et al.* (2001) Role of GABA$_B$ receptors in the sedative/hypnotic effect of gamma-hydroxybutyric acid. *European Journal of Pharmacology* 428, 315–321.

Carai, M. A., Vacca, G., Serra, S. *et al.* (2004) Suppression of GABA$_B$ receptor function in vivo by disulfide reducing agent, DL-dithiothreitol (DTT). *Psychopharmacology* 174, 283–290.

Dalvi, A. and Rodgers, R. J. (1996) GABAergic influences on plus-maze behaviour in mice. *Psychopharmacology* 128, 380–397.

Drake, R. G., Davis, L. L., Cates, M. E. *et al.* (2003) Baclofen treatment for chronic posttraumatic stress disorder. *Annals of Pharmacotherapy* 37, 1177–1181.

Humeniuk, R. E., White, J. M. and Ong, J. (1994) The effects of GABA$_B$ ligands on alcohol withdrawal in mice. *Pharmacology Biochemistry and Behavior* 49, 561–566.

Krupitsky, E. M., Burakov, A. M., Ivanov, V. B. *et al.* (1993) Baclofen administration for the treatment of affective disorders in alcoholic patients. *Drug and Alcohol Dependence* 33, 157–163.

Nava, F., Premi, S., Manzato, E. and Lucchini, A. (2006) Comparing treatments of alcoholism on craving and biochemical measures of alcohol consumption. *Journal of Psychoactive Drugs* 38, 211–217.

Schweitzer, P., Roberto, M. and Madamba, S. G. (2004) Gamma-hydroxybutyrate increases a potassium current and decreases the H-current in hippocampal neurons via GABA$_B$ receptors. *Journal of Pharmacology and Experimental Therapeutics* 311, 172–179.

Letter to the Editor and Reply

The American Journal of Drug and Alcohol Abuse vol. 34, no. 2, pp. 235–238, 2008

Are the effects of gamma-hydroxybutyrate (GHB) treatment partly physiological in alcohol dependence?

Olivier Ameisen, M.D.

ABSTRACT

It has been hypothesized that the therapeutic effects of gamma-hydroxybutyrate (GHB) in alcohol dependence could be related to ethanol-mimicking action of the drug and that GHB could reduce alcohol craving, intake, and withdrawal by acting as a "substitute" of the alcohol in the central nervous system. Nevertheless, alcohol being the strongest trigger of craving and intake, it is difficult to ascribe reduction of craving and intake to the ethanol-mimicking activity of GHB. I have recently proposed that alcohol/substance dependence could result from a GHB-deficiency-related dysphoric syndrome in which alcohol/substances would be sought to "substitute" for insufficient GHB effect. GHB is the sole identified naturally occurring gamma-aminobutyric acid B ($GABA_B$) receptor agonist. Here, I propose that exogenous GHB might in fact "substitute" for deficient endogenous GHB and represent true substitutive treatment for GHB deficiency and that baclofen and GHB could both compensate for deficient effect of the physiological $GABA_B$ receptor agonist(s).

KEYWORDS

alcohol dependence, $GABA_B$, gamma-hydroxybutyrate deficiency

Dr. Nava and colleagues, quoting work that gives fresh significance to Dr. Gessa's team's landmark findings on gamma-hydroxybutyrate (GHB), suggest that the "mechanisms of GHB effects on alcohol intake, craving, and withdrawal may be related to the ethanol-mimicking action of the drug . . . and that GHB may act as a 'substitute' of the alcohol in the central nervous system."[1] An alcohol-like effect is of course certain to be beneficial for withdrawal. But alcohol being the strongest trigger of alcohol craving and intake makes it difficult to ascribe the reducing effects of GHB on alcohol craving and intake to the alcohol-mimicking activity of GHB. A GHB receptor has been recently identified in the human brain.[2] Could exogenous GHB in fact also "substitute" for itself (deficient endogenous GHB)? GHB is currently the sole identified naturally occurring gamma-aminobutyric acid B ($GABA_B$) receptor agonist. And of all sedative-hypnotics used for the treatment of alcohol dependence, the only two shown to reduce or suppress motivation to consume alcohol—GHB and baclofen—are also the only two that have $GABA_B$ receptor-mediated effects.[3] I have recently proposed that alcohol/substance dependence could result from an adaptive phenomenon in response to an underlying GHB-deficiency-related dysphoric syndrome (anxiety, insomnia, depression) in which alcohol and related substances would be sought to "substitute" for insufficient GHB effect.[3] At the later stage of dependence, exogenous GHB could, in addition to "substituting" for the alcohol (as proposed by the authors), also represent true substitutive treatment for GHB deficiency.

Interestingly, while baclofen—a *synthetic* molecule—is characterized as the prototypic $GABA_B$ receptor agonist, the *physiologic* $GABA_B$ receptor agonist(s) is (are) yet to be identified (aside from GHB, which possesses such *physiologic* activity). So baclofen and GHB could in fact both compensate for *deficient effect of the physiological $GABA_B$ receptor agonist(s)*.

REFERENCES

1. Nava F, Premi S, Manzato E, Campagnola W, Lucchini A, Gessa GL. Gammahydroxybutyrate reduces both withdrawal syndrome and hypercortisolism in severe abstinent alcoholics: an open study vs. diazepam. *Am J Drug Alcohol Abuse* 2007; **33**(3):379–392.

2. Andriamampandry C, Taleb O, Kemmel V, Humbert JP, Aunis D, Maitre M. Cloning and functional characterization of a gamma-hydroxybutyrate receptor identified in the human brain. *FASEB J* 2007 Mar;**21**(3):885–895. Epub 2006 Dec 28.

3. Ameisen O. Gamma-hydroxybutyrate (GHB)-deficiency in alcohol-dependence? *Alcohol Alcohol* 2007;**42**(5):506. Epub 2007 Aug 1.

Reply to the Letter "Are the Effects of Gamma-Hydroxybutyrate (GHB) Treatment Partly Physiological in Alcohol Dependence?"
by Olivier Ameisen

Felice Nava, M.D., Ph.D., Department of Addiction Medicine, Hospital of Castelfranco Veneto, Treviso, Italy

We find Dr. Ameisen's comment appealing. The gamma-hydroxybutyrate (GHB) antialcohol molecular effects are yet largely obscure. Clinically speaking, the GHB seems to act as a true "substitute" of alcohol[1] and this aspect may explain two of the major effects of GHB for the treatment of alcoholism: the suppression of both withdrawal syndrome and craving.[2,3]

We know that several of the pharmacological effects induced by GHB are due to a potentiation of GABAergic transmission.[4] This effect may be due to a simple brain conversion of exogenous GHB in gamma-aminobutyric acid (GABA) and/or to a direct GHB activation of own receptors that have been recently identified in the human brain.[5] Moreover, since some of the most important central effects of GHB, that is also a naturally occurring $GABA_B$ receptor agonist, are shared with the $GABA_B$ agonist baclofen, we may suppose that several of the GHB actions may also be mediated through the activation of $GABA_B$ receptors.[4]

In light of the above evidence and considering our recent work,[3] Dr. Ameisen is correct in pointing out that alcoholism may be a disease characterized by a GHB deficiency in the brain. In accord with this hypothesis, in alcoholics the ethanol would act as a "substitute" for the insufficient effects of GHB. In other words, it is the alcohol that may act as a "substitute" for GHB and not the contrary. Furthermore, since baclofen has been demonstrated to suppress both in animals and humans the intake of several drugs including alcohol,[6-9] we may suppose a key role of the endogenous GHB not only in the alcoholism but also in several other forms of drug dependence. If the previous hypothesis will be demonstrated, the role of endogenous GHB will be elucidated and the potential properties of GHB as medication will be better developed.

REFERENCES

1. Gessa GL, Agabio R, Carai MA, Lobina C, Pani M, Reali R, Colombo G. Mechanism of the antialcohol effect of gamma-hydroxybutyric acid. *Alcohol* 2002;20:71–76.

2. Nava F, Premi S, Manzato E, Lucchini A. Comparing treatments of alcoholism on craving and biochemical measures of alcohol consumptionists. *J Psychoactive Drugs* 2006;**38**:211–217.

3. Nava F, Premi S, Manzato E, Campagnola W, Lucchini A, Gessa GL. Gamma-hydroxybutyrate reduces both withdrawal syndrome and hypercortisolism in severe abstinent alcoholics: an open study vs. diazepam. *Am J Drug Alcohol Abuse* 2007;**33**:379–392.

4. Wong CG, Gibson KM, Snead OC. 3rd. From the street to the brain: neurobiology of the recreational drug gamma-hydroxybutyric acid. *Trends Pharmacol Sci* 2004;**25**:29–34.

5. Andriamampandry C, Taleb O, Kemmel V, Humbert JP, Aunis D, Maitre M. Cloning and functional characterization of a gamma-hydroxybutyrate receptor identified in the human brain. *FASEB J* 2007;**21**:885–895.

6. Addolorato G, Caputo F, Capristo E, Domenicali M, Bernardi M, Janiri L, Agabio R, Colombo G, Gessa GL, Gasbarrini G. Baclofen efficacy in reducing alcohol craving and intake: a preliminary double-blind randomized controlled study. *Alcohol Alcohol* 2002;**37**:504–508.

7. Haney M, Hart CL, Foltin RW. Effects of baclofen on cocaine self-administration: opioid and nonopioid-dependent volunteers. *Neuropsychopharmacology* 2006;**31**:1814–1821.

8. Spano MS, Fattore L, Fratta W, Fadda P. The GABA$_B$ receptor agonist baclofen prevents heroin-induced reinstatement of heroin-seeking behavior in rats. *Neuropsychopharmacology* 2007;**52**:1555–1562.

9. Walker BM, Koob GF. The gamma-aminobutyric acid-B receptor agonist baclofen attenuates responding for ethanol in ethanol-dependent rats. *Alcohol Clin Exp Res* 2007;**31**:11–18.

NOTES

CHAPTER 1. MOMENT OF TRUTH

1. K. A. McCormick, N. E. Cochran, A. L. Back, et al., "How primary care providers talk to patients about alcohol: a qualitative study," *Journal of General Internal Medicine* 21(9) (2006): 966–972.

2. For physician rates of alcohol and other substance dependence, see J. Brewster, "Prevalence of alcohol and other drug problems among physicians," *Journal of the American Medical Association* 255 (1986): 1913–1920; J. Anthony et al., "Psychoactive drug dependence and abuse: more common in some occupations than in others?" *Journal of Employee Assistance Research* 1 (1992): 148–186; and F. Stinson et al., "Prevalence of DSM-III-R alcohol abuse and/or dependence among selected occupations," *Alcohol Health Research World* 16 (1992): 165–172. For rates of alcohol dependence in the general population, see B. F. Grant, "Prevalence and correlates of alcohol use and DSM-IV alcohol dependence in the United States," *Journal of Studies on Alcohol* 58 (1997): 464–473. For rates of problem drinking, see "Results from the 2006 National Survey on Drug Use and Health: National

Findings," U. S. Department of Health and Human Services, Substance Abuse and Mental Health Services Administration, Office of Applied Studies, p. 3, www.oas.samhsa.gov/NSDUHlatest.htm. For rates of liver cirrhosis among physicians, see BBC One's *Real Story with Fiona Bruce*, June 16, 2005.

CHAPTER 2. A REMEDY GONE WRONG

1. B. F. Grant et al., "Prevalence and co-occurrence of substance use disorders and independent mood and anxiety disorders: results from the National Epidemiological Survey on Alcohol and Related Conditions," *Archives of General Psychiatry* 61 (2004): 807–816.

2. R. Yehuda et al., "Maternal, not paternal, PTSD is related to increased risk for PTSD in offspring of Holocaust survivors," *Journal of Psychiatric Research*, February 15, 2008, e-publication ahead of print. Regarding genomic imprinting, I am grateful to Jerome B. Posner, M.D., for bringing this phenomenon to my attention as the possible means of transmission of PTSD risk from parent to child and suggesting that it "is probably caused by epigenetic mechanisms, as for example, DNA methylation"; personal communication, August 17, 2008.

CHAPTER 4. DOING GREAT AND FEELING AWFUL

1. For relapse rates after rehab for alcoholism, see J. M. Polich, D. J. Armor, and H. B. Braiker, "Stability and change in drinking patterns," in *The Course of Alcoholism: Four Years After Treatment* (New York: John Wiley & Sons, 1981), 159–200. For relapse after rehab for other substance abuse, see W. A. Hunt, L. W. Barnett, and L. G. Branch, "Relapse rates in addictions programs," *Journal of Clinical Psychology* 27 (1971): 455– 456, and G. A. Marlatt and J. R. Gordon, "Determinants of relapse: implications of the maintenance of behavior change," in *Behavioral Medicine: Changing Health Lifestyle*, ed.

P. O. Davidson and S. M. Davidson (New York: Brunner/Mazel, 1980), 410–452.

CHAPTER 6. AGAINST MEDICAL ADVICE, OR, THE LIFE OF AFTERWARD

1. Linda Carroll, "Genetic Studies Promise a Path to Better Treatment of Addictions," *New York Times*, November 14, 2000.
2. D. C. Roberts and M. M. Andrews, "Baclofen suppression of cocaine self-administration: demonstration using a discrete trials procedure," *Psychopharmacology* 131(3) (June 1997): 271–277.
3. B. A. Johnson et al., "Oral topiramate for treatment of alcohol dependence: a randomised clinical trial," *Lancet* 361 (2003): 1677–1685.

CHAPTER 7. CUTTING THROUGH CRAVING

1. C. R. Smith et al., "High-dose oral baclofen: experience in patients with multiple sclerosis," *Neurology* 41 (1991): 1829–1831.
2. R. Gerkin et al., "First-order elimination kinetics following baclofen overdose," *Annals of Emergency Medicine* 15 (1986): 843–846.
3. B. F. Grant et al., "Prevalence and co-occurrence of substance use disorders and independent mood and anxiety disorders: results from the National Epidemiological Survey on Alcohol and Related Conditions," *Archives of General Psychiatry* 61 (2004): 807–816.

CHAPTER 8. THE END OF ADDICTION?

1. Megan Barnett, "The New Pill Pushers," *U.S. News & World Report*, April 18, 2004, citing these statistics and quoting Nancy Nielsen, speaker of the American Medical Association board of delegates.
2. O. Ameisen, "Naltrexone treatment for alcohol dependency," *Journal of the American Medical Association* 294(8): (August 24/31, 2005): 899–900; author reply 900.

CHAPTER 9. HOW BACLOFEN WORKS: WHAT WE KNOW, AND
NEED TO KNOW

1. The wording of the criteria is my own, based on American Psychiatric Association, *Diagnostic and Statistical Manual of Mental Disorders*, Fourth Edition, Text Revision (Washington, D.C.: American Psychiatric Association, 2000), 197.

2. George F. Koob and Michel Le Moal, "Addiction and the brain anti-reward system," *Annual Review of Psychology* 59 (2008): 29–53, and A. Markou, T. R. Kosten, and G. F. Koob, "Neurobiological similarities in depression and drug dependence: a self-medication hypothesis," *Neuropsychopharmacology* 18(3) (March 1998): 135–174.

3. O. Ameisen, "Naltrexone treatment for alcohol dependency," *Journal of the American Medical Association* 294(8) (August 24/31, 2005): 899– 900; author reply 900.

4. For topiramate's association with glaucoma, see G. L. Spaeth and Anand V. Mantravadi, "Topiramate as treatment for alcohol dependence," *Journal of the American Medical Association* 229(4) (January 30, 2008): 405; for topiramate's effect on suicide risk, see Gardiner Harris and Benedict Carey, "F.D.A. Finds Increase in Suicide for Patients Using Seizure Medications," *New York Times*, February 1, 2008.

5. D. T. George et al., "Neurokinin 1 receptor antagonism as a possible therapy for alcoholism," *Science* 319(5869) (March 14, 2008): 1536–1539; for the commentary by M. Heilig, see story posted February 14, 2008, at abcnews.go.com/health/drugs/story?id=4291394&page=1.

6. G. Addolorato et al., "Effectiveness and safety of baclofen for maintenance of alcohol abstinence in alcohol-dependent patients with liver cirrhosis: randomised, double-blind controlled study," *Lancet* 370(9603) (December 8, 2007): 1884–1885.

7. P. Greene, "Baclofen in the treatment of dystonia," *Clinical Neuropharmacology* 15(4) (August 1992): 276–288.

8. G. Addolorato et al., "Baclofen efficacy in reducing alcohol craving and intake: a preliminary double-blind randomized controlled study," *Alcohol and Alcoholism* 37(5) (September–October 2002): 504–508.

9. P. C. Waldmeier et al., "Roles of GABA$_B$ receptor subtypes in pre-synaptic auto- and heteroreceptor function regulating GABA and glutamate release," *Journal of Neural Transmission*, July 30, 2008, e-publication ahead of print.

10. P. Fadda et al., "Baclofen antagonizes nicotine-, cocaine-, and morphine-induced dopamine release in the nucleus accumbens of rat," *Synapse* 50(1) (October 2003): 1–6.

11. O. Ameisen, "Are the effects of gamma-hydroxybutyrate (GHB) treatment partly physiological in alcohol dependence?" and F. Nava, "Reply to the letter 'Are the effects of gamma-hydroxybutyrate (GHB) treatment partly physiological in alcohol dependence?' by Olivier Ameisen," *American Journal of Drug and Alcohol Abuse*, 34(2): 235–238.

12. N. H. Naqvi et al., "Damage to the insula disrupts addiction to cig-arette smoking," *Science* 315(5811) (January 26, 2007): 531–534.

13. H. Harwood, *Updating Estimates of the Economic Costs of Alcohol Abuse in the United States: Estimates, Update Methods and Data.* National Institute on Alcohol Abuse and Alcoholism. Bethesda, Maryland: National Institutes of Health, 1998.

14. See chapter 1, note 2.

15. Personal communication, February 27, 2008.

ACKNOWLEDGMENTS

First of all, I thank my parents for their boundless love and for showing me by their example the power of dreams when everything appears to be lost. In my biological prison, I heard the greatest experts say that my alcoholism was in one of the disease's most severe forms. They told me that addiction was chronic and irreversible, that no medication existed or would ever exist to change its course. I was ready to accept everything that was happening to me, brutal though it was, but the word *irreversible* I could not accept. I always found it extraordinary that when a whole continent had capitulated to the Nazis, my father and mother, though on the list for programmed death, never for one moment doubted the Allied victory. In view of their situations at the time—my father a French army officer transferred, as a Jew, from a normal prisoner of war camp to a forced labor camp, and my mother in Auschwitz—their conviction was absurd. But without it, neither one nor the other would have survived. That is what they taught me: for a miracle to happen, one needs to have dreamed it.

I thank my brother, Jean-Claude, and his wife, Fabienne, and my sister, Eva, and her husband, François, for keeping their love for me intact despite the damage that addiction inflicts on families. And I thank my cousin Steve Israeler for being on my side and believing in me all along.

There is not space to name here all those who gave me much-needed support and encouragement during my illness. Thanks especially to Joan (at her request I have not used her real name) for sending me a newspaper article about baclofen as described above. Without that act of kindness, I would probably have died from alcoholism and would never have been able to write this book.

Thanks to Rebecca, for her friendship during and after my disease; to Vanessa, for her inspiration and empathy during the final phase of my alcoholism; to Anne, who believed in my recovery and my treatment model; to Michèle, for her support; to Jean-Luc and Martial, for their persistence on my behalf; to the late Raymond Barre and his wife, Eva; to the late Arif Mardin, his wife, Latife, and their children, Joe and Julie; to Murat and Ayse Sungar; to the late Maurice Blin and his wife, Melita; to Ladislas and Clare Kerenyi; and to Yvette Nicolas and her sons, Olivier and Renaud.

The late Jean Bernard and the late Philippe Coumel inspired me with their passion for medical research and instilled something of that same spirit in me. My colleagues John Laragh, Jeffrey Borer, and Paul Kligfield contributed to reinforce this passion in our work together, as my friends Jean and Rosita

Dausset and the late Joshua Lederberg and his wife, Marguerite, did in our many conversations. I am grateful to them all.

I feel the deepest gratitude to the physicians who treated me during my illness, especially Drs. John Schaefer and Elizabeth Khuri in New York and Dr. Jean-Paul Descombey in Paris, whose friendship and concern particularly touched me, and Drs. Dorothée Lecallier and Françoise Georges for their kindness and compassion.

Without prolonged close contact in Alcoholics Anonymous and rehab with many fellow acoloholics and other addicts, I would never have been able to understand my disease, and I thank them all for the inspiration and insight they gave me.

My efforts to understand how baclofen could be so useful in the treatment of addiction, and to further research its effects and mechanisms of action, have brought me into contact with many outstanding figures in the medical and scientific community. I am grateful to all those who have discussed the science and treatment of addiction with me, especially George F. Koob, Eliot L. Gardner, David C. Roberts, Anna Rose Childress, Giancarlo Colombo, Giovanni Addolorato, Fabio Caputo, Mary Jeanne Kreek, Charles O'Brien, and Antonio Damasio. My brother, Jean-Claude Ameisen, and Jerome B. Posner gave me particularly valuable feedback on some of my papers.

Thanks to Boris Pasche for urging me to write my self-case report on the suppression of my alcoholism, and to Georges Moroz for his encouragement as I sought to bring attention to baclofen.

Alain Coblence first suggested that I write this book and gave me the benefit of his considerable acumen, both legal and otherwise, as it progressed to publication. He put me in touch with my literary agent, Michael Carlisle of Inkwell Management, whose belief in the importance of the baclofen story, unwavering support, and penetrating judgment ensured that these pages saw the light of day. I am grateful to them both not only for their consummate professionalism, but also for their friendship.

I also wish to thank Michael Carlisle's associate at Inkwell Management, Elisa Petrini, for her initial editorial help and suggestions. Hilary Hinzmann gave me invaluable assistance in the writing of the book, and I am happy for the friendship that has developed between us.

No one could ask for a more astute, passionate, and creative editor and publisher than Sarah Crichton. She has made this a far better book than it otherwise would have been. I am also grateful for the work of her colleagues at Farrar, Straus and Giroux who helped usher the book into the world on a very tight schedule, including Cailey Hall, Debra Helfand, Susan Goldfarb, Don McConnell, Peter Richardson, Abby Kagan, Jeff Seroy, and Sarita Varma.

Last but not least, thanks to Noëlle from the bottom of my heart for her affection, her infinite patience and willingness to listen, her counsel, and her understanding, which have been so precious to me.

PERMISSION ACKNOWLEDGMENTS

Grateful acknowledgment is made to the following for granting permission to reprint these articles and abstracts in the appendix:

Alcohol and Alcoholism vol. 40, no. 2, pp. 147-150, 2005. "Complete and prolonged suppression of symptoms and consequences of alcohol-dependence using high-dose baclofen: a self-case report of a physician." Olivier Ameisen. By permission of the Medical Council on Alcohol and Oxford University Press.

Alcohol and Alcoholism vol. 42, no. 2, pp. 158-160, 2007. "Suppression of symptoms of alcohol dependence and craving using high-dose baclofen." William Bucknam. By permission of the Medical Council on Alcohol and Oxford University Press.

Journal of Clinical Psychopharmacology vol. 27, no. 3, 2007. "Baclofen suppresses alcohol intake and craving for alcohol in a schizophrenic alcohol-dependence patient: a case report." Agabio, R., Marras, P., Addolorato, G., et al. By permission of Lippincott, Williams & Wilkins, and Wolters Kluwer Heath.

Alcohol and Alcoholism vol. 37, no. 5, pp. 504-508, 2002. "Baclofen efficacy in reducing alcohol craving and intake: a preliminary double-blind randomized controlled study." Giovanni Addolorato, Fabio Caputo, Esmeralda Capristo, Marco Domenicali, Mauro Bernardi, Luigi Janiri, Roberta Agabio, Giancarlo Colombo, Gian Luigi Gessa, and Giovanni Gasbarrini. By permission of the Medical Council on Alcohol and Oxford University Press.

Reprinted from *The Lancet*, 370(9603) (8 December 2007-14 December 2007), 1915-1922. "Effectiveness and safety of baclofen for maintenance of alcohol abstinence in alcohol-dependent patients with live cirrhosis: randomised, double-blind controlled study." Addolorato G., Leggio L., Ferrulli A., et al. With permission from Elsevier.

American Journal of Psychiatry 146, 353-356, 1989. "Role of gamma-aminobutyric acid in antipanic drug efficacy." Breslow, M. F., Fankhauser, M. P., Potter, R. L., et al.

HEAL THYSELF

A Doctor at the Peak of His Medical Career,

Destroyed by Alcohol — and the Personal Miracle

That Brought Him Back

Olivier Ameisen, M.D.

ABOUT THIS GUIDE

The questions and discussion topics that follow are designed to enhance your reading of Olivier Ameisen's *Heal Thyself*. We hope they will enrich your experience as you explore his poignant, insightful, and provocative story, which is already transforming the treatment of addiction.

Heal Thyself is both a riveting personal memoir of battling addiction and the inspiring scientific saga of an extraordinary physician who bravely used himself as a guinea pig to find an effective medication for this deadly disease—and then shed his anonymity as a physician with addiction and campaigned against all odds to bring this breakthrough treatment, which produces complete, rapid, and effortless freedom from addiction, to the attention of a dogmatic medical establishment. Astonishingly, the medication he found, baclofen, has been hiding in plain sight of the addiction treatment community for years. Yet despite baclofen's sterling safety record and compelling evidence of its effectiveness, most addiction specialists and researchers continue to ignore it.

The first book to combine the personal experience of addiction with the science of addiction, and the first to bring the healing potential of baclofen to the public at large, *Heal Thyself* is also a compassionate call to action that could herald the end of addiction for tens of millions of people with this disease, until now deadly and irreversible.

QUESTIONS FOR DISCUSSION

1. The book's narrative weaves together a personal and a scientific story. Did you find the combination of these elements effective and compelling? What was the most powerful personal moment in the book for you? What part of the science of addiction most intrigued you?

2. The book reports that one in four U.S. deaths is caused by alcohol, tobacco, or illegal drugs, and observes that addiction to nicotine is the single biggest cause of cancer. Were you aware that addiction is such a huge public health problem? Would you support changing public health priorities to provide more funding for addiction research and treatment?

3. The rates of alcoholism and illegal substance dependence among physicians equal those in the general population. Based on what you've read in the book, do you think medical and governmental authorities are taking the right measures to identify and treat physicians with substance-dependence problems in order to help them and safeguard the public?

4. Dr. Ameisen describes how the moral stigma of addiction pervades our society, despite overwhelming evidence that addiction is a biological disease that manifests itself in imbalanced neurotransmission in the brain. Studies cited in the book also show that the likeliest explanation for vulnerability to addiction is a preexisting imbalance in neurotransmission associated with chronic anxiety and depression, post-traumatic stress disorder, or related problems. Before reading the book, were you inclined to see addiction as a failure of moral character or self-control? Has reading it changed your view of addiction and those who suffer from it?

5. Dr. Ameisen explores the possibility that his mother's traumatic experiences as a Holocaust survivor may have predisposed him to chronic anxiety and thus made him vulnerable to addiction. Have you observed similar patterns in your own family or in friends' families?

6. Addiction has both direct and indirect victims—not only alcoholics and other addicts, but also their families, loved ones, and friends. Has the book deepened your understanding of how the disease drives a wedge between the people who suffer from it and those around them? After reading it, do you feel any better equipped to reach out to a friend, relative, or coworker who is struggling with substance dependence?

7. As the book explains, studies show that people with anxiety, depression, and post-traumatic stress disorder or with so-called nondrug addictions—gambling addiction, binge eating, sex addiction, and compulsive shopping, among others—have the same imbalanced neurotransmission as

people with drug addiction. Given this shared pattern, does it seem reasonable that a single medication might be effective against all these problems?

8. The history of medicine reveals that whenever medicine has lacked an effective treatment for an illness, it has blamed the patient for supposed immorality or a lack of positive attitude and willpower. Were you surprised to read in the book that victims of tuberculosis and cancer were once seen in this way? What can each of us do to change the way addiction is viewed by society?

9. The book reports studies documenting that physicians most often miss the signs of addiction in their patients, and even change the subject when patients bring it up. What should be done to encourage honest discussion between doctors and patients about addiction?

10. Serendipity—a lucky break—made Dr. Ameisen aware of baclofen, and many other important medical and scientific breakthroughs have depended on chance. Has luck ever played a dramatic role in your own life? Do you think medical and scientific authorities are as open to serendipity as they should be?

11. When Dr. Ameisen first heard about baclofen and began self-experimenting with it, he did not know how safe it was. What do you think of his decision, as a patient and a physician, to prescribe himself baclofen?

12. After baclofen ended Dr. Ameisen's craving for alcohol and completely freed him from addiction, he was astonished to learn that neurologists have safely used high doses of baclofen for comfort care of patients with mus-

cular spasms and similar problems since the 1960s, but that largely because of the specialization of modern medicine, addiction researchers and caregivers did not know anything about this. What should medical authorities and organizations do to encourage doctors in different fields to learn from one another?

13. Baclofen has been documented to be non-euphoric and nonaddictive. Do you agree with Dr. Ameisen that taking baclofen for addiction should be seen in the same way as taking a medication for any chronic condition, such as a beta-blocker for high blood pressure?

14. Before he found baclofen, Dr. Ameisen tried every available form of treatment for alcoholism. But as the book discusses, the existing treatments are not enough on their own to help the vast majority of alcoholics and other addicts to quit. Given the extremely high failure rate of existing treatments, and in light of baclofen's excellent safety record and documented effectiveness in both animals and humans, do you think addiction specialists' resistance to prescribing baclofen is reasonable?

15. Following Dr. Ameisen's example and treatment protocol, some other physicians are already prescribing baclofen to alcoholics and other addicts. Is this a good thing, or should more studies be done first?

16. The usual medications for addiction—disulfiram, naltrexone, acamprosate, topiramate, and varenicline—have shown only limited benefit in repeated trials, and all except acamprosate can have serious side effects. What do you think of pharmaceutical companies that continue to push

these medications, and of doctors who continue to prescribe them? What is your reaction to seeing advertisements for these medications?

17. Prescribing baclofen for addiction is an "off-label" use. Before reading the book, did you know that more than 23 percent of all prescriptions are off-label? Has a physician ever advised you that he or she is prescribing something to you or a family member off-label?

18. A randomized clinical trial of baclofen for addiction would cost about $500,000. Because baclofen is out of patent and has been available as a generic prescription medication since the 1980s, no pharmaceutical company has a financial incentive to fund such a trial. Given the enormous cost to society of treating substance abuse—alcohol abuse-related costs have been estimated at $200 billion a year in the U.S. alone—should government step in to fund randomized clinical trials of baclofen?

19. Dr. Ameisen observes that AIDS activists had a decisive influence on changing AIDS treatment to incorporate lifesaving medications, and he calls on patients, their families, and concerned physicians to lobby for clinical trials of baclofen for addiction. How much influence do you feel patients with addiction and their advocates should have on the direction of medical research and treatment?

20. A bill is pending in Congress to change the name of the National Institute on Drug Abuse to the National Institute on Diseases of Addiction and the name of the National Institute on Alcohol Abuse and Alcoholism to the National Institute on Alcohol Disorders and Health. As the book discusses, many scientists and physicians support this as part of

the new understanding of addiction as a biological disease, but others criticize it as diminishing the importance of personal responsibility in recovery from addiction. Before reading the book, would you have supported the name changes? Has reading the book changed your opinion?